COMRADES IN ART

The Correspondence of Ronald Stevenson and Percy Grainger 1957–61

with Interviews, Essays and other Writings on Grainger by Ronald Stevenson

COMRADES IN ART

The Correspondence of Ronald Stevenson and Percy Grainger 1957–61

with Interviews, Essays and other Writings on Grainger by Ronald Stevenson

Compiled and Annotated by Teresa Balough

Musicians in Letters No. 2
Musicians on Music No. 8

TOCCATA PRESS

First published in 2010 by Toccata Press.

British Library Cataloguing in Publication Data
A Catalogue record for this book is available from the British Library.

ISBN 978-0-907689-67-6
Musicians in Letters ISSN 0960-0094
Musicians on Music ISSN 0264-6889

This publication has been supported by The Australian Music Foundation, The Ida Carroll Trust, in association with The Manchester Musical Heritage Trust, and The Ronald Stevenson Society.

THE MANCHESTER
MUSICAL HERITAGE TRUST

AUSTRALIAN
MUSIC
FOUNDATION

Set in 11 on 12 point ITC New Baskerville
by Imprimata Publishers Ltd
Printed and bound in Great Britain

Contents

Illustrations

To Marjorie Stevenson and Owen Peagler

Introduction

Percy Grainger and Ronald Stevenson – 'Camerado, I Give You My Hand!'[1]

TERESA BALOUGH

In 1957 the Australian-American pianist and composer Percy Grainger was 75 years old and in failing health when he received a letter from a young Scottish composer named Ronald Stevenson. Stevenson requested Grainger's reminiscences of his former piano-teacher Ferruccio Busoni,[2] to be included in a book Stevenson was writing on Busoni. Grainger's reply, dated 2 August 1957, would lead to 32 letters exchanged between the two men over the four years leading up to Grainger's death in February 1961. Stevenson was 29 years old at the time, living in West Linton just south of Edinburgh, with his wife Marjorie and their two small children and teaching in various Edinburgh schools and in the Extra-Mural Department of Edinburgh University. He recalled that Grainger 'gave me companionship through correspondence at a time when I needed it because there wasn't a great deal of stimulation, cultural stimulation, in my life'.[3]

Stevenson had performed and admired Grainger's folk-music settings as a young piano student and learned of Grainger's involvement with Busoni when doing research on Busoni in 1955 while in Rome on an Italian government scholarship. The two men soon found that despite their 46-year age-difference, they had affinities in many areas. Both were pianists of staggering abilities and composers who combined a love for folk-music and demotic, working-class art with an aesthetic that proposed a 'world music' which would include the farthest reaches of humanity. Both made an art of piano transcription

[1] 'Song of the Open Road' (*Leaves of Grass*) by Walt Whitman. *Cf.* also pp. 197 and 247, below.

[2] Busoni (1866–1924), Italian pianist, composer and author of *Sketch of a New Aesthetic of Music* (1907), was, like Grainger, a musical pioneer. At Busoni's suggestion, Grainger studied piano with him briefly in 1903.

[3] Ronald Stevenson in an interview with the author, 10 November 1998; *cf.* p. 60, below.

Grainger photographed in Aarhus, Denmark, in 1957, the year in which his correspondence with Ronald Stevenson began

of a wide variety of works and were champions of little-known music and composers. Both were authors, striving to share their knowledge of musics of many times and places in the printed word and in lecture-recitals. And both revered the work of Walt Whitman, that great poet of inclusivity, the pioneering spirit and the open road.

As the correspondence of the two men grew, their mutual admiration deepened. So impressed was Grainger with Stevenson's writing that in 1959 he requested that all of Stevenson's articles be sent to the Grainger Museum: 'You are a magnificent worder [...]. Your complete articles (now or in a near future) ought to make an impressive collection'.[4] Stevenson soon realised that he wanted to write at length on Grainger and in his last letter to him, dated 7 February 1961, wrote: 'My work on your music is growing out of hand and can now only assume the form of a book'. It is a correspondence which sheds light on the thoughts of one man coming to the end of his creative life and the other just entering into his most fertile period of productivity. They were like messengers crossing in the night, passing a torch.

Percy Grainger was born on 8 July 1882, in Melbourne, Australia to the architect John Grainger and his wife Rose Aldridge Grainger. His first piano teacher was his mother, followed by Louis Pabst[5] and Adelaide Burkitt. In 1895 he and his mother travelled to Frankfurt am Main, Germany where he was enrolled at the Hoch Conservatory, studying piano with James Kwast and composition with Iwan Knorr. During his years at the Hoch Conservatory he first began composing in an experimental style, working with the word-rhythms of natural speech (*Love Verses from 'The Song of Solomon'*) and extended melody and irregular rhythms (*Hill-Song No. 1*).[6] In 1901 the Graingers moved to London where he embarked on a successful career as a concert artist. During this period he became interested in British folk-song, collecting his first songs with the aid of an Edison-Bell phonograph in 1906. In that same year he met and was befriended by Edvard Grieg, of whose Piano Concerto he became the leading exponent. In 1909

[4] Letter 12, dated 12 June 1959; *cf.* p. 88, below. In the event, it was to be half a century before an anthology of Stevenson's writings appeared: *Song in Gold Pavilion: Ronald Stevenson on Music*, ed. Chris Walton, University of Pretoria Press, Pretoria, 2009. *Busoni: Aspects of a Genius*, the first volume (of two) of *Ronald Stevenson on Music and Musicians*, is in preparation from Toccata Press.

[5] Born in Germany in 1846, Louis Pabst had studied in St Petersburg under Anton Rubinstein and moved to Melbourne in 1884. Grainger began studying with Pabst around 1891 and often referred to him as 'the best piano teacher of my life'.

[6] First composed in 1901–2 'for large room-music ensemble' (24 solo instruments), the *Hill-Song No. 1* was rescored in 1921 and revised two years later.

he first allowed some of his folk-music settings to be publicly performed at a concert of contemporary British music, and their success encouraged him to release more of his works.

In 1914 Grainger and his mother moved to the United States, where he made a stunning recital debut at New York's Aeolian Hall. In 1916–17 three of Grainger's large-scale works, *In a Nutshell, The Warriors* and *Marching Song of Democracy*, received their premieres. In 1917 his father died in Melbourne, and Grainger enlisted in the United States Army Band. After being discharged from the army in 1919, he began an association with the Chicago Musical College summer school which would last until 1931. In 1921 Grainger and his mother purchased a home in White Plains, New York, and the following year Rose Grainger committed suicide, as a result of mental illness brought on by syphilis (contracted from her husband before Grainger's birth). In 1926 Grainger undertook a concert tour of Australia and on board ship returning home met his future wife, Ella Viola Strom, whom he would marry in 1928.

In 1932 Grainger spent a year as associate professor and head of the music department at New York University and the following year travelled to Australia to found the Grainger Museum as a repository for musical memorabilia and a centre for the study of Anglo-Saxon, Nordic and ethnic music on the grounds of the University of Melbourne. (The Grainger Museum would be officially opened in 1938.) It was also in 1932 that Grainger met the English musicologist Dom Anselm Hughes and began a 28-year collaboration with him which would result in eighteen editions of *English Gothic Music*, music dating from around the year 1000 to the first half of the fifteenth century in England. In 1937 he joined the teaching staff of the National Music Camp at Interlochen, Michigan and would spend most summers there until 1944. From 1941–45 Grainger travelled widely, giving concerts for the American Red Cross and the war effort.

In 1945 Grainger met Burnett Cross, a science teacher and science editor for the publisher Harcourt Brace, with whom he would enjoy a fifteen-year partnership in creating instruments for the production of Grainger's 'Free Music', music freed from the limitations of fixed pitch, harmony and rhythm which he had first heard in his mind as a boy and written about as a man.[7] In 1953 Grainger underwent the first

[7] Between 1946 and 1961 Grainger and Burnett Cross developed a number of experimental machines for the production of Grainger's 'Free Music', music freed of the tyranny of set pitches and able to glide, with precision, to any microtonal space. Grainger called these instruments 'Tone Tools' in keeping with his desire to free the English language of any words of foreign derivation, in this case replacing the Latin-derived 'instrument'. The first to be developed was the

of many operations for prostate cancer. During the time that he was corresponding with Stevenson (from 22 August 1957 until 18 October 1960), Grainger was experiencing much physical pain and distress but also rejoiced in the successful completion of several Free Music machines, the publication in full of his *Kipling 'Jungle Book' Cycle*, and the recording of many of his band works by Frederick Fennell and Richard Franko Goldman. Shortly after Christmas 1960, his health had deteriorated to the extent that he had to be admitted to the White Plains Hospital, and he died there on 20 February 1961, only thirteen days after Stevenson had written his last letter to him.

Ronald Stevenson was born on 6 March 1928 in Blackburn, Lancashire, to a working-class family of Scottish descent. He studied piano from the age of eight and began accompanying and composing for the Blackburn Ballet company at fifteen. He received an open scholarship to the Royal Northern College of Music in Manchester in 1945, studying piano with Lucy Pierce and Iso Elinson and composition with Richard Hall, and graduated with distinction in 1948. As a conscientious objector in the years after World War II, he was imprisoned and later sent to Freighting Hall Farm, Colchester, during which time he set all of William Blake's *Songs of Innocence* for voice and piano. After the War he spent a year-and-a-half teaching music at Boldon Colliery School, Durham, before moving to Edinburgh in 1952, where he would teach at a number of schools and lecture for the Workers' Educational Association until 1963.

'Solovox-and-Melanette Tone-Tool' which played from a perforated paper roll operating in a silenced reproducing piano. No sooner had they perfected this instrument than an improvement came to mind, represented by the 'Reed-Box Tone-Tool' played by suction controlled by perforated-wrapping paper rolls; it was on this device that the first precisely planned gliding chords were executed and recorded. Next came the 'Hills-and-Dales Oscillator-Player' in which a vacuum-tube oscillator is played by a lever moved up and down by a roll of wrapping paper stood on end and cut with 'hills' and 'dales' for high and low intervals and capable of producing perfect glides. The 'Kangaroo Pouch Tone-Tool' of 1952 incorporated eight vacuum-tube oscillators operated by their own pitch- and volume-control graphs connected by metal arms to sheets of wrapping paper. This very tall machine nearly reached the ceiling of Grainger's living room, and they were seriously considering cutting a hole in the ceiling to extend its reach when they decided to use photocell technology instead. The final constructions were the only ones to bear the title 'Free Music Machine' and were much more compact, using rolls of clear plastic painted with bands of black plastic ink to denote pitch and volume which was then read by photocells. The final machine, completed in 1960, not long before Grainger's death in February the next year, was capable of seven-part polyphonic glides and instantaneous leaps. *Cf.* also note 6 on p. 29.

Ronald Stevenson at his desk in West Linton, around the time he began his correspondence with Percy Grainger

In 1952 Stevenson married Marjorie Spedding, and their son Gordon was born in 1953. In 1955 Stevenson received an open scholarship from the Italian government to study in Rome at the Conservatorio di Santa Cecilia and research the work of Ferruccio Busoni. In 1956 the Stevensons made their home in West Linton, Peeblesshire, where their daughters, Gerda and Ella Savourna,[8] were born. On Christmas Eve 1960 Stevenson began work on his monumental work for piano solo, the *Passacaglia on DSCH* dedicated to Dmitri Shostakovich, and completed it in 1962. From 1963–65 he occupied the position of Senior Lecturer in Composition at the University of Cape Town before returning to Scotland, where

[8] Ella Savourna was, in fact, named for Ella Grainger, who, after Percy's death, became a close friend of the Stevensons. The other two Stevenson children had famous namesakes as well: Gordon was named after the British actor, producer, director and scenic designer Edward Gordon Craig (1877–1966), and Gerda after Gerda Busoni, Ferruccio Busoni's widow. On Craig, *cf.* also p. 60, below.

he received an Arts Council award the following year. Deciding to devote himself exclusively to composing, performing and lecturing, he embarked on a series of world-wide concert tours, while receiving commissions from, among others, Yehudi Menuhin and the BBC. In 1971 his book *Western Music: An Introduction* was published by Kahn & Averill, London.

During the 1970s and '80s Stevenson continued to perform and lecture widely, his many broadcasts including three series of programmes for Radio Scotland on Scottish traditional music. In 1982 he was artist-in-residence at the University of Melbourne in Australia, in 1985 Visiting Professor in Shanghai Conservatory, and in 1987 composer-in-residence at the University of York. In 1986 the first of a series of recordings by Stevenson of his own works and music by Grainger, Busoni, Liszt and others were released by the Altarus label.[9]

Throughout his career Stevenson has composed in a wide variety of styles, working in almost every musical form,[10] although the majority of his works (as were Grainger's) are for piano solo, solo song or chorus. The one exception has been his avoidance of sonata form or any structure rooted in 'musical conflict'. As a song-writer he has enjoyed a tremendous range of literary inspirations, from settings of Rabindranath Tagore to Chinese verses by Ho Chi Minh, Vietnamese miniatures and Japanese haiku, the Gaelic works of Sorley MacLean and the radical poetry of Hugh MacDiarmid. His Piano Concerto No. 2, *The Continents*, first performed in 1972 at the Henry Wood Promenade Concerts in London (the composer was the soloist), provided further amplification of his ideal of world music, travelling through the world's musics in five continental sections. As he wrote in *Western Music*, 'the sum of world music is the complete music of mankind'.[11]

As was Grainger, Stevenson too is an enthusiastic practitioner of the art of transcription, the art of arranging a pre-existing work for another medium. Stevenson's transcriptions encompass an enormous range of styles, from the *Peter Grimes Fantasy* on themes from Benjamin Britten's opera (commissioned by BBC TV with Britten's approval) to

[9] *Percy Grainger 'Salute to Scotland'*, Altarus AIR-CD-9040; *The Essence of Busoni*, Altarus AIR-CD-9041; *Twentieth-Century Operatic Fantasias*, Altarus AIR-CD-9042; *Cathedrals in Sound*, Altarus AIR-CD-9043; *Ferruccio Busoni: Music for two pianos and piano duet* (with Joseph Banowetz), Altarus AIR-CD-9044.

[10] The List of Works compiled by Martin Anderson in Colin Scott-Sutherland (ed.), *Ronald Stevenson: The Man and his Music* (Toccata Press, London, 2005), occupies no fewer than 85 pages.

[11] *Op. cit.*, p. 208.

Percy and Rose Grainger (on left) with a group at Pension Pfaff, Frankfurt, 1895

the *Ragmaster* written as a tribute to the jazz musician Eubie Blake. From his very earliest years also, Stevenson has numbered among his output many 'homages' to 'artist comrades' who have touched his life, from the 1949 *Fantasy on Doktor Faust* (from Busoni) to the 1989 *Corroboree for Grainger.*

In more recent years Stevenson has concentrated his attention on efforts toward world peace. His *Peace Motets* for four-part mixed chorus (1984–87) set various Biblical texts, ending with 'Blessed are the Peacemakers'. His sixtieth birthday in 1988 was celebrated with two 'Concerts for Peace' in Edinburgh and Glasgow. He has been part of the Edinburgh Peace Festival and gave a recital to celebrate the United Nations' decision to refer to the World Court the question of the legality of the manufacture of nuclear weapons. It was in 1987–88 that he wrote the *Motus Perpetuus Temporibus Fatalibus* on the theme of the threat of nuclear catastrophe, combining the monograms BACH, DSCH (Shostakovich), FB (Busoni) and ASCH (Schoenberg) in a twelve-note series.

During the time of his correspondence with Grainger, Stevenson was enjoying an extremely fruitful creative period. He had not long moved into the house that is still his home, in West Linton, and his second child had been born. The following year he would embark on a series of tours, lectures and essays. In his last letter to Grainger, dated 7 February 1961, he wrote: 'I have been engulfed and deluged with work on all sides, and, in the middle – no in the *vortex* – of it all – I have been (and still am) embroiled in the best creative period of my 33 years'.[12]

The themes of the Grainger-Stevenson correspondence range from Busoni to Delius and Bach, English-speaking innovations in art, the music of little-known composers, Grainger's compositions and his intense dislike of the piano as an artistic medium. It was Busoni that brought them together and yet their views on Busoni as a composer differed in the extreme. Grainger responded to Stevenson's request for memories of Busoni by remarking, 'I have a lot to remember of Busoni, but I am not sure it is the kind of thing anyone who admires Busoni would want. His behavior to me ranged from great generosity to sharp spitefulness. The fact was that I didn't admire his compositions in the least'.[13] Stevenson replied with surprising generosity of spirit: 'You say your memories of Busoni may not be the kind of thing an admirer of his would want. Then I say "Hurrah" – that is *just* what I want; for the *last* thing I intend to do is to write a hagiography'.[14] Their views on the place of Johann Sebastian Bach in music history differed as well and led to a highly creative essay by Stevenson in which he juxtaposed their positions in an 'Imaginary Conversation'[15] based on Grainger's correspondence and published articles.

They found common ground in their championing of little-known music, and Grainger wrote to Stevenson 'I consider very noble your championship of undervalued or overlooked talents, such as Busoni & Maurice Emmanuel'.[16] Likewise, they were united in their appreciation for English-speaking innovation and advancement in the arts, a theme which Grainger had been promoting for many years.[17] Early on in the

[12] *Cf.* Letter 33, p. 119, below.

[13] Letter 1, dated 22 August 1957; *cf.* p. 76, below.

[14] Letter 2, dated 13 September 1957; *cf.* p. 77, below.

[15] *Bach and Wagner: A Journey in Music (An Imaginary Conversation between Percy Grainger and the Author)*, published in 1980 in *The Grainger Journal*, Vol. 3, No. 1, pp. 10–13; reproduced on pp. 176–80, below.

[16] Letter 12, dated 12 June 1959; *cf.* p. 88, below.

[17] As in his 'English-Speaking Music and the War Effort', a radio broadcast given for the Australian Broadcasting Commission on 21 October 1943, and 'Characteristics of Nordic Music', a radio broadcast given on WEVD (New York) on 4 July 1933, published in Malcolm Gillies and Bruce Clunies Ross (eds.), *Grainger on Music*, Oxford University Press, Oxford, 1999, pp. 258–66.

correspondence Stevenson suggested a Percy Grainger Festival and offered to write clean copies of some of Grainger's scores. Grainger was touched by this generosity but replied: 'I *have* to write them all out myself – this is the way I work them up (you have lovely music-writing & letter-writing, by the way)'.[18] In 1960 Stevenson prepared a piano transcription of Grainger's *Hill-Song No. 1* for the celebration of his 78th birthday 'because I wanted to hear as often as I like this music which I love and admire'.[19] On 20 July Grainger replied:

> I was looking at your piano solo transcription of my *Hillsong No. 1* this morning & admiring it. You are a splendid craftsman, indeed [...]. I feel *greatly* honored that you should wish to investigate my music so thoroughly, & I congratulate you on your mastery of graceful details – in wording, in your handwriting, in your transcribing.[20]

The correspondence contains insight into Grainger's views of himself as a composer as he explains himself to his young friend. When Stevenson wrote suggesting that he would like to write an article on Grainger, the older man replied:

> My main view is this: that I am essentially an experimental composer, & that several of my innovations have been caught up into the body of 'modern music', things such as my discordant harmony (leading by way of Cyril Scott's to Schoenberg's atonalism), my irregular rhythms (leading by way of C. Scott's sonata Op. 66 to Stravinsky's irregular rhythms in The Rite of Spring), my large chamber-music (Hill-songs I, etc.) leading to Vaughan Williams's, Schoenberg's, Stravinsky's, Hindemith's large chamber music.[21]

He added: 'it should be clearly understood between us that what I send is strictly "one man's opinion only" & that I will not expect you to agree with me on any point'.[22] But in his last letter to Grainger, dated 7 February 1961, Stevenson wrote, 'I am convinced of the *rightness* of your claims as the first innovator of the 20th century and shall seek to attest to them.'[23] It is to be hoped that Grainger was able to read this letter before his death on 20 February: it would undoubtedly have given him much satisfaction.

[18] Letter 6, dated 10 August 1958; *cf.* p. 83, below.

[19] Letter 28, dated 5 July 1960; *cf.* p. 111, below.

[20] Letter 30; *cf.* p. 116, below.

[21] Letter 14, dated 4 July 1959; *cf.* p. 93, below.

[22] *Ibid.*

[23] Letter 33; *cf.* p. 121, below.

Stevenson in his 'Den of Musiquity' in West Linton, around 1995, with Whitman's Leaves of Grass on the desk before him

Speaking of his affinity for Grainger, Stevenson considers that 'I'm in collaboration with his spirit and always have been!'[24] He has often remarked that he looked on Grainger as a mentor: 'he gave me the confidence to pursue Scottish music. After all, he said that Scottish music, Scottish folk music, was his emancipation'.[25] It was in the 1950s that Stevenson began to immerse himself in Scottish traditional music, creating settings of poems by the Scots Sorley MacLean and Hugh MacDiarmid and embarking on a series of *Scottish Folk-Music Settings* patterned after the *British Folk-Music Settings* of Grainger, to whom he dedicated the works. In 1998 Alastair Chisholm would write of these early works: 'it is worth remembering that thirty years ago Stevenson stood alone as a nationalist Scottish composer, scorned by the establishment'.[26] In 1915 Grainger wrote of his own *British Folk-Music Settings,* 'I thought a few years ago that folk-music was not paid enough attention in England, and on that account I devoted

[24] In an interview with the author on 10 November 1998; *cf.* p. 53, below.

[25] *Ibid.*

[26] 'Stevenson's Soutar Settings in the Context of Some Personal Memories', *Chapman,* Nos. 89–90 (double issue), Summer 1998, pp. 74–76.

myself exclusively to arranging folk-music for a time'.[27] Grainger and Stevenson both believed, as Grainger wrote, that 'music should belong to the people, and we can best bring them to an understanding and enjoyment of the greatest music thru folk-music, the natural expression of the people'.[28]

Grainger and Stevenson were both advocates of universalism but realised that the way must be nourished by local roots. Grainger felt that 'the basis of all art is racial'[29] and that the way of great creative art is from the local to the national to the universal. Stevenson once wrote: 'I think all great art aspires beyond nationalism, as an exploration of occult regions of experience. But I am convinced that a people's culture cannot get beyond nationalism until it has *realised* it'.[30] In 1925 Grainger expressed his view that 'art should be one of the meeting-places of all races, without racial, national or local prejudices, jealousies, or smallnesses'.[31] In 1933 – after the Nazis had seized power in Germany – he wrote: 'As I see it, the greatest need of music today is the need of universalism in every aspect of the word. The only healthy thing to-day is to be able, as far as possible, to admire the products of all ages, all races, all styles, and all schools'.[32] Just as Grainger believed that music should be used to bring the people of the world together, Stevenson wrote that 'Music [...] is one, as the human race is one. As humanity achieves unity [...] music will achieve unity also, because it reflects reality [...].'[33] In such works as the *Passacaglia on DSCH*, the Piano Concerto No. 2 (*The Continents*) and the Violin Concerto, he incorporated the diverse elements of many forms of music to create his own 'world music'.

[27] Quoted by William Armstrong in 'Percy Aldridge Grainger: Australian Composer and Pianist', *The Musician* XX/8, August 1915, p. 496.

[28] In interview with Edna Horton, 'Rare Music of Early English Age Restored', *Musical Courier*, 1 October 1939.

[29] Quoted in John Kennedy, 'Anybody Can Play the Piano: An Interview with Percy Grainger', *Collier's*, No. 80, 24 September 1927.

[30] Ronald Stevenson in a letter to Ateş Orga dated 30 April 1968, quoted in Malcolm MacDonald, *Ronald Stevenson: A Musical Biography*, National Library of Scotland, Edinburgh, 1989, p. 95.

[31] Letter to Nathaniel Dett, 6 March 1925, published (as Letter 20) in Malcolm Gillies and David Pear (eds.), *The All-Round Man: Selected Letters of Percy Grainger, 1914–1961*, Clarendon Press, Oxford, 1994, p. 74.

[32] 'Percy Grainger's Fighting Creed: His Guiding Principles as a Composer', *The Australian Musical News*, 1 October 1924, pp. 17–18.

[33] Ronald Stevenson, *Western Music: An Introduction*, *op. cit.*, p. 197.

Both men were involved in what Grainger called the 'Walt Whitman business', 'trying to relish and tally the myriad attractiveness of a million different arts and expressions'.[34] The 'great grey poet' was a source of inspiration and another meeting point for Stevenson and Grainger. Both admired his pioneering spirit, love of life and the common man, delight in nature and the human body, openness, expansiveness and the comradery that he evoked. Stevenson claimed that Grainger was 'wide', 'Whitmanesque', 'inclusive'; 'Whitman is so essential to Grainger and to an understanding of Percy. [...] he was [...] a pioneer, a Whitmanesque pioneer'.[35] Of his own relationship to Whitman, Stevenson said 'I'm devoted to Walt Whitman. I feel such a relationship with his ideas'.[36] The influence of Whitman on the two composers went far deeper than the mere setting of words to music: it infused their outlook on life and art.

The two men exchanged many manuscripts, articles and recordings during the four years of their correspondence. Stevenson consistently championed Grainger's music, writing about it and performing it in concert. In his recorded performances of Grainger's piano works, he has something of the wild dash and fearless boldness that characterised so many of Grainger's own recordings. He has captured the Grainger spirit as well as the notes and is, in my opinion, the supreme interpreter of many of Grainger's works. Grainger wrote in admiration of Stevenson's abilities as composer, author, speaker and performer, elaborating in 1959: 'What a delightful lecturer you are & what an exquisite pianist! Your tone-differentiation (bringing out middle melodic lines) is superb'.[37] Had they been age-mates, met when Grainger was actively engaged in promoting the work of other composers, I have no doubt he would have championed Stevenson's music as well.

Stevenson's immersion in Grainger's work and psyche has given him insights into his art that are profound. He was perhaps the first to realise that Grainger, like Whitman, had his art rooted in nature: 'he called for "humanity" music. [...] His music was related to people, not only the folk music collection, but everything he did'.[38] He called him '"Music's Mowgli", the natural man of music, more than anybody else.

[34] Letter to Cyril Scott dated 19 November 1947.

[35] In interview with the author on 10 November 1998; *cf.* p. 33, below.

[36] *Ibid.*

[37] Letter 11, dated 6 May 1959; *cf.* p. 88, below.

[38] In interview with the author on 10 November 1998; *cf.* p. 51, below.

[...] He wanted music to be a natural expression'.[39] Stevenson was the first to illustrate the incredible aural relationship between Grainger's *Free Music No. 1* and the sound of a pack of wolves howling.[40] He saw Grainger as a prophet of 21st-century music, an experimenter whose roots reached far down into the folk soul:

> Percy had his roots as deep down as possible in the reality of folk music and shot above that as high as possible to the abstraction of the stars. [...] I think that Percy was a prophet of this century because he did not get bogged down in experiment. [...] I believe that Percy experimented from experience.[41]

Stevenson added his own prophetic note when he stated:

> He was really an instigator and true revolutionary who had a great knowledge of the past; and his revolution was based on the knowledge of the accumulation of past history and perspective, like a triangle, two angles of which, the past and the present, were given which predetermined the third angle, the future.[42]

At a time when much prurient interest has been attached to Grainger's personal life, sexual behaviour and purported anti-Semitism, Stevenson raises the voice of a sage: 'He did have a morality about art and indeed about life. Whatever are considered aberrations he was very honest about, very open, too open I think for most people'.[43] To the charge of racism Stevenson offers the response that Grainger is no longer here to provide:

> he was a racist in the non-pejorative sense. [...] He was interested in races. [...] he made a profound study of music and peoples. [...] One shouldn't have to justify him because he's the justification of himself, his work is his own justification. [...] His published articles [...] give ample proof that he was totally open to American Jewish composers and admiring of their work'[44]

[39] *Ibid.* In 'Music's Mowgli' (*Books and Bookmen*, Vol. 22, No. 6, March 1977, pp. 18–19) Stevenson compares Grainger to Kipling's natural boy of *The Jungle Book* stories; *cf.* p. 134, below.

[40] *Cf.* p. 139, below.

[41] *Ibid.*

[42] *Ibid.*

[43] *Ibid.*

[44] *Ibid.*

Grainger railed against the establishment and the powers-that-be, but his support of individual composers, whether the African-American Nathaniel Dett or Jewish composers such as Ernest Bloch and George Gershwin among many others, was unstinting.

Ronald Stevenson has often dreamed about writing his own book on Percy Grainger, a book that would provide insights into the man and his art from the perspective of a 'comrade in art'. In one of his later letters to Grainger, Stevenson wrote:

> It is strange that a composer of your years should still provide an article writer with something new to say. Stranger still when one reflects that some of the music that is 'newest' was written 60 years ago! [...] But if it is strange, it is also inspiring, for it means that your music still presents a challenge.[45]

Two weeks later Grainger sent Stevenson a similar endorsement: 'my conviction is that anything & everything written by you is certain to be print-worthy in the extreme'.[46]

The correspondence, interviews, lectures and articles which follow are indeed 'print-worthy in the extreme' and offer insights into the philosophies and artistic methods of two outstanding creative artists of the twentieth century. These two comrades in art, united by their love of the natural and the free, with a passion for the roots of folk art combined with a love of experimentation and joyful embrace of the new, a desire to spread the knowledge and understanding of the world's musics and convinced of the uses of music for world peace, never meeting in the flesh yet continually meeting in the mind, offer to a world in dire need the message of a freer, more democratic, all-embracing vision of the future of art. As Grainger wrote, music should

> refine our emotional susceptibilities, thereby making music-lovers (and perhaps mankind, in general) more receptive to all those delicate stirs that make for world-peace and for a gentler and happier life on this globe. I look on music as a religious art, a form of devotion, and essentially an art in which many different personalities blend into one harmonious whole.[47]

Stevenson concludes:

> I believe that the future will see – or rather, hear – musical multilingualism [...]. This music will wait, as truth waits, to be discovered. It cannot

[45] Letter 22, dated 14 May 1960; *cf.* p. 106, below.

[46] Letter 23, dated 18 May 1960; *cf.* p. 107, below.

[47] Percy Grainger, 'Percy Grainger to Broadcast', undated press release, c. 1934.

> be forced [...]. Goethe spoke of 'world citizenship'. Such a concept implies the necessity of world music. The epic artist [...] as a man [...] will know that conflict is the law of divided society; but as a musician, he will know that unity is equally a law of that great harmony which is music and which one day will reflect the reality of society united.'[48]

The correspondence is reproduced here as in the letters themselves, with idiosyncratic spellings (a hallmark of Grainger's writing) uncorrected. The only editorial license I have allowed myself is the conversion of underlined words and phrases into italics. In Part III, Stevenson's Writings on Grainger, Stevenson's original footnotes are indicated with '–RS'.

Teresa Balough
Old Lyme, Connecticut
14 February 2009

Acknowledgements

This book could never have been completed without the active involvement of Ronald Stevenson and his wife Marjorie. It had its incipit during a visit to the Stevensons' home in West Linton, below Edinburgh, in 1996 when Ronald and I were discussing his long-harboured desire to publish a compilation of his correspondence with Percy Grainger. Finding a publisher in Martin Anderson of Toccata Press, the work eventually grew to include Stevenson's scholarly writings on Grainger, buttressed by two lengthy interviews, one from autumn 1998 and the other from summer 2005, in which Stevenson was given an opportunity to expand upon and summarise his thoughts on Grainger. Marjorie Stevenson was an active part of the entire process and also went to considerable length to elucidate obscure references; many of the footnotes bear silent witness to her assiduous detective work. My husband, Owen Peagler, who accompanied me on each of the visits to West Linton, was also a constant support and editorial advisor. It is because of Marjorie's and Owen's firm belief in the project and their warm encouragement at every step that this book is dedicated to them. Last but not least, very warm thanks are due to our publisher, Martin Anderson, who went far beyond the call of duty in helping to track down elusive information and making helpful suggestions about the text. This book has benefited considerably from his input.

The photograph on p. 19 was taken by Colin Scott-Sutherland, to whom go thanks. I took the one on p. 8, and Ronald Stevenson supplied the one on p. 31. All the others are reproduced by permission of the Estate of Percy Aldridge Grainger, with thanks to Barry Ould.

[48] *Western Music: An Introduction, op. cit.*, pp. 207–8.

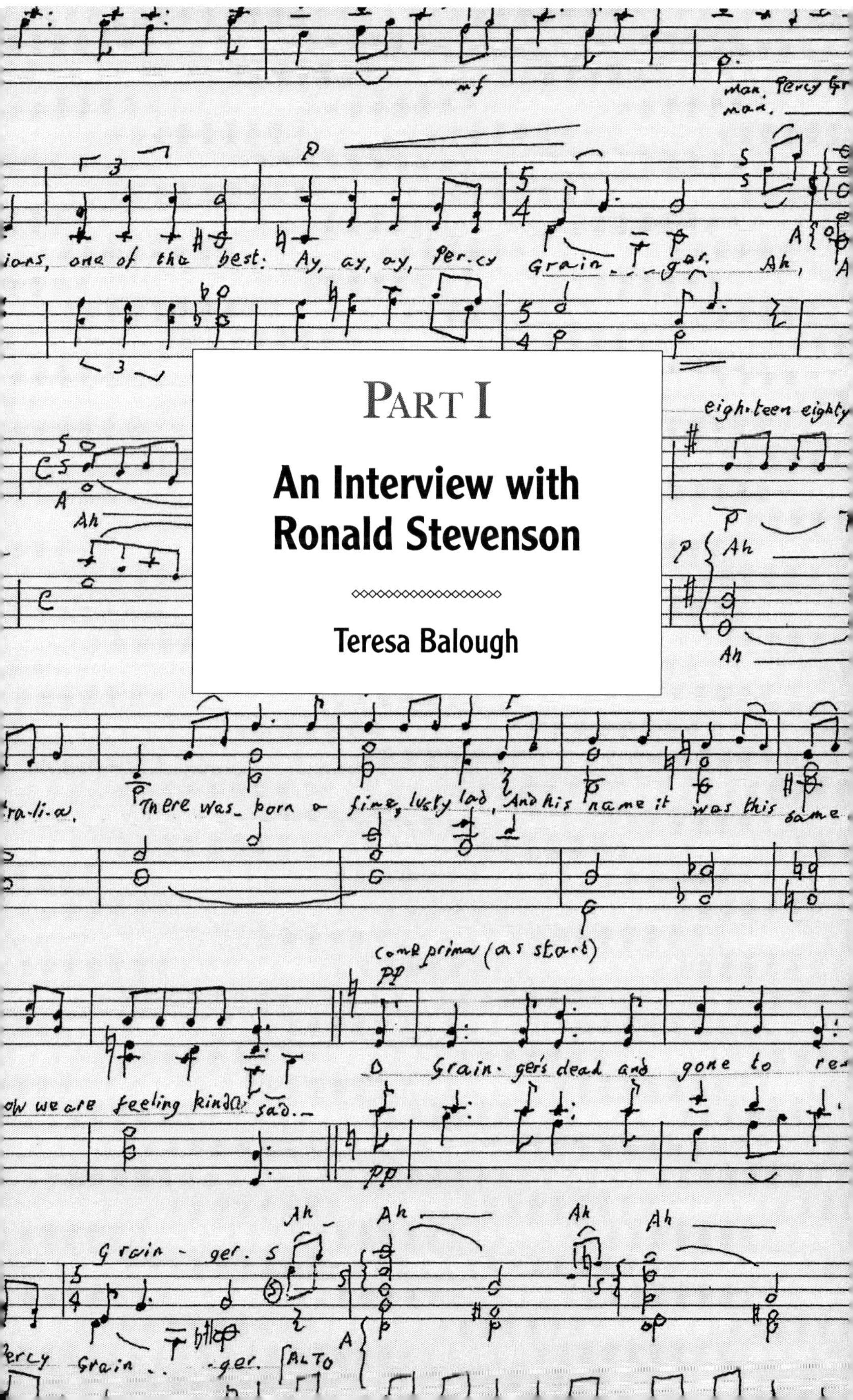

Part I

An Interview with Ronald Stevenson

Teresa Balough

If you were writing a book or an essay about Grainger today, what would you like to say about him?[1]

Well, I think I have more perspective about his work. I think I would describe him as a composer of the 21st century; at least if the 21st century aspires and achieves half of what he implied, I think that would be marvellous. I think that art is essentially aristocratic. In Percy's case he was concerned about its being democratic in a very wide, broad sense. I think he was both actually. I mean, K. K. Nygaard[2] told me how keen he [Grainger] was about checking all sorts of musical article details and running out of the room and bringing a book in at meal time and finding the quote that he wanted and so on. I think he was scholarly, though he wore his scholarship very lightly so that people thought he was a playboy. Perhaps that was his own fault, that he allowed people to think that; or perhaps he even enjoyed that view of himself, that persona.

I have written a good deal about him, and I hold to everything I've written about him. I think it's true when I described him as 'Music's Mowgli',[3] the natural man of music, more than anybody else. But I think there are other things one could say as well as that. I think his aesthetic predated all the discussions about Soviet socialist realism and went much further than that because it wasn't limited to a specific political viewpoint or a biased viewpoint. It was wide; it was Whitmanesque; it was all-inclusive. I have an interview about all the stramash that was caused in America about Shostakovich, and Percy was asked about it; and his reply to the press would have made many people think that Percy was a communist, which he wasn't.[4]

[1] Recorded on 10 November 1998; **M** indicates a contribution from Marjorie Stevenson, the composer's wife.

[2] Kaare Kristian Nygaard (1903–89), Norwegian-American sculptor and surgeon, began a surgical practice in White Plains, New York in 1940 and became physician and close personal friend to Grainger.

[3] *Cf.* p. 134, below.

[4] An article by the violinist Louis Krasner ('Crisis in the Arts', *Syracuse University Alumnus News,* May 1969, p. 14) recorded Grainger's skilfully oblique defence of Shostakovich who, on an official visit to the United States in 1949, had naturally been constrained to defend Soviet cultural policy in his public pronouncements, polarising opinion in the American press. Krasner, who was concert-master of the Minneapolis Symphony Orchestra at the time, was then touring with the

You know, there's been so much said and written and so much, I personally think, nonsense perpetrated about Percy and his ideas; and it seems to me that you have had all along what I view as the correct understanding of what Percy was doing, which so many people couldn't fathom or took in the wrong direction, or they didn't bother to look at the whole picture. What are your views on the direction that's being taken towards his work today? I know there are so many recordings, there's a lot of performance; but what about the ideals, the idealism of the man? Do you think that's being addressed?

No, I think it's the mountain top, and people can't see it.

So most people are not seeing what Percy was really doing. What do you feel should be the next step, or what would you ideally see as the next step?

---

orchestra, Dimitri Mitropoulos, its conductor, and Grainger, their concerto soloist. Krasner's recollections contain a brief but perceptive character-sketch of Grainger:

> After a long night on the train, we arrived in Winnipeg. Mitropoulos and I taxied to the hotel together. As we entered the hotel lobby, several reporters rushed up to the Maestro, informed of the heated debate among musicians as it was carried in the national news media and pressed him for a statement. The issue was so presented that it seemed necessary to attack Shostakovich in order to uphold the right of an artist's freedom of expression.
>
> Mitropoulos hesitated and searched for words. Any defense of the composer would, it seemed, uphold Communist dictatorship. (And he was aware that the orchestra's manager and its board of trustees were becoming concerned about his public statements.)
>
> Just at that moment Mr. Grainger [...] strode into the hotel lobby and greeted us enthusiastically. It was a pleasure to see this open, joyous spirit of a man. Mitropoulos reacted instantly.
>
> 'Here,' he urged the reporters, 'you have our soloist, our pianist, he is a famous composer – he writes music. Do ask him. As an Australian he is unbiased and non-partisan. He can tell you from personal experience how a composer reacts to the question.'
>
> All eyes turned to the thin, wiry frame of Percy Grainger, who stood with ruddy complexion and beaming, questioning eyes. He had walked from the railway station, rucksack on his shoulder. Grainger was an eternal boy scout, a nature-lover, a vegetarian, and a practicing Spartan; he was no theorist. He lived a hardy life – no luxuries, no special needs, no services. He was a self-sufficient character and had not heard of the controversy. The reporters explained what had happened in recent days in New York City and then asked him what he thought of Shostakovich, who seemed willing to accept the idea that his government could tell him what to write.
>
> 'Huh,' shrugged Grainger, responding in his well-known singular, non-conformist manner, 'I wish my government would care what I write. They don't give a hoot if I ever write a note!'

I discussed this with our dear friend, Percy's dear friend, Burnett;[5] and Burnett thought that the Free Music[6] should be introduced in a strategic way, and he asked me if I had any ideas about how it might be done. I thought perhaps a surreptitious way of introducing it was in the interval of a concert or maybe in the beginning before people have gone to their seats, and to have a recording playing softly, even without any announcement, and from time to time to introduce the music like this without any announcement so that people could have open minds about it as far as they could. And then, if and when, hopefully when, it was performed in a concert, the context they would remember. It wouldn't seem entirely unfamiliar. Burnett agreed. He thought that was an excellent idea which had not been suggested by anybody else. I thought that Burnett's recordings could be played on tape. And perhaps it doesn't only apply to Percy, it could apply to other music as well, but I think particularly to his because he was doing something so radically new that the method of presentation becomes very important. That came out of a discussion between Burnett and myself, and he was very pleased about it. He agreed very much.

Yes, I think you thought alike in many ways.

[5] William Burnett Cross (1914–96), teacher, author, photographer and Senior Science Editor for Harcourt Brace Jovanovich, was Grainger's collaborator in the production of instruments for the performance of Grainger's 'Free Music' from 1945 to 1961 and became one of his closest friends.

[6] From the time he was a young boy Grainger dreamed of a form of music freed from the restrictions of traditional melody, harmony and rhythm, music that could make use of any and all microtonal pitches and rhythmic variations. This music, which he heard in his mind, he called 'Free Music'. Grainger spent a good portion of the last twenty years of his life trying to duplicate this inner music through the development of machines he created in collaboration with Burnett Cross – *cf.* note 7 on pp. 12–13. The first of these Free Music machines were mechanical, but the final one completed just before his death in 1961 was almost entirely electrical – although, unlike the early forms of electronic music, Grainger's scores were meant to reproduce a pre-existing thought rather than make use of a new tonal resource. The Grainger Museum in Melbourne houses 31 recordings made by Cross and Grainger of sketches for Free Music, including experiments with solovoxes, reed box, reed organ, oscillators, piano rolls and butterfly piano. Two completed works, *Free Music No. 1* and *Free Music No. 2*, have been realised since Grainger's death using computer technology by Les Craythorn and Barry Conyngham, respectively. A version of *Free Music No. 1* prepared by Grainger for four theremins has been recorded by Lydia Kavina for the album *Music from the Ether: Original Works for Theremin* (Mode 76).

Grainger with his doctor and friend K. K. Nygaard, mid-1950s

Yes, I felt that Burnett was a kind of brother of mine. Really, I felt immediately at home with him. And he was the son that Percy Grainger never had.

I love that. That's beautiful. You've often had insights into Percy's music that I've never heard anyone else venture until after you had mentioned it. One of those was the relationship between Free Music and nature, the sounds of nature, such as those wolves howling that you unearthed.[7] *How did you come to that?*

Well, I first of all felt that Percy was so near to nature that he was music's natural man. And he did not have a sentimental view of nature as perhaps some impressionist painters did. He had a very realistic view of nature; one might say 'nature red in tooth and claw'. And he could tally, to use Whitman's phrase, he could tally what was in nature by his own music, by his own character. It was in him as well. I think

[7] In a 1982 lecture recital for the Percy Grainger Centenary Celebration at The University of Western Australia (*cf.* pp. 159–67, below), Stevenson presented a recording of wolves howling followed by a recording of Grainger's *Free Music No. 1* (realised on synthesiser at the University of Melbourne). The resemblance in sounds was uncanny.

Stevenson with Nygaard and his second wife, Gail, three decades later

Whitman is so essential to Grainger and to an understanding of Percy.

Have you written about the relation of Whitman and Grainger?

No! That's something I'd like to do!

That probably only you could do.

I'm devoted to Walt Whitman. I feel such a relationship with his ideas.

And obviously Percy did, too.

Yes. You know, working together to produce this book about Percy, combined with the letters, these thoughts about Percy, is a 'Graingeresque' thing to do! I'm delighted.

Less literary and academic!

Yes. More of what would appeal to the honest-to-goodness music-lover and less, thank goodness, of what would appeal to the dull academic!

There's a wonderful poem by Vachel Lindsay,[8] who was a friend of Percy. I think I have a letter from Percy in which he speaks of Vachel Lindsay. No, is it a letter from Vachel Lindsay?[9] I can't remember. There is a reference somewhere[10] about Percy falling asleep when Vachel was reading his poetry, and then Vachel Lindsay couldn't bear this so he dropped the book very heavily and Percy awoke. (LAUGHTER)

K. K. Nygaard's bust of Grainger

I thought you were going to say he threw the book at him.

No, Percy admired Vachel Lindsay very much. But there is a poem, I think it's 'Eagle under the Snow', and the last line or two of it I think are so apposite to Percy Grainger:

> To live in mankind is far, far more than to live in a name.

And that's what Percy did and what he will continue to do, what the spirit, the Graingeresque spirit will continue to do, to live in mankind. And it will be far more than his name.

M Who is the man who did the book, *The Arts of Mankind* – is it Van Loon?

Van Loon,[11] yes. Van Loon wrote beautifully about all the arts

[8] Nicholas Vachel Lindsay (1879–1931) was an American poet who played the part of a modern troubadour, walking across the country to perform dramatic readings of his works in exchange for bed and board. He is most well known for *General William Booth Enters into Heaven* and *The Congo*, in which he expresses his concern for racial harmony.

[9] Stevenson's correspondence is now preserved in the National Library of Scotland in Edinburgh.

[10] In a letter, now lost, from Victoria Greenwood to Ronald Stevenson. Victoria Greenwood and her husband George were friends and frequent house-guests of Percy and Ella Grainger and accompanied them on a hiking trip on their honeymoon. George Greenwood was also a good pianist and would join Percy in impromptu two-piano recitals at home. (*Cf.* Eileen Dorum, *Percy Grainger: The Man behind the Music*, published by the author, Melbourne, 1986, pp. 129.)

[11] Hendrik Willem van Loon (1882–1944) was a Dutch-American historian and journalist, best-known for *The Story of Mankind,* who wrote many popular history books aimed at young adults. His *The Arts* appeared in 1937.

contributing to the art of life. I think that's what Percy did. The great art is the art of life, very much. Twentieth-century art, I believe, does not contribute to life at all; it's something apart from life. Yes, Vachel Lindsay was a great friend of Percy's.

He [Vachel Lindsay] must have had something in common with the ideas of Walt Whitman as well. That statement sounds almost Whitmanesque.

Yes. 'The Eagle under the Stone' is that poem.[12] I have it somewhere in the house, but I do remember that final couplet which is in some ways the best part. It's the climax of the whole poem. And it delighted me to know that they were friends, you see, that they had met. I feel this very strongly about Percy Grainger that I think of kindred spirits at least having some kinship with Percy; and before I knew it, I find that they had! They did meet. Of course, he met so many people; he was so outward-going. He was far more than a pianist. He was quite right in his attitude to the piano. Of course, he was far more than that, but a very great pianist, especially about 1925, and a pioneer, a Whitmanesque pioneer. He made the first modern recording in the sense of the recording technique. It was the first electrical recording.

[12] 'The Eagle That is Forgotten' was published in *The Little Book of Modern Verse*, ed. Jessie Rittenhouse, Houghton Mifflin, Boston, 1917:

> Sleep softly ... eagle forgotten ... under the stone.
> Time has its way with you there, and the clay has its own.
> 'We have buried him now,' thought your foes, and in secret rejoiced.
> They made a brave show of their mourning, their hatred unvoiced.
> They had snarled at you, barked at you, foamed at you, day after day.
> Now you were ended. They praised you ... and laid you away.
> The others, that mourned you in silence and terror and truth,
> The widow bereft of her crust, and the boy without youth,
> The mocked and the scorned and the wounded, the lame and the poor,
> That should have remembered forever,... remember no more.
> Where are those lovers of yours, on what name do they call,
> The lost, that in armies wept over your funeral pall?
> They call on the names of a hundred high-valiant ones,
> A hundred white eagles have risen, the sons of your sons.
> The zeal in their wings is a zeal that your dreaming began,
> The valor that wore out your soul in the service of man.
> Sleep softly ... eagle forgotten ... under the stone.
> Time has its way with you there, and the clay has its own.
> Sleep on, O brave-hearted, O wise man that kindled the flame—
> To live in mankind is far more than to live in a name,
> To live in mankind, far, far more than to live in a name!—

Percy was the first in so many ways. That was the Chopin Sonata in B Minor, which I heard with my friend Lawrence Glover.[13]

That was the first electrical recording?

Yes, it was. It's historic. Yes.

Not many people know this.

No. That is an important fact historically. They'd all been acoustic recordings before then. That was the first electric.[14]

M And you know Percy's recording of the B minor Sonata. Benjamin Britten told Ronald and me, 'He was the Daddy of them all!' He thought it was so wonderful, that recording.

And Ben Britten also said that he believed the recording which Percy had made in Aarhus, Denmark, of the Grieg Concerto[15] was the most creative recording he'd ever heard and that the avalanches of wrong notes in the cadenza were an appendix to the true art of pianism. (LAUGHTER)

That's the best description of his 'appendixes' I can think of! If you were going to sit down and write a book or an essay about Percy, how would you open it?

Well it depends on the context, for whom I was writing it. I do consider my audience.

[13] The Ulsterman Lawrence Glover was a pianist and fellow student with Stevenson at Manchester College of Music; *cf.* also p. 228 and 249, below.

[14] The Columbia Graphophone Company issued Grainger's recording of the Chopin Sonata in B minor, Op. 58, in 1925 as its first complete electrical recording set.

[15] When Grainger was 75 years old, a live recording was made (on 25 February 1957) of his performance of Edvard Grieg's Piano Concerto in A minor with the Aarhus Municipal Orchestra conducted by Per Dreier. Released by Vanguard Records in 1963, it is considered to be a pinnacle of emotional response over technical mastery. *Cf.* also p. 137, below. The English composer, conductor and pianist Benjamin Britten (1913–76) was also an admirer of and advocate for Grainger's music. In 1966 he presented an entire evening of Grainger music at the Aldeburgh Festival and in 1968 directed the English Chamber Orchestra, the Ambrosian Singers, Peter Pears and John Shirley-Quirk in a recording for Decca of Grainger's folk-music settings.

Burnett Cross with Ella and Percy Grainger, 1951

For yourself.

Ah! Yes, I think it's true that if one is true to oneself, one may contribute to others. But the first thing is to be true to oneself, so what would I say about Percy? Well, I have said a number of things about Percy; but a lot remains to be said. I would try to address myself to young composers of perhaps the future, and I would say that this is an indication of what would be truly progressive, more than anything I know from the twentieth century because Percy had his roots as deep down as possible in the reality of folk-music and shot above that as high as possible to the abstraction of the stars. But there are so many young composers now who like to think that they are being modern by beginning in abstraction, and they never reach reality.

Burnett Cross and Percy Grainger working on Free Music experiments in the early 1950s

M Yes, that reminds me, Ronald; can I interrupt?

You're not interrupting.

M That reminds me that the thing about Percy was that he used electronics and things, he only used it in order to visualise the music that he'd already had in mind. He didn't have the mechanics and then think: 'What can I do with it?'

What toy I can play with? No.

M He used it as a tool to what he envisaged, which is quite the converse with what has happened with some composers, isn't it?

Yes, and he kept the equilibrium between the reality of folk-music, an interest in folk-music, in many folk-musics really, and his appetite for experiment, which I think was considerable. I think that's an important statement, isn't it?

It's a very important statement.

To hold things in equilibrium.

I remember you once told me that you felt that Grainger and Busoni had in a sense held you in equilibrium, the fact that you had these two mentors, so to speak. Would you care to elaborate on that?

Well, I think that Busoni was a grand European; but he did explore, through Natalie Curtis,[16] American Indian music; and he was drawing very near to Percy's aesthetic when he did that. Percy himself collaborated with Natalie Curtis later on. Busoni was in touch with her first, I believe. Certainly they were all together at the American performance conducted by Stokowski of Busoni's *Indian*, Amerindian, *Fantasy*,[17] and Percy wrote about it with great approval. So they did come to the unison of agreement on that issue, on Amerindian music. But I think that Percy struck up for America, for a new world, for the new world, and for Australia, a new world; and Busoni was such a Dantesque European, Italian, that his interests did not extend to so-called primitive music – that's an unpardonable phrase, I think, 'primitive music', it's such a superior voice.

M Well, if you use the word, you must mean it historically, Ronald, mustn't you?

For Busoni, you see, culture was high culture, it was European culture; and yet, you see, Busoni would probably say – I can't prove this but I would guess that he would say – that Dante was at the height of European culture. And yet it was Dante who was the first to write in the vernacular. Everyone before Dante had written in Latin. Dante himself wrote in Latin also, but when he came to write *La Commedia*, when he wrote that, he wrote in the vernacular and he created the

[16] Natalie Curtis Burlin (1875–1921) was an American ethnomusicologist whose *The Indians' Book*, songs and tales from eighteen native American tribes, and *Songs and Tales from the Dark Continent*, transcriptions of works recorded by African students at Hampton Institute in Virginia, Grainger much admired. He arranged for the performance of her *Memories of New Mexico* in 1925 and arranged two of the songs she collected, 'Lullaby' and 'Zulu Song', for vocal ensemble.

[17] Curtis studied briefly with Busoni, and he was aware of her work with American Indians. In 1911 he asked her to send him a selection of Indian melodies, which he incorporated into a work for piano and orchestra called *Indian Fantasy*. It was performed by the Philadelphia Orchestra in 1915 with Leopold Stokowski conducting and Busoni at the piano. For Grainger's comments, *cf.* p. 166, below.

Italian language in doing so. What Dante had to say was so unpalatable to Rome, because he had to free – you know this, there was a price on his head – it was so unpalatable that he had to disguise it, he had to secrete it, and he did it by writing in what was called *terza rima.* He wrote three lines in each stanza, and the form was *a b a,* the next one began *b c b,* and so on; and Dante did that because he wanted to develop a method of writing which would ensure that his poetry could not be curtailed, because people would know that the form had something missing. I think that it is important that this background, the origin of popular culture, truly popular culture, was from a very great intellectual.

M I don't think Percy traversed this, did he? I don't think he got into this territory.

Well, Percy didn't have this feel, but he would have been very interested if we could have conversed about this.

It would have been a great conversation.

It would, it would. Well, I don't think it's irrelevant at all to mention Dante and in doing so I somersault over the map and relate Dante to any so-called primitive person you can quote or to an Amerindian poet writing in his or her vernacular or an Australian Aborigine doing the same in his or her own way. Those are some new thoughts of mine. I don't think I've thought that before. So I don't really think that Busoni and Percy were as different as people think. I mean, they were united through the Amerindian. My picture is that an Indian took Busoni's hand and Grainger's hand, one on each hand, and united them in this interest in Amerindian music.

Yes. On the other hand, you might think that now that Busoni and Grainger are both in the spiritual realms, maybe they've been united by Ronald Stevenson!

M I think that Terry means that sometimes it takes a third party to bring things together.

I believe so.

Well, it's unusual. I know that this is very unusual in my own life, if I may just invoke the first person singular, which all art does according to Walt Whitman (*Song of Myself*). Why not? I do think that it has been my lot to, lot is perhaps too heavy a word, it has been my joy, it *is* my joy to and will be to unite what have been considered to be opposites, to find the harmony, the resolution of the discord, if there is any, if there is any discord. And it's interesting that Natalie Curtis was really the medium for the meeting place of Busoni and Grainger. Percy dealt with Natalie Curtis' work a little later than Busoni did. Percy was very keen on who had the right to do something first and who should be acknowledged to do something first. That doesn't interest me very much personally. It was a point of honour with him because he knew that he'd done some things [first] and the right was for Australia; they should have been given that right, you see. He felt that. But I don't think it matters all that much who did something first. All that matters is that something necessary should be done and should be seen or heard to be done and continue to be done. I think also that Percy was a prophet of this century because he did not get bogged down in experiment. He kept his feet on the ground. He kept his realism. Etymologically, 'experiment' and 'experience' have the same root; and I believe that Percy experimented from experience. And what has happened now in the twentieth century, late in the twentieth century, is that there are people attempting to experiment without experience, without relating it to experience. They have no experience. They haven't won the right to experiment. They've gone berserk, which is unfortunately a Scandinavian-Norse word which doesn't apply to them, although it applies to Percy.[18] You see, Percy's experiments were based on a huge experience. It must have been inherited to some extent; I don't know to what extent. Some of this experience is experience of Australian Aborigines, his experience of being the son of that remarkable mother, perhaps the son also of a very remarkable father if we knew more about the father apart from his drunkenness. The fact that his father, I think, came originally, or his father's family came originally, from Newcastle – and, indeed, if you go to Newcastle, you'll find a Grainger Street (now I don't know, I haven't explored the origin of that Grainger, but it could relate) – and Newcastle has a great musicality. I know: I've worked there, I've lived there. And, you see, it's a kind of borderland, frontier land between the north of England and the south of Scotland and has, indeed, features of both cultures, very Scottish culture. You take the song 'The Keel Row'. Now it's pronounced in Newcastle in the Scottish manner 'The Keel Rau', not 'The Keel Row' (r-o-w). And so it's no wonder that Percy looked north; and his first liberation,

[18] Grainger's love of all things Nordic was pronounced, as was his admiration for the Viking sagas and the courage and fortitude of the Berserker warriors whose single-minded focus on the battle led to a near-unstoppable force. To Grainger's mind this unquenchable frenzy should apply to a true 'warrior' of art as well.

as he wrote, as you well know, was *The Songs of the North,*[19] and they were Scottish songs. And he understood the language very well, the musical language. I believe it is possible to learn a language, a foreign language, a language which is not one's native language, as it is in verbal language that it's possible to learn musical language. Benjamin Britten did it repeatedly because, like Percy, he had a great love of Scotland and Benjamin Britten has a significant number of Scottish works. And he can speak Scots in his music, Benjamin Britten. And Percy could. I think Percy found it less of a jump than Britten did probably because of his Australian background, I would guess, and perhaps because of his friend in Germany from whom he claimed to have one or two composition lessons, Karl Klimsch.[20] Klimsch had these volumes, you see. I have the volumes. I think Percy probably did it more directly than Britten did, but Britten wrote a Scottish Rhapsody for two pianos and orchestra.[21] Some of his last music was settings of Robert Burns, very beautiful, dedicated to the Queen Mother, a very appropriate dedication because she was Scottish, is Scottish. Benjamin Britten, therefore, had a very strong connection with Percy's interest in Scotland. I think that would appeal to him very much. Benjamin Britten is not just to be considered a south English composer. He was that, of course, but he also mastered musical language in such a way that he became multilingual. And I think that is in the true Grainger tradition, to be a multi-linguist in music. And Percy was doing that before Britten did it, and he continued to do it. And I think it is a way that will be shown, I would guess (this is a hazard of mine), I would guess that it is a way that will, should be, or perhaps even must be considered in the next century, considering the history of music in the twentieth century. What has happened, what is the role of folk music, what about Bartók and Kodály.

[19] In 1900, following a three-day walking tour of the Scottish Highlands and while still a student at the Hoch Conservatory in Frankfurt-am-Main, Germany, Grainger made fourteen settings of Scottish folksongs from the collection *Songs of the North (Gathered Together from The Highlands and Lowlands of Scotland)*, edited by A. C. MacLeod and Harold Boulton and first published in London towards the end of the nineteenth century. *Cf.* pp. 160–61, below.

[20] Karl Ferdinand Klimsch (1841–1926) was a lithographer and landscape painter living in Frankfurt with whom Grainger studied composition in addition to his classes at the Hoch Conservatory. According to Grainger, Klimsch was not only his only really helpful composition teacher but also 'interested P.G. in folksong by showing him "Songs of the North", around 1898–1900' (inscribed by Grainger on the edge of the score of *Scotch Folksongs from 'Songs of the North'*).

[21] Britten's *Scottish Ballad* was composed in 1941.

Do you feel that young composers – by looking at Grainger's music, his work, his output, his wide interests – would benefit in seeing this vision?

I think they can only benefit. I think it's bound to happen. I'm not a prophet, but I can't see how it can't happen. But I don't think it's... We can't force it. I think it will happen as an evolutionary process. I don't think it will be a forced birth. I think it will happen naturally through a reassessment of folk-music. Folk-music has become very commercialised in the twentieth century. I think it is not folk-music as it was, and it is a serious question. If there is a valid folk-music now at the end of the twentieth century, who are the folk? Who are the folk making folk-music? They are mainly middle-class students who play at making folk-music just as they play, the middle-class students, some of them from comfortable backgrounds although their university courses are not comfortable financially these days; and they play at 'tearing the trousers' on purpose. That is a caricature of the working class. As a matter of fact, the old working class were photographed in their Sunday best, a very different matter. I don't know where I'm leading myself!

(LAUGHTER) *You're having rambles like Percy did!*

Yes, it is a Graingerous and dangerous modulation into a far-distant key!

And you never know quite where it's going to land you!

Well, back home I think.

Well, there you are. Burnett used to say that Percy was fond of making a statement, kind of leaping with both feet out into thin air and seeing where it landed him. Sometimes it wasn't a palatable place, and he had to move back. Sometimes it was a great insight. It led to many things. How do you view the current craze, it seems like mania, for sensationalising Percy's life? Do you view that as being a detriment to his message or not?

I think he will survive. I'm sure he will survive that. If it is a fault, it was his own fault, I think. But his honesty is very rare. And I think that should be valued, that he was honest about himself. I don't think he intended any sensation at all. I'm sure he did not, and it's very complex.

M He had an ingenuousness, didn't he, in this way that wasn't around in his time?

I think you're absolutely right. He set an example, in a sense, that you were open about things. If they didn't work to your benefit, so be it.

I think far too much is being spoken and written about the so-called aberrations. You see, when I was staying with Ella[22] at the time leading up to the publication of John's[23] Grainger book, I had the proofs. The proofs had been sent to Ella, and she asked me to read them; and I had very busy days, and the only time I could read was late at night. And she would very sweetly come downstairs, counting because of her eyesight, counting in Swedish; and she would say in a very maternal way: 'Ronald, you must go to bed, you mustn't stay up late like this', you see. That was very, very sweet of her. I said, 'Look, Ella, this is the only possibility I have to read this text'. [She said:] 'I believe they're saying terrible things about Percy'.

She said that to you?

Yes. She said, 'I only want you to know one thing: that he never did me any harm'. Those were her words.

I remember you saying that to me many years ago, and I've always thought of it.

Yes, now I regretted that there were some things in the book, and I wrote to John about it; and I said, 'Look, you don't invite a person to a party (making a comparison with placing a book in public) and say "Here is Mr. Percy Grainger, the famous flagellant"'. You just don't do that. Well, there were two issues about that book. I suggested to John that he miss this out completely for a first book; perhaps it could be considered in a later book. I think it would create a wrong impression. I don't think it would present the whole of Percy Grainger, the whole Percy Grainger, whole in every sense. And it was interesting that Peter Pears and Ben Britten had contacted John because they wrote a preface.[24] They had read the book. They were perturbed about one

[22] Ella Viola Strom (1889–1979), Swedish artist and poet, married Percy Grainger in 1928 (*cf.* p. 154). Stevenson was in New York in 1976, visiting Ella at the Grainger home in White Plains, giving recitals at the Liederkranz and for Ella's 87th birthday.

[23] The first published full-length biography of Grainger, *Percy Grainger* by John Bird (Elek Books, London), appeared in 1976; a revised and expanded edition was published by Faber & Faber, London, in 1982.

[24] Benjamin Britten and Peter Pears, 'Prefatory Note,' *ibid.*

Stevenson with Ella Grainger in the Grainger home in White Plains, New York, c. 1978

thing in the book which was a dream that Percy had, a sadomasochistic dream. And I thought, I said to John: 'In my opinion' (well, I disagree with Ben Britten in particulars) 'I think this dream, as a dream, a very deep thing, should be included in the book and should be related to Amerindian practice'.[25]

That would be a brilliant thing to do.

In fact, I have (you haven't seen the dream in this book because it isn't there – it's a very terrible passage in some ways), but I have Amerindian drawings, paintings which have exactly the same thing in them.

[25] In this dream Grainger experienced the equivalent of the practice of American Plains Indians known as the Sun Dance. Outlawed by the American government for many years but now making a return as one of the traditional sacred rites, the Sun Dance is viewed as a form of sacrifice during which male participants undergo the piercing of their chest and securing of a skewer beneath their skin. The skewer is then attached by a thong to a central tree around which the dancer circles, dancing and praying until the skin breaks and the skewer is freed. In some cases, participants in this sacred ritual have been known to actually hang from the tree until the rod breaks free. I have had the privilege of witnessing this rite among the Lakota and found it very moving.

Fascinating.

Exactly the same thing. This is violent, and I never dreamed of introducing violence in this context. I'll show you the pictures of the Amerindians, and they're practising exactly what Percy writes about. I'll find it now. It was a dream of Percy's. What is in the dream is very deep, really very, very deep in character; and it's extraordinary to think that a so-called civilised person, which means a person living in a city, like the word 'civic', and that kind of civilisation wasn't Percy Grainger's culture. He was living in a culture, not a civilisation. And I think it shows a great kinship of spirit with so-called 'primitive' peoples. He was in that sense a 'primitive' man, I shouldn't use the word 'primitive', a primitive man who was highly sophisticated, highly educated, self-educated really.

They didn't understand.

They were squeamish. They didn't want it to be included in the book. I saw the letter that Peter Pears wrote, a photocopy of it that John Bird sent to Ella; and I saw that. He said, 'Please omit this dream. We find it very unpleasant'. But as a matter of fact, it was one of the most quintessentially Graingeresque things in the book. And also John Bird doesn't at all understand the relationship between Busoni and Grainger, not at all. It's very incomplete what he's written, but it's a good book in spite of that. It's a ground-breaking book.

It's a ground-breaking, pioneering book.

Yes, it is, it is, open to gross misunderstanding, especially the time when it came out at first.

It's always dangerous, I think, for someone to attempt a psychological biography.

Yes. The patient is not on the couch anymore! (LAUGHTER)

It's not fair, is it? He's not there to explain his interest.

It's metaphysical!

Is there anything in regard to Percy that you feel needs to be addressed that hasn't been particularly?

Well, his last work, the question of the Free Music. My own view is

Percy and Ella Grainger working on the 'Kangaroo Pouch' Free Music Machine, 1950s

that it could be introduced (and I discussed this with Burnett and he agreed and thought it was a very good idea) by playing recordings, tapes in the interval of a concert and not announcing it so that the audience who have come out in the intermission will be talking and one or two of them would say, 'Hey, what's that? What's this?' And perhaps if it were done not too often but regularly, but infrequently, it would gradually infiltrate and then one day could be performed in

concert. That was one of my ideas, and Burnett approved of that idea; he thought it was very good. It's using psychology, really.
Are you thinking, for example, of the realisation of Free Music *No. 1?*[26]

Yes.

To play it once, or to play it in a loop continuously?

During interval it would be played in a loop.

To keep on playing it, you mean.

Yes, it would need to be that because people will be talking, and then the intelligent ones or the musical ones would eventually think, 'Oh, this is coming again. Oh, I recognise this. Yes, interesting'. That was one idea I had. I think that could be put into practice: the how to, the technique, the method of introducing Free Music. I think it would be much better to do it gradually like that than to... That is familiarising it in the best sense. [It] would be much better than to make a special issue of it because after all Percy's vision of Free Music came very early in his life when he was rowing on the water in Australia.[27] I think it would be historically incorrect if his Free Music had to be programmed with, for instance, Stockhausen. I know that Percy once went to a Stockhausen concert and was very positive in his reaction. My own interpretation of that, as I am not an enthusiast for Stockhausen, my own interpretation, I must say in honesty, is that Percy wanted to accept all the new things. It was a principle of his. The principle, I think, has some positive and good aspects to it, but I (now I dare to criticise Percy in this regard) think it was actually a weakness in him later on in life that he wanted to accept the new and wanted to be in the vanguard of the new; and he always was prepared to champion new work and young work. Well, Stockhausen didn't need championing because he had a great publicity stunt going for him from West Germany. I performed some Stockhausen in Edinburgh. I played some of the published piano music. It's supposed to be piano music. It's not piano music. He wrote, for instance, a chord with a different dynamic for each finger. Now, Percy had done something like that, many people have done something like that; but there are so

[26] EMS Synthi 100 realisation by Les Craythorn.

[27] Grainger wrote that as a young boy of nine or ten in Australia he watched the waves while boating on the Albert Park Lagoon in Melbourne and dreamed of a music that would reflect the freedom of movement of the waves.

many dynamics in that particular piece that it's utterly impossible to play it on the piano whether one's name is that of a leading, brilliant virtuoso or a beginner. It's equally impossible to play it: to have a different dynamic for every finger, ten dynamics, which may indicate the necessity of electronic music, of electronic control. And I made some *musique concrète*[28] (how ancient this appears now); I made it in Edinburgh. I took a tape recording along to the railway station; and in those days trains had whistles, very high-pitched whistles, so I decided to record this whistle at a very low speed. We speak of 78 revolutions per minute, don't we (it sounds very 'revolutionary'); but it was recorded at a very low speed, I think even with the finger working it so that it was very, very slow (I'm going slower and slower!). Then I recorded an engine (in those days we still had the old railway trains), the sound of the train chugging away; and I recorded at a very high speed. So the sounds that resulted were sounds that were unfamiliar; people didn't know what it was. And I took it to a lecture on the new music (this was ages and ages ago). It was really an exercise in audience reaction, and I got it. In Edinburgh I might not have got it, because Edinburgh is a very understated city, understated culture. They pride themselves on their good taste. But there was a Yorkshireman in the audience (I could tell from his accent that he came from Yorkshire). First of all I played Stockhausen's piano piece. I tried to do as well as I could do. And then at a sign from my hand (my hand went up, you see, from the keyboard), a well-concealed tape recorder under the grand piano was switched on and we heard these strange sounds, this *musique concrète.* And the Yorkshire man with a big voice at the back of the audience stood up and said 'What a bloody din!' and walked out. I thought that was wonderfully honest. (LAUGHTER) At least he reacted; Edinburgh people didn't react. They wouldn't react to anything; even if there had been an earthquake, they wouldn't react. So I did that years and years and years ago. Stockhausen was born in the same year that I was, 1928; and he has had a great publicity behind him and formed his own music-publishing company, but now he is in a kind of desuetude. Articles have been published about it; he's not getting anywhere. This is bound to happen. I think if this rubbish is performed as often as possible, intelligent people surely will waken up to the fact. I'm all for as much performance of the new music as possible, to get rid of it as quickly as possible, most of it. Yes, I would say most of it. After all, what was done very early in this century is continuing to be done. Stravinsky is regarded as a modern composer, but *The Rite of Spring* was 1913. If you think of the nineteenth century, if you think

[28] Music using natural or 'concrete' sound sources recorded on tape.

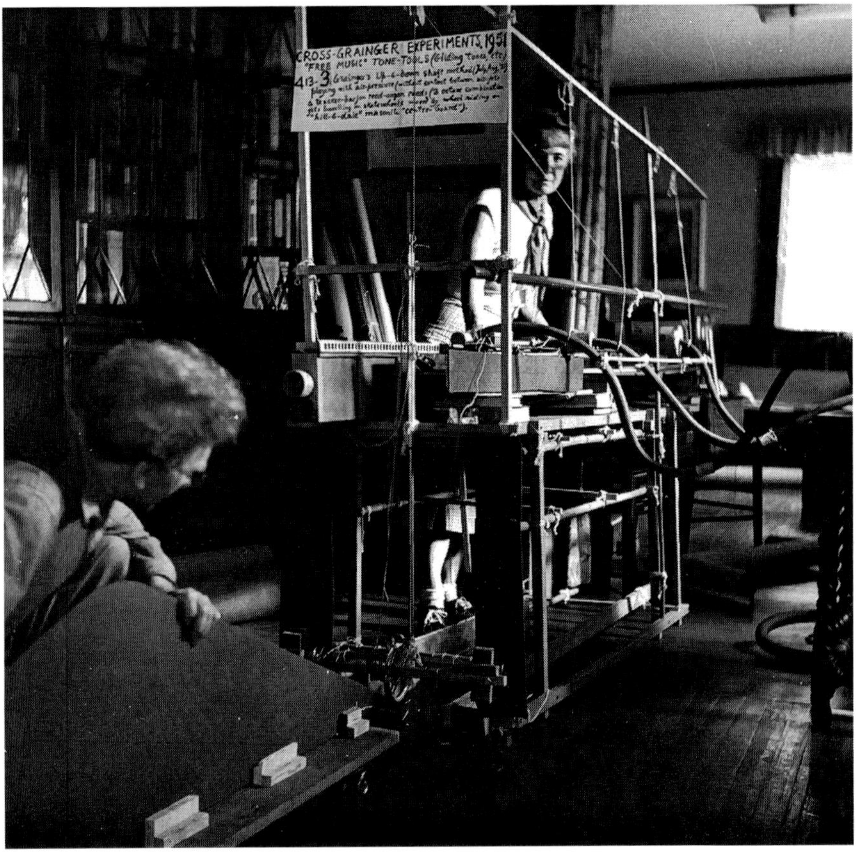

Ella and Percy Grainger working with a Free Music 'Tone Tool' in 1951

of any century, take the nineteenth. At the beginning of it we had very great composers. We had Chopin, Mendelssohn, Schumann, all born within a very short period from each other; and they were true contemporaries. Think of that music and then think of the end of the century. Think of Wagner. Think of late Verdi, remarkable music, perhaps more remarkable even than Wagner when you consider the whole of the career of Verdi, what was happening at the end. Now in the twentieth century we are still thought to be revolutionary, and Stravinsky from 1913 is still considered the way music should go: modern, modern music. It's phenomenal. It's never happened, to my knowledge, in any previous century that music considered ultra-modern at the beginning of the century should still be considered that at the end of the century. Now I think Percy wanted to include the new music; and he wanted to be a part of it, even a leader in it.

But what he did in fact, in practice, was to conserve the good. He kept on with his interest in folk-music and wind-band music. Those were constants in his life. And I don't think there is any fundamental difference between Percy Grainger's music written in his teenage and later on. He himself felt that. And I think that is very good. It's honest. There is a principle at work there; he's not trying to [be] modern but he always wanted to appreciate the modern and the new. That was his principle. It was very open-hearted. But the way things went, I think it was an expression of his wish to be a 'yea-sayer'.

Percy was never negative, I think. He wanted music to be a natural expression. He wanted to play *Turkey in the Straw*[29] with the New York Phil, I think it was. Now I think that may have been a bit of cheek. With anybody else it could have been a cheeky joke, but with Percy I think it was simply straightforward: he'd like to do that. I think he meant it and he would have done it splendidly and people would have enjoyed it; but it was refused, of course. If he'd offered the Schoenberg Piano Concerto, a piano concerto written by a cellist who couldn't play the piano himself, it would have been accepted. He was even offering to play for a very reduced fee or no fee at all on condition that not only his own music be included in the programme but music of friends, Cyril Scott[30] and others, Sparre Olsen[31] and so on. Marvellous, marvellous open-heartedness.

There's been a lot of nonsense written about Grainger's so-called racism. Would you like to say something about that?

[29] The American folk-song 'Turkey in the Straw' was arranged for piano solo by Texas-born composer and one-time cowboy David Guion (1892–1981). Guion, a modern-day troubadour who travelled the country performing his music, was one of the first composers in America to collect and transcribe folk-music for the concert stage.

[30] English composer and author Cyril Meir Scott (1879–1970) was a student at the Hoch Conservatory when Grainger arrived there in 1895 and became a life-long friend. His 1916 article for *The Musical Quarterly*, 'Percy Grainger: The Music and the Man', Vol. II, No. 3 (July 1916), pp. 425–33, remains one of the finest assessments of Grainger's early work (it is reprinted in *A Musical Genius from Australia: Selected Writings by and about Percy Grainger*, ed. Teresa Balough, University of Western Australia Press, Perth, 1982 (2nd edn. 1997), pp. 92–97.

[31] Carl Gustav Sparre Olsen (1903-84) was a Norwegian violinist, composer, conductor and music-critic especially noted for his work in the development of Norwegian choral singing. He and Grainger met in the 1930s and became close friends. Grainger arranged Olsen's 'Mountain Norway' for mixed chorus and his 'When Yuletide Comes' for saxophone choir. In 1963 Olsen published a memoir of their friendship: *Percy Grainger*, Det norske samlaget, Oslo.

Well, I think he was a racist in the non-pejorative sense. There's nothing of the Nazi about Percy Grainger. He was interested in races. In fact, as you well know, he made a profound study of music and peoples; and I think that some of the writing in recent years has been sensational and un-Graingeresque. There is ample evidence. One shouldn't have to justify him because he's the justification of himself; his work is his own justification. I mean, which anti-Semite would champion the work of George Gershwin, and not only Gershwin, other composers, too? His published articles, particularly in the American magazines, music magazines, give ample proof that he was totally open to American Jewish composers and admiring of the work. There's an article, for instance, in which he eulogises about Ernest Bloch, an American Jewish composer who has been grossly neglected by his fellow Jews.[32] There is only one work of his that people know at all, that is *Schelomo;* but there are many other works, and some of them are very near to the aesthetic of Percy Grainger, I think. I have the piano music of Ernest Bloch, but I don't think it's his major music. I think some of the chamber music is wonderful. I'm disappointed really that America, a country which has welcomed so many peoples including the Jews (think only of New York for one thing) should have in some regards raised the bogie that Grainger was an anti-Semite. It's utterly at variance with his whole aesthetic and his whole principled morality really. He did have a morality about art and indeed about life. Whatever are considered aberrations he was very honest about, very open, too open, I think, for most people. The article that he wrote with a very definite, a very positive paragraph on Ernest Bloch, I think that should go down. And also many friendships. I've only recently been reading the notes which were in Melbourne. They were brought back by a friend of mine. He had a photocopy made of his notes on an American-Jewish pianist who was a great friend of his. I think this was Harold Bauer.[33]

This is often one of the erroneous charges that's levelled at Grainger.

[32] 'Impressions of Art in Europe, Part I,' *Musical Courier*, Vol. 98, No. 22, 1 June 1929. The twelve articles which comprised Grainger's survey, undertaken on tour in Europe and covering Finland, Sweden and Norway, and England, were published in four instalments in the *Musical Courier* between then and October 1929; they are republished in Gillies and Clunies Ross (eds.), *Grainger on Music, op. cit.*, pp. 188–213.

[33] The Anglo-American pianist Harold Bauer (1873–1951) studied with Paderewski and became principal teacher of piano at the Manhattan School of Music.

Percy was a racist in the unpejorative sense.[34] He was like Whitman. I think we could find a wonderful quotation from Whitman about admiring all races. There is a poem in *Leaves of Grass* about that, and it would apply to Percy. He was profoundly interested in Black American music, in Amerindian music. He was the first to notate Australian Aboriginal melody.[35] That is a fact: he notated it. We see this annotation of transcripts of Aboriginal music for the first time. He was the first in many regards. He was really an instigator and true revolutionary who had a great knowledge of the past; and his revolution was based on the knowledge of the accumulation of past history and perspective, like a triangle, two angles of which, the past and the present, were given which predetermined the third angle, the future. I think that's what he understood very well; that's how he worked. I haven't expressed that before, I think.

That's a very beautiful thought. What would you say is the supreme significance of Grainger after all these years, amongst all the things he did.

Well, in an age which in many ways has become dehumanised, unhuman, I think Percy struck up, he called out for 'humanity' music and not omitting any aspect of humanity if it was humanity honestly. His music was related to people, not only the folk-music collection but everything he did. And now at the end of the twentieth century, I think we have music that is unrelated to people. Percy was a great admirer of the open air, fresh air; and the old-fashioned English word for melody is 'air'. Without air there is no life, without melody there is no music; and Percy loved melody and was a great melodist of many-voiced music. He wouldn't use the word 'contrapuntist', but he was a great democratic melodist: free opportunities for all to sing and play. He was a wonderful natural contrapuntist, not an academic

[34] Grainger lived during an age in which western European forms dominated the arts. As an avid supporter of British and Nordic culture, he railed against this western European domination and often wrote scathingly of it. But he was a strong supporter of individual artists from both western European and other ethnic backgrounds such as the Jewish composers Ernest Bloch and George Gershwin and the African-American musicians Nathaniel Dett and Duke Ellington. And in a letter to Nathaniel Dett, dated 6 March 1925 (published in Gillies and Pear (eds.), *The All-Around Man, op. cit.*, pp. 73–76), he wrote that 'art should be one of the meeting places of all races, without racial, national or local prejudices, jealousies or smallnesses'.

[35] In 1909 Grainger met the British anthropologist Baldwin Spencer (1860–1929) and transcribed three songs from his cylinder recordings of Central Australian Aboriginal music. Spencer's were among the first field recordings of non-western music to be documented.

Grainger with the Norwegian composer Sparre Olsen, Norway, 8 June 1939

contrapuntist. A free flow of wonderful melody, I think that's one of his great contributions. Air, he let the air into music. And now at the end of the twentieth century, there is very little air and it's not clean air that we have either in the physical world or in music. You see, his choice of, his preference, his own predilection was for the human voice in choral writing and the extension of the human voice in woodwind-writing, in wind-writing, because that is as near as we can get to the human voice. String-writing is not near to the human voice. I mean the human voice is a wind instrument, it's like a bagpipe, the volume is the bag. He has been from my early years (I'd be a child when I first encountered the name Percy Grainger and the idea Percy Grainger), he has constantly been, I feel, a member of my own family – of course, it's the human family; [I feel] that I have been related to him somehow more than simply a physical relationship. I really feel that I've been related to him; and there are one or two others who have as well. I'm not trying to say that I have achieved more than anybody else. I think there have been people who are near to the spirit of Grainger. Even among his friends I think there were one or two who didn't really comprehend the idea of Percy Grainger. I personally feel that Cyril Scott[36] didn't. Cyril was a great friend and he wrote very well, but his aesthetic was very different from Percy's. I've no right to say this except from my study of Cyril Scott's music, which I love; but I think he didn't show anything in his music to prove that he was aesthetically near to Percy Grainger. I think he was as a friend; I think he was as a fellow musician. I think Sparre Olsen came nearer to one corner of Grainger's work. I think the spirit of Grainger wasn't far removed from the spirit of that very great film star Danny Kaye[37] who was once asked if he would play the role of Grainger in a film but never did. I think there was something in common. I imagine so. I'm a great admirer of Danny Kaye's films.

Perhaps the humanness, large-heartedness.

Yes, oh yes.

That brings me to the next question I had: what is the major linking influence that you see, as a young composer yourself, that Grainger had upon your work and your life?

Well, he gave me the confidence to pursue Scottish music. After all, he said that Scottish music, Scottish folk-music, was his emancipation. And when I studied the work he did on Scots folk-music (in 1900 he did it, very early)[38] that was really like having a wonderful teacher. And he gave me the courage to be free with folk-music in a way that nobody else did because before that I had studied Bartók's involvement with folk-music, and Bartók very often was a purist in the question of harmonising folk music. Now Percy was very radical. He believed it was possible to harmonise folk music in many different ways if one didn't do violence to the actual folk-material, which he never did because he understood it so well. He didn't belittle folk-music. He thought there were many possibilities there. I think that Bartók

[36] *Cf.* note 30 on p. 49, above.

[37] Danny Kaye (born Daniel Kaminsky in Brooklyn, New York) (1913–87) was an award-winning actor, musician and comedian best known for his gift of rapid-fire singing and monologue and his skillful spoofing of orchestra conductors. During the 1940s he was one of the screen's biggest comedy and musical stars. A committed philanthropist, he donated the proceeds from many of his concerts to supply pension funds for musicians. He also toured widely for The United Nations Children's Fund (UNICEF), for which he was a permanent ambassador-at-large.

[38] Fourteen *Scotch Folksongs from 'Songs of the North'* were set by Grainger for voice and piano in 1900 when he was only eighteen years old: *cf.* note 19 on p. 40, above.

had, in comparison, a narrower view. I don't want to underestimate Bartók, who did very important work and was a wonderful composer in many ways; but he didn't have the openness and the freedom approach that Percy had, nothing like it. And yet Bartók, because he went to America at a time when the new music academically was very interesting and very well advertised, promulgated and so on, I think Bartók has probably a higher rating in American universities than Percy has.

Oh yes, that's certainly true.

That's a guess of mine.

You're right on the head!

I personally don't think (I don't want to spend too much time talking about Bartók, though they did cross swords so to speak, didn't they, in print.[39] If it's possible to cross swords in print, they did)...

The best way to do it, probably!

Yeah, I think so (LAUGHTER). Yes, let's keep it to print all the time. Well, I think that because Kodály[40] did not live in America as Bartók did, he didn't have the means of his work being taken up in America and broadcast in a very real sense. But I believe that Kodály is nearer to Percy's way of thinking than Bartók was. For one thing, Kodály

[39] The edition of the American music-magazine *The Music News* published on 29 September 1933 carried an article by Grainger entitled 'Melody versus Rhythm' (a slightly different version, first published in *Australian Musical News* in August 1933 (Vol. 24, No. 1, pp. 12–14), is republished in Gillies and Clunies Ross (eds.), *Grainger on Music, op. cit.*, pp. 251–57), in which he advocated the supremacy of the melodic or emotional response over the rhythmic element, citing the spiritualising effect of melody versus the materialistic effect of rhythm. This article was shown to Bartók by Storm Bull, who had been one of Grainger's students. Bartók responded by publishing a refutation in the same publication ('Béla Bartók Replies to Percy Grainger', January 1934), arguing that melody and rhythm never could or should be in conflict (Bartók's rejoinder was republished in Benjamin Suchoff (ed.), *Béla Bartók Essays*, Faber & Faber, London, 1976, pp. 224–24).

[40] Although Zoltán Kodály (1882–1967) remained in Hungary and his mature compositional output is less well-known than that of Bartók, his development of a way of training children in music based largely on his experience in folk-music (known as the Kodály Method) has been widely influential throughout the western world.

was very scientific, and Percy had a great ambition to be scientific about folk-music and to be honest about it, to annotate everything; and Kodály did that. Kodály didn't compose a great deal, but what he did compose is very significant; and the *Children's Dances*,[41] I think, are very near to Grainger, the published *Children's Dances.* Percy would have been delighted with Kodály's very simple solution to pianistic pentatony because Kodály simply said: 'Practise these tunes on the white keys (they're all pentatonic, minor pentatonic, Hungarian pentatonic) and when you have learned these pieces on white keys, just slide your hand down to the black keys and you can play the whole thing'. It works. Now that kind of very simple, very basic solution to a problem would be very near to Percy's heart. He would admire that surely, a short cut not missing out anything, the short cut to the essential, like jumping over a five-bar gate into nature.

M Like he did so many times.

I said five bars because of the pentatony, of course, a pentatonic gate!

I remember reading that when you were quite young you'd heard things like Shepherd's Hey.

Oh yes, and played them on the piano.

But at first did they have an immediate reaction for you?

Oh, yes, yes, of course. Of course, I loved it. Percy could speak to children in music very well and speak to natural people in music. Yes, I loved it. I had a very, very strong feeling about Percy Grainger. When I went on country walks I could feel something of the spirit of Percy Grainger as I heard it in the music even as a child, you see. When I say a child, I suppose about ten years of age, something like that, quite early.

So you were playing some of the piano pieces at that stage already?

Yes. I found it for myself; my teacher didn't suggest that I play Percy Grainger. She would suggest that I take Royal Associated Examinations and play little-known composers from the eighteenth century. That would be thought to be high-class.

[41] Kodaly's *Children's Dances* for piano solo consist of pentatonic melodies arranged to be performed entirely on the black keys of the piano.

How did you discover the early folk-music settings, the Scottish folk-music settings of Grainger's, because those weren't published.

In White Plains.[42]

When you were there visiting Ella?

Oh yes. Yes, I saw manuscripts.

That must have been a wonderful feeling to come across these.

Oh, it was. It was. It was indeed. It was wonderful, and I made copies by hand of them. Yes, that really was; and I'm very glad that three of them were published.[43]

But you've been playing them ever since you discovered them.

Oh yes. Surely. I think they're very fine. I rearranged the order because I think that Percy, because he wasn't giving as many concerts latterly, and because that's the revision of those three folksongs that he did later in his life, didn't consider the best programming possibility. You find the order is different in the manuscript. I've given it in my edition, I've given his order; but I've changed the order because I think that it's better to have a slower movement in the middle and a quick movement at the end.[44]

To round it off.

To round it off and to ensure a reaction from the audience! (LAUGHTER)

[42] In 1921 Grainger and his mother purchased their first and only permanent home in America on the outskirts of New York City: 7 Cromwell Place, White Plains, New York. After his mother's death in 1922, Grainger continued to live there; and after his marriage to Ella Strom in 1928, he and his wife made it their home. Since Ella Grainger's death in 1979, 7 Cromwell Place has been the headquarters for the International Percy Grainger Society.

[43] In 1954 Grainger arranged three of his fourteen voice-and-piano settings of Scottish folksongs from MacLeod and Boulton's *Songs of the North* (*cf.* note 19 on p. 40, above, and pp. 160–61, below) for piano solo as *Three Scotch Folksongs from 'Songs of the North*; they were published in 1983 by C. F. Peters, edited by Stevenson.

[44] *Cf.* Stevenson's comments on p. 171, below.

The Grainger home at 7 Cromwell Place, White Plains, New York

Well, that you do!

But, you see, he didn't do that. I think he put the slow piece at the end. I've given the original order; and if people want to stick to it, they can do so. I think that's only fair for an editor to do that, and only honest. And I wanted a photograph of the young Percy when he first discovered all this[45] because I think the photograph should link with the music, with all the background, although, of course, these later pieces, these rewritings, were at the end, near the end of his life. But I still think that the origin of it is what we need, and the spirit is there in any case. The youthful spirit was there right to the end, and the illness didn't matter really.

Now a lot of people have written about how bitter he was towards the end and how unhappy and so forth, but you apparently didn't see that in your correspondence with him.

No, no, no. I think he had attempted so much and there had been in later years comparatively little feedback compared to what there was earlier on. No, I think whatever bitterness there might have been at certain moments, certain times, his spirit would somersault over it.

I like that! That's very good. Now is there anything else you would like to say? If Percy were alive today what would you see him doing, what kind of work?

[45] A photograph taken of Grainger in 1900 by Marx of Frankfurt and given by Grainger to Karl Klimsch who had originally inspired his interest in folk-music was used to illustrate the publication.

Well, this is a difficult question. I think he would be very interested in the United Nations; and it wouldn't surprise me if he worked for the United Nations individually, as a free worker. After all, Yehudi Menuhin did. And when I met and worked with Menuhin on my Violin Concerto,[46] I was rather hesitant to mention Percy Grainger in case he had a received opinion about Percy, because Menuhin does not respond to received opinion as many people do. He has his own opinion. For instance, one might think that Menuhin as an American-born Jew would be very interested in Gustav Mahler. He is not. He was very critical of Mahler's music. He thinks it has cheapness in it, it has vulgarity without a true spirit of vulgarity, of the people. I was interested in that. So Menuhin does have his own opinion, you see. But when I dared to mention, when I thought: 'Yes, I'll try it, I'll mention Percy Grainger', he said: 'Of course I love Percy Grainger's music. It was the very first music I ever played on the violin'.

Did he? That's wonderful.

Yes, he said, 'Everybody knew it when I was a child'. It was in the 1920s, you see. And he said, 'I played *Country Gardens,* of course, and *Shepherd's Hey.* I love *Shepherd's Hey.* I love the titles and I love the music. The music was even better than the titles'. (LAUGHTER) Oh, he was very enthusiastic. He said, 'Why did you think I don't love the music of Percy Grainger?' I said: 'I didn't think that. I didn't know because there are people who have different opinions of Grainger who don't really know about Grainger'. But he said, 'I grew up with Percy Grainger's music, the first music I ever heard, and I loved it. I still love it'. He's very open-hearted.

He must be a wonderful man.

Oh, he is indeed. Yes. Always prepared to learn.

That's the mark of a great man.

Yes. Very youthful even well into his eighties, he's still very youthful. People would use the word 'naive'. Well, I think it's an achievement to be as knowledgeable, as experienced, and as naive as Menuhin is

[46] Stevenson's Violin Concerto, *The Gypsy,* composed in 1977–79 was commissioned by Sir Yehudi Menuhin. It received its world premiere on 21 May 1992 with the soloist Hu Kun and the BBC Scottish Symphony Orchestra under Menuhin's direction.

all those things. I think it's lovely. The child is there still somewhere in his heart, very beautiful.

A leading question about Percy.

Well, I hope I can give you a following answer. (LAUGHTER)

I'm sure you can.

If you'll lead me, I'll follow. (LAUGHTER) I hope!

I always think of Rudolf Steiner's[47] *leading statements. What does he call them, leading questions?*

Yes, yes.

If Percy were still living today, what, if any, collaboration would you like to have done?

I'd like him to have started all over again in Scotland because Scotland hath great need of Percy Grainger.

(LAUGHTER) *But it has Ronald Stevenson!*

Well, it would do even better with a collaboration with the two of us! And indeed it's already happened because I'm in collaboration with his spirit and always have been! And I mean that in the most positive sense. Yes, because, you see, Scotland is a peripheral country in Europe; and I think, I'm sure of this, that in the periphery you have the possibility of preservation more than you have in the big centre. That may be why Percy was so interested in Scandinavia, which is peripheral to central Europe. Percy was interested in small countries, and the paradox is that he went to live in one of the largest countries. (LAUGHTER)

[47] Rudolf Steiner (1861–1925) was an Austrian-born scientific, literary and philosophical scholar and lecturer. In 1924 he founded the General Anthroposophical Society devoted to the scientific study of the spirit. He was the author of many books and lectures on a wide variety of subjects from science to education, economics, religion and agriculture. He was responsible for the instigation of Waldorf Schools based on a holistic approach to education and left behind many ideas, which he called 'leading thoughts', such as biodynamic agriculture and anthroposophical medicine, which were meant for others to take up and develop.

Of course!

Well, I think Scotland has great need of this. There's still a vast amount of Scottish folk-music preserved as if under snow. There is still a very great deal. People have said it's all been done, but it hasn't all been done by any means; and the School of Scottish Studies in Edinburgh University, which in some ways is a sarcophagus of culture (I used that phrase some years ago and it caused great offence because it was true) (LAUGHTER), they haven't done much of this really compared to what [they might have done]. Really they've done very well, but there's a great deal of it still to be done. The fact that Scotland is so far away from London, I say far away in every sense, means that things have been ignored but preserved through ignorance, preserved through being ignored. And the trouble is that too many Scots have followed the best road, as Samuel Johnson said 'the road to London', and not stayed here, not worked here.

When you wrote to Percy you were a very young man.[48] *How did you view your relationship with him? Did you view him as a mentor in any sense or was it simply a friendship that developed?*

I was aware, even as a young man, that I had contacted a kindred spirit, and that he gave me companionship through correspondence at a time when I needed it because there wasn't a great deal of stimulation, cultural stimulation, in my life. In fact, I relied very much on correspondence at that time. I relied very much on correspondence of creative people who were still alive and with whom I could [relate], with whom there was a relationship in my ideas and in my work. I felt that. The other correspondence I had, a much longer correspondence, was with Edward Gordon Craig,[49] the great genius of the theatre; and that has been developed not so much by me as by our daughter Gerda,[50] who, as you know, is in theatre. I think Gordon Craig's books are really worth reading, particularly his masterpiece *On the Art of the Theatre.*[51]

[48] When they began their correspondence in August of 1957, Stevenson was 29 years old and Grainger 75. *Cf.* also p. 9, above.

[49] *Cf.* note 8, p. 14, above. Craig developed new theories of scene design which strove to capture the essential spirit of the play in a poetic manner.

[50] Gerda Stevenson (b. 1956) is an award-winning actress, writer, director and founding member of Stellar Quines Theatre Co. (a group founded to facilitate the creative work of women in Scottish theatre).

[51] Methuen, London, 1911.

Yes, and who else were you corresponding with at the same time?

Well, I did correspond with a few musicians. Oh, I corresponded with many. I corresponded with Cyril Scott, with Luigi Dallapiccola[52] in Italy, with Roman Vlad,[53] whom I met actually but I corresponded with him before we met and wrote a big article on Vlad. The connection there was with Busoni because Vlad had written a very intelligent article on Busoni's music; and that was the beginning of our correspondence, the correspondence with Roman Vlad. And then I met him at the Summer School, the Dartington Hall Summer School,[54] and I liked him very much. And he showed me his *Studi dodecafonici,* the Dodecaphonic Studies for piano; and he asked me if I would play them and what I thought about them. I liked them and I wrote them out; I made my own copy of them in pen. And I rewrote the piano-writing, not changing a single note but the distribution of the hands. All that was revised, you see. I didn't know whether I would cause offence to him, because composers can be very egoistic. But he did a wonderful thing, or at least half a wonderful thing. First of all, he more than approved it. He approved it very positively and thanked me. And I had really edited that work, and he published it and dedicated it to me; and it was my edition that he published.

Do you remember what year that would be?

Oh, it is a hard question. Well, I was in Italy in 19, I think, 58 (Marjorie will remember better than I); and Vlad was coming to the Dartington Hall Summer School, I think in 1959, or maybe 1960, and I met him there.[55] Oh, I'd met him in Rome, I'd been in his home in Rome; but I met him again at the Dartington Summer School and I played his Dodecaphonic Studies. I admired them because he had a liberal attitude to twelve-note composition. He wasn't a fanatic about it, and he related twelve-note composition to the history of music.

[52] Luigi Dallapiccola (1904–75), Italian composer and professor at the Florence Conservatory, renowned for his rigorous yet lyrical use of the twelve-tone technique and his profound humanism.

[53] Italian composer and music historian of Romanian origin, Roman Vlad (b. 1919) is best-known for his works in serial, aleatoric and electronic styles and his writings on twentieth-century music and composers.

[54] The Dartington Hall Summer School takes place on the Dartington Hall Estate in South Devon. It was founded in the 1920s to bring together amateur and professional musicians for five weeks of summer school/music festival.

[55] Vlad taught at Dartington in 1954 and 1955.

I was almost going to wonder if Vlad had introduced you to the fact that Percy had studied with Busoni.

No. Vlad didn't know a thing about Percy Grainger.

So you brought that to him?

Yes.

How did you discover that Percy had studied with Busoni?

Because of my Busoni research.[56] I did research for many years. Marjorie and I visited Busoni's widow Gerda Busoni, or in the Swedish pronunciation 'Yerda'. And Gerda invited Marjorie and myself, after we had corresponded for some years, to visit her in Stockholm, in Lidingo which is really a village. And she was living very simply with her old sister: two very old ladies, two wise old ladies of the North. We went there every day; and they cooked for us, especially Helme, Gerda's sister, because Gerda was blind, you see. She'd been blinded by British bombs in Berlin because she remained in Berlin; and she was very frightened leaving Berlin, the idea of leaving it because that was her home. She had lost everything, including her sight, because it was the flash of the bomb that took her sight, the optic nerve, you see. And yet she was so positive, and she remembered Percy very well. She'd given him gifts when he came to study with Busoni, with her husband. She'd given him Scandinavian gifts of books, and she told me a wonderful anecdote about Percy which I think has never been published anywhere. She said that Percy was with them in London about 1900 or in the early 1900s; and Busoni said you must come to Berlin and you have lessons with me. No question of money [was] involved. Busoni never taught for money; he wouldn't accept any money from anybody. And he didn't teach by the clock. He would teach for very long periods, and then they'd go out to a cafe and he'd introduce young musicians to other people in the arts and so on.

[56] Stevenson's research on Busoni has led to a number of published articles, including 'Busoni and Mozart' (*The Score*, No. 13, September 1955, pp. 25–38), 'Busoni: The Legend of a Prodigal' (*The Score*, No. 15, March 1956, pp. 15–30), 'Busoni e la Gran Bretagna' (*Bolletino Storico Empolese*, Vol. 1, anno II, No. 4, 1958, pp. 303–13), 'Busoni's Great Fugue' (*The Listener*, Vol. 87, No. 2238, 3 February 1972, p. 157), 'Busoni – Doktor Faust of the Keyboard' (*EPTA Piano Journal*, Vol. 1, No. 1, 1980, pp. 14–15), and 'Busoni and Melody' (*Chapman*, Nos. 89–90, Summer 1998, pp. 81–86). It is these and other articles that form the basis of *Busoni: Aspects of a Genius* (*cf.* note 4 on p. 11); Stevenson's *magnum opus* on Busoni, the work of a lifetime, awaits publication.

Wonderful pedagogue, an actual pedagogue. Gerda Busoni told me that the young Grainger saw them off in a cab (that would be a horse-drawn cab in London in those days); and Percy was talking a great deal very enthusiastically. He'd more to say, and the cab driver was becoming very impatient. So Percy said to the cab driver, 'Just drive along, just go along, and I'll continue, I'll run beside and continue the conversation.' (LAUGHTER) A very Graingeresque story! She admired Percy Grainger very much, and Busoni admired him. He wrote in the letters to Gerda when he met Percy in London before Gerda had met him. He describes him in the most wonderful way. And Busoni was very modest. He pursued culture by being modest and honest and not showing off his own culture but being quite prepared to admit his shortcomings and wanting to know more; and he always asked people 'What should I read?' Now for a Tuscan who lived in Berlin and spoke German to ask to read great works in other literatures was very unusual. And Percy said to him: 'You should read, in my opinion, Walt Whitman and Kipling'. Now they met again in New York in about 1914 or '15; and Busoni's first comment was: 'Percy, you were right about Whitman and, in my opinion, for me, wrong about Kipling'.

He wanted to learn, you see; and when Busoni met the Irish conductor Hamilton Harty,[57] conductor of the Hallé Orchestra (there was a cartoon in the newspaper, 'Hallé and Harty' and they crossed out one 'l' in Hallé so it was 'Hale and Harty'), when Busoni worked with Harty he admired Harty very much because Harty was also a composer, a very, very fine composer. He was Irish and he was a conductor, an outstanding conductor, particularly of Berlioz, one of the pioneers in the twentieth century of Berlioz's music because Berlioz was ignored for a long time even in France, especially in France. When it came to the Berlioz centenary, there was none of his music available in France. People had to write to Germany to get it. Now Busoni asked Harty, Hamilton Harty, which Irish writer he should read. He said: 'I know Bernard Shaw. We've met a number of times'. They had a mutual friend, Bernard Shaw and Busoni, and they spent a long time with each other in discussion. Busoni describes Shaw in a very interesting way, a summing-up which was very perceptive. He described Bernard Shaw as a minister of religion disguised as a clown. Wonderful. And only from a few meetings he could see that, you see. Now, Harty said: 'I think you might read the playwright John Synge, John Millington Synge, *The Playboy of the Western World*. And Busoni read Synge, which is Anglo-Irish actually. There's a great deal of Irish in the language,

[57] Sir Herbert Hamilton Harty (1879–1941), Irish conductor, composer and accompanist, was principal conductor of the Hallé Orchestra from 1920 to 1933.

you see; and he wrote to Harty. (The letter is in Dublin in Trinity College Library, Dublin. I know it is, but I haven't been able to consult it.) And he said: 'You are absolutely right about John Synge. What a great writer'. Now for a great European, in the Goethean sense, to read an Irish playwright when he, Busoni, was a sick man (he was very ill: he had a heart condition, a liver condition and was really desperately ill), to read that and to be able to appreciate it shows a very hospitable culture.

Well it seems to me that you throughout your life have formed a community of minds.

That's a wonderful phrase. Thank you.

Did you feel that after Grainger passed on, shortly after your correspondence began, did you still feel this wonderful connection to him continue?

Oh yes, very strong.

What would you say are the major connections, points of contact, between you and Grainger?

Well, perhaps number one should be Scottish music because he said this interested him as much as anything and more than most folk-musics. I've been supported, I've been encouraged by that statement of his; and I have devoted my work to the cause of Scottish music and I think I've done it, I know I've done it, in a Graingeresque way. That is to say that I have performed the music and I have broadcast. I've practiced aesthetic propaganda on the radio. I've broadcast talks, you see, and I've taken the three indigenous instruments or styles of instrumental music and the vocal music of Scotland, I've taken the bagpipe music; the clarsach, the harp music; and the vocal folksongs and I've actually broadcast talks on these subjects for the BBC Radio 3 and for Radio Scotland. Largely a waste of time as far as Radio Scotland is concerned, but one hopes that one or two, as Gordon Craig would have said, five or four or three, no, or two or one perhaps might have listened.

Well, of course, you've done lecture-recitals much in the same way, I think, that Percy did them, which was not common when he was doing them.

That's right. And I think they speak of a piano *recital,* you see, and I think the true recital includes the pianist reciting. Paderewski did it. He spoke very movingly. He was a great orator, in fact, and raised a great deal of money for Poland, from America particularly. And I know that the audience doesn't know a thing; the honest people know that they don't know a thing about the music. These days there are sophisticates compared with what they used to be; and the sophisticates learn even less because they think they know when they don't, whereas people years ago didn't know and they knew they didn't know and were ready to know, ready to learn. But I hope I don't speak down to an audience. I always have spoken at a recital a little, spoke a little; and I think I honed it to a fine art. In my latest recitals I've just said enough and not too much.

And you also have this love of early music in common with Percy, don't you?

Oh yes, indeed. Yes, yes, yes.

And I was so amazed in hearing your Summer is icumen in[58] *that some of the phrases are very much in the Grainger style, but that was before you even heard* Rosenkavalier[59] *wasn't it?*

Oh yes, I didn't know *Rosenkavalier* at all when that was written. *Rosenkavalier Ramble*? Didn't know a thing about it.

But it's a ramble.

Yes, it is a ramble. That's right. Yes. I'm very lucky to have lived at the time when Percy was still alive.

Well, you keep him still alive, I think.

Well, I try to meet him. I haven't embalmed him. That's another terrible Russian thing. No, he's a blithe spirit. And I'm very glad I met Ella because I think that she had something of the spirit of Percy.

Yes. She became a very close friend of yours, didn't she?

[58] In 1951 Stevenson set the old English round from the mid-thirteenth century, 'Sumer is icumen in', for piano solo as the first of *Two Eclogues* (named for the collection of pastoral poems by Virgil) and dedicated it to Grainger.

[59] Grainger began his *Ramble on Love* (which he subtitled 'Ramble on the last love-duet in the opera "The Rose-Bearer"') for piano solo before 1920 and completed it in 1927 (Furstner, G. Schirmer). It was recorded by Stevenson for Altarus Records in 1996 (*cf.* Appendix, p. 256, below).

I think it's reasonable to say that, yes.

You met many times.

I think I could say that without exaggeration. We had a correspondence. I wouldn't expect her to be the letter writer that Percy was. We have many letters from Ella, yes. Ella didn't like what I wrote about Gerda Busoni. I sent her my chapter about Gerda Busoni.

She didn't like it? Why was that?

No, she didn't. She wrote about that, and she was quite frank and told me that she didn't like it. And I took that to mean that she wouldn't like anybody to write like that about her in relation to Percy.

That's very interesting.

You see, I wrote from, I would say, a young idealist's point of view about Gerda Busoni. But, you see, there is no scandal in Busoni's life. Nobody has turned up scandal.

They've tried to but...

Oh, they've tried to, yes.

Of course, they would try to.

Yes. You see, Beaumont[60] published on Busoni, and he discovered the dedicatee, a young American lady, well, a girl really, a teenager, a dedicatee of the I think it was the *Sonatina ad usum infantis*, the Sonatina for the use of children, which was written originally for the harpsichord, I think. And Beaumont found a photograph of this young girl and published it in his book; and he, in correspondence with me before his book was published, thank goodness, he wanted to claim that there was an affair, that Busoni had an affair with this young girl. Well, actually the young girl [was a girlfriend of Busoni's son]. I questioned Busoni's student the American Edward Weiss – Weiss was in the Busoni house a great deal – he knew this young American girl and he said this girl was actually a girlfriend of Busoni's son Rafaello, who had many girlfriends. They were almost all Jewish

[60] Antony Beaumont's *Busoni the Composer* was published in 1985 (Faber & Faber, London/Indiana University Press, Bloomington) and *Ferruccio Busoni: Selected Letters* in 1987 (Faber & Faber, London/Columbia University Press, New York).

girlfriends as it happened. And I have many photographs of the Busoni household. Busoni was very free as a father, very unmoralistic. This American girl was often in the Busoni house to see the son, and there are photographs and so on. So Beaumont makes this out that there was a love affair with this girl, you see. It's ridiculous. Edward Weiss told me, this is a bit silly in a way, but he told me the silly young men's approach that he and the famous Egon Petri[61] and another student of Busoni, a piano student, [took] when they were with each other [and] sometimes talked about Busoni's relationship with his wife, with Gerda. He seemed to be so monastic, Busoni seemed to be so monastic that these young, silly idealistic young men couldn't believe that he'd fathered children, two sons, you see. Ridiculous. They couldn't imagine it. They seemed to be so... Well it's almost a religious comment, really. He seemed to be almost monk-like. He wasn't. He was very, very funny.

Edward Weiss said: 'I did see Busoni once in the kitchen' – Edward Weiss used to go for coffee in the morning, you see, very welcome – 'with a young woman who was helping in the house' (a kind of servant for Gerda because Gerda didn't always enjoy very good health). He said: 'I saw Busoni with his arms around this young woman and patting her on the back, so I quickly disappeared from the picture when I saw this. It was an intimate moment. I later learned that this girl's mother had died'.

You see how easy it is to misinterpret things. He was comforting her.

Yes.

I would like to get your thoughts on Rose Grainger,[62] *because I think you have a different insight than many people have.*

Well, I've discussed this with Marjorie and we both tend to be what Percy wouldn't like us to be, critical of Rose Grainger. Complex, complex because, I mean he did owe a very great deal to her and it was a wonderful companionship. She was an amazing mother, especially for that time in history, to be so liberated.

[61] Egon Petri (1882–1962), German pianist of Dutch descent, was widely recognised as Busoni's most important pupil and interpreter.

[62] Percy's mother, Rose Grainger (1861–1922), is a controversial figure. She was devoted to her son but was fiercely possessive and tied him to her in many emotional ways. A victim of syphilis which she contracted from her husband, she committed suicide in 1922 by jumping from the eighteenth floor of the Aeolian Hall Building in New York City.

Grainger with his mother, Rose, in 1916

M I think it's difficult for us today to emphasise with Rose living in Edwardian times. Our knowledge of psychology and awareness about how one should be and not be as a parent these days is, I think, quite advanced compared with what I can remember about my parents. When a child grows into puberty, adolescence and then adulthood, it's difficult for a mother to turn oneself into a friend from a mother. It should be a very gradual process. It needs a lot of thought on the part of mothers to let go in a way that we know we must in these days.

Well, she was protective, wasn't she?

M Yes, but when that protectiveness gets into the territory of emotional blackmail, it's very tricky, isn't it? And I'd only go this far.

She puzzled Percy's friends. I think some of them were outraged by her behaviour, particularly Scandinavian friends who tend to be freer in relationships. I think aesthetically Rose Grainger has not been paid the tribute she deserved. For instance, when you had a Sir Thomas Beecham[63] (and there's only one of that ilk) who told Percy that the *Australian Up-Country Song* was the worst piece of music he knew, that Percy's mother, not just in response to that but always from the beginning of that work, that piece of music, had been convinced it was one of the best things Percy had ever done. I think that's wonderful. I think she was right. But, you see, Beecham couldn't understand the popular, the truly popular voice in that music. Beecham was a wonderful man in many ways, a wonderful conductor. What he did for Delius one must always remember; and having done for Delius what he did, one would like to think that he would have understood Percy, Percy was so near to Delius.[64] Yes, I love that in Rose Grainger that she appreciated the Australian voice in *Australian Up-Country Song*[65] as it was called at one time, wasn't it. And that's very important. Many mothers, wanting the best for a child, especially at that time, especially from a middle-class background (which she had with a husband who at one period was a good earner as an architect, although a squanderer also), many people would go for the classics and the high class and would say: 'That is the music to which you should aspire'. But the fact that she realised the Australian voice, I think, is a marvellous testimony to Percy. It speaks volumes because there must have been other things too. I mean, they read together; and it could be (I've no proof of this, perhaps it's an area of research to be done), it could be that Rose Grainger was the beginning of his love of Kipling and of Whitman. I don't know, that's a guess because they read together so much.

I think his father sent him his first Kipling. That's not to say that Rose didn't deepen that by reading it with him. Certainly, he dedicated all of his Kipling settings to her.

[63] The English conductor Sir Thomas Beecham (1879–1961) was a champion of British composers, especially Frederick Delius, many of whose works received their first performances at his hands. His recordings of Delius works set the standard for later interpretations. He also wrote an extensive biography of the composer which was published in 1959 (*Frederick Delius*, Hutchinson, London).

[64] Percy met the English impressionist composer Frederick Delius (1862–1934) in 1907 and was amazed to find that their musical vocabulary was so similar. They became life-long friends and supporters of each other's music.

[65] Also known as *Australian Up-Country Tune*, the work was composed by Grainger for *a cappella* mixed chorus in 1928 based on a tune written in 1905. The melody was also employed by him in *Colonial Song* (1911–14) and *'The Gum-Suckers' March* (1905–16).

Yes, yes.

So he related it to her.

Yes. They are wonderful songs, the settings. That's a very powerful song, 'If I Were Hanged on the Highest Hill, Mother o' Mine'.[66] That's a very great song. That is shameless emotion, very passionate without being overtly sexual. It is not sexual in the way that, for instance, Richard Strauss can write very sexual music. Strauss himself said that; he said that he could put into music the difference between a blond and a redhead. Nonsense.

M It's saying that you know that whatever happens in life, your mother's going to stand by you. It's that.

You know, what's so touching about that is that it comes at the beginning of The Light that Failed *by Kipling; and that story is about an orphan boy. The boy in that story was an orphan, but there's a lot behind it. It's a wonderful, wonderful song.*

It's a great song. You see, Percy never wrote an opera; and I think never wished to write an opera.

M Well, I think you also have one thing that we haven't actually said, and it occurs to me because we're talking about song. One of the things you have in common with Percy is that [song is important to you both]. Everybody knows, well now they do, about Percy's pianism and everything, everybody knows about your pianism; but Percy's genius was with choir and voice, and song is at least as important to

[66] Grainger's 22 numbered Kipling settings (there are 33 settings in all) are dedicated to his mother. No. 1, 'Dedication', a setting for tenor and piano composed in 1901, is of a poem from Kipling's novel *The Light that Failed* (1891):

> If I were hanged on the highest hill,
> *Mother o' mine, O mother o' mine!*
> I know whose love would follow me still,
> *Mother o' mine, O mother o' mine!*
>
> If I were drowned in the deepest sea,
> *Mother o' mine, O mother o' mine!*
> I know whose tears would come down to me,
> *Mother o' mine, O mother o' mine!*
>
> If I were damned of body and soul,
> I know whose prayers would make me whole,
> *Mother o' mine, O mother o' mine!*

you in your output as the piano music. So that is another [thing you have in common].

In Percy's case I would say windband and choir.

M Yes, that is his genius.

That's the real genius. The electronic music was an essay. He bequeathed it as Walt Whitman bequeathed it, an adventure to you for the future.

How do you see that music of the future? How do you envision that? What's coming?

Well, I think it's bound to come. Busoni also wrote about it. Should I show you the passage? It may be that Percy knew about this. It may be that this was an indication of future possibilities that Percy picked up from Busoni when nobody else did. It may be. There's a little book, *The Aesthetic*,[67] which is published and is in Dover paperback with other writings of other writers, Debussy and the American composer (supposed to be the greatest American composer ever) Ives. *The Essay before a Sonata* by Charles Ives, that's in the same volume as Busoni's *New Aesthetic* and the other thing I mentioned. Now I'll just get the little book.

The New Aesthetic *was published in what year? 1906?*

1906. It was an Insel Verlag book published in, I think it was, Berlin. Curiously enough, it doesn't say here; but I think, I'm almost sure, it was Berlin. And in that book Busoni quotes a magazine article that he had been reading entitled 'New Music for an Old World', not 'Old Music for the New World'! And this article was about Dr Thaddeus Cahill,[68] an Irish name, Dr Thaddeus Cahill's 'dynamophone,' 'an extraordinary invention for producing scientifically perfect music',

[67] In his book *Sketch of a New Aesthetic of Music* (1907; Dover edition, New York, 1962) Busoni wrote: 'Music is born free; and to win freedom is its destiny', a sentiment which Grainger had developed as a young boy in Melbourne long before his meeting with Busoni – whose enthusiasm for new art and experimentation with microtones and new scales must have been encouraging to Grainger, who was only twenty years old when they first met.

[68] Cahill (1867–1934) was an American lawyer and inventor who created the first electromechanical musical instrument, the Telharmonium or Dynamophone, a giant electronic music-generator, the first version of which he patented in 1898.

an article by Ray Stannard Baker in *McClure's* magazine, July 1906. Now when did Percy go to study with Busoni?[69] It was before that, wasn't it?

Yes, it was.

Well, the thing is that it was translated and published in New York in 1910 in the English edition, and that is now a Dover paperback, the English edition. Busoni had also written about micro-tonal music and given a demonstration of micro-tonal music, of thirds of tones; and this is a very beautiful book. Rainer Maria Rilke[70] had met Busoni in the early years of the century, and he had read this book in typescript. He said that it is extraordinary that a Tuscan can write such beautiful, almost Goethean, German; and Busoni dedicated it to Rilke. It is an unusual dedication to dedicate a book on music to a poet. And when the book came out in New York, I would guess that Percy knew that book in the English translation, although Percy could have read it in German. I think it's a very, very interesting link with Free Music.[71] As far as I know no one has investigated this, simply because Busoni is not known. He is a great master who is almost unknown really. He's only known as the transcriber of Bach. Mrs Busoni told me that she was known in America as Mrs Bach-Busoni and in all seriousness introduced at parties, 'Oh you must meet Mrs Bach-Busoni!' (LAUGHTER) That's the only Busoni they knew.

[69] Grainger studied briefly with Busoni in Berlin during the summer of 1903.

[70] Rainer Maria Rilke (1875–1926) is considered to be one of the greatest of modern German lyric poets.

[71] In his Free Music, conceived by Grainger around 1892 (*cf.* note 6 on p. 29, above), 'melody is [...] free to roam thru tonal space [...] melodic lines may each have their own rhythmic pulse (or not) [...] there are no scales–the melodic lines may slide & glide from & to any depth & heights of (practical) tonal space [...] harmony will consist of free combinations (when desired) of all free intervals [...]' (Grainger in a letter to Olin Downes dated 10 September 1942.

PART II

The Correspondence

1957–61

The 33 letters which follow cover the period from 22 August 1957 to 7 February 1961. Unfortunately, the letter from Ronald Stevenson to Percy Grainger which precipitated the correspondence is missing and can be found neither in the Grainger Museum in Melbourne, Australia which houses correspondence to Grainger, nor the archives of the Ronald Stevenson Society, nor in the National Library of Scotland where the originals of Grainger's letters to Stevenson are deposited. From Grainger's first letter to Stevenson, it is clear that Stevenson had written to Grainger requesting his memories of Busoni for a book which Stevenson was preparing to write on Busoni and that he had enclosed a copy of his recently published article 'Busoni: The Legend of a Prodigal' and the score of a song by Grainger's wife, Ella, which he had transcribed for piano solo. Grainger's response was warm and laudatory; and over the course of the next three years he would write eighteen letters to Stevenson, who responded with fourteen more of his own missives. Stevenson's last letter to Grainger, written only days before Grainger's death, acknowledged a Christmas card and photo which had been sent by Ella: 'Best wishes, Percy! My work on your music is growing out of hand and can now only assume the form of a book. *This I shall certainly do*' (*cf.* p. 121). What follows is the fulfilment of that promise given nearly a half century ago.

Letter 1

August 22, 1957

Dear Mr. Stevenson,

Thank you so much for your kind letter & your splendid article on Busoni.[1] I am most grateful for your good wishes, & your generous remarks about my music. My wife thanks you warmly for your gracious remarks about her & the piece written for her.[2]

By what time would you need to have my memories of Busoni,[3] to be

[1] 'Busoni: The Legend of a Prodigal': *cf.* note 56, p. 62, above.

[2] A song by Ella Grainger entitled 'Love at First Sight' was transcribed for piano solo by Stevenson.

[3] Grainger met Busoni in 1903 and at Busoni's invitation studied with him in Berlin that summer.

of any practical use to you? I have been ill for some years (undergoing 10 operations[4]) & therefore got behind hand with my work, which consists of finishing some scores for 'Grainger Festivals' in Australia & Texas: the works being a *Kipling 'Jungle Book' Cycle*[5] for small chorus & large chamber music (about 15 movements) a *Random Round*[6] for large chamber music, & several other numbers that need revision. These *have* to be done before I can tackle other jobs. I have a lot to remember of Busoni, but I am not sure it is the kind of thing anyone who admires Busoni would want. His behavior to me ranged from great generosity to sharp spitefulness. The fact was that I didn't admire his compositions in the least, which is a situation not unlikely to arouse the worst in a composer – particularly in an ignored composer. This I, also an 'ignored composer', have been able to study in myself!

Please tell me the latest date, to be of any use.

Yours admiringly,
Percy Grainger

Letter 2

13 IX 57
Townfoot House
West Linton
Peebleshire
Scotland

Dear Mr. Grainger,

Many thanks for your kind letter of Aug. 22nd and for your generous remarks about my article on Busoni. But, most of all, thank you for your cooperation in offering to let me have some memories of Busoni to incorporate in my book on him. There is no hurry for this; if you could let me have a few paragraphs sometime before next summer, I should be very grateful.

[4] In August 1953 Grainger underwent the first of a series of painful operations for prostate cancer.

[5] Grainger's *Kipling 'Jungle Book' Cycle* for mixed chorus and chamber ensemble was begun in 1898 and completed in 1947. In 1957 he was preparing the work for publication by Schott & Co. the following year.

[6] *Random Round*, a 'join-in-when-you-like' round for vocal and instrumental ensemble based on the polyphonic improvisational techniques Grainger had observed in South Sea Islanders, was originally composed in 1912–14; but further sketches were made in 1943, 1946 and 1957.

Already, you have whetted my appetite by the few words on Busoni contained in your letter ('his behavior to me ranged from great generosity to sharp spitefulness'). You say your memories of Busoni may not be the kind of thing an admirer of his would want. Then I say: 'Hurrah' – that is just what I want; for the last thing I intend to do is to write hagiography. *Entre nous*, I have met a number of Busoni's circle and can say quite candidly that I have never met a more queer lot of people, with one or two notable exceptions. They would be hard to beat for possessiveness and *Schwärmerei*[7]. As I never met the man himself (I am now in my 30th year), after meeting a cross-section of his entourage and positively not liking them, I begin to wonder whether I would have liked Busoni himself. Probably the answer would have been: yes and no. I hazard that the scornful Dantesque mask must have hidden a sometimes too vulnerable compassion.

To make a wholesome change of subject: the best bit of news in your letter was that you are busy composing.

All success for the 'Grainger Festivals' in Australia and Texas!

In November, I go on an Arts Council tour of concerts (piano) in Argyll. I want to include a piece of yours and am thinking of the *Strathspey & Reel*, unless something more recent. Apropos this, would you object to my playing the last few bars of the Scottish piece as I have written them on the enclosed ms.?[8] Speak up and put me in my place, if I have spoken out of it.

I also have an idea to propose a talk on you to the BBC. Enclosed is the script of a talk on Busoni, which I broadcast on June 4th, 1956 (BBC Third Programme). I am sorry I have to ask you to return this, as it is the only copy I possess. But there is no hurry for its return. I have a tape-recording of this talk, which is at present in the hands of

[7] German: excessive or unwholesome sentiment.

[8] *Scotch Strathspey and Reel* for chamber ensemble of winds, strings and voices was composed by Grainger in 1901–11 and published by Schott & Co. in 1924. It is a combination of six Scottish and Irish tunes with the sea chanty 'What Shall We Do With a Drunken Sailor?' of which Grainger wrote in a programme note:

> If a room-full of Scotch and Irish fiddlers and pipers and any nationality of English-speaking chanty-singing deep-sea sailors could be spirited together and suddenly miraculously endowed with the gift for polyphonic improvisation enjoyed, for instance, by South Sea Island Polynesians what a strange merry friendly Babel of tune, harmony and rhythm might result!

Stevenson's edition of the work remains loyal to the melody and harmony of the original and consists of alterations only in the piano writing in terms of Stevenson's own personal pianism, having to do with the 'size and shape of the hands' (RS). It was prepared as 'an appreciation or homage to the composer' (RS).

Hamburg Radio. When I get it back, I could have it copied and send it to you, if you would like to hear it.

The Atlantic Ocean is magnificent, but in a case like this its 3,000 miles do get in the way! Would it be too much to ask you to send me a recent photograph of yourself and your wife?

In closing, I want to thank you for your article on Grieg in the current issue of *The Musical Times*,[9] which I read with reverence and relish. To you, I believe those two adjectives will not be incompatible. The enclosed photo of a Grieg concert in London I send to warm your heart and fan the fire of memory.

All greetings.
Ronald Stevenson

Letter 3

Townfoot House - W. Linton - Peebleshire
Scotland

Dear Mr. Grainger,

I wonder if you ever received a copy of a BBC talk of mine on Busoni[10] which I sent to you last Sept., with some cuttings from the British press apropos last year's Grieg Festival at the London Proms? I shall be very glad if your silence means that you have been busy working on the new Kipling Cycle and all the other things; tho' I hope you have not had a recurrence of illness.

Would you please be so kind as to return the typescript of my talk on Busoni, *which I need urgently*?

When are the Grainger Festivals in Texas and Australia to be held? Is there any literature (pamphlets, previews, etc.) on these festivals available?

Would you be opposed to the idea of a Grainger Festival in London? Even a single —— Grainger concert would blow the dodecaphonic cobwebs off the decadent top-hats! I am sounding Cyril Scott about this idea.

On a concert tour of the Scottish islands last year, I met an old Mod[11] singer who remembered meeting a young fellow called Grainger at the beginning of the century up in the Scottish Hielands.

[9] Percy Grainger, 'Edvard Grieg: A Tribute', *The Musical Times*, Vol. 98, September 1957, pp. 482–83.

[10] Broadcast on the BBC Third Programme, 4 June 1956. The letter he mentions (Letter 2) was actually dated 13 September 1957.

[11] A Mod is a festival of Scottish Gaelic song, arts and culture.

I played your *Scotch Strathspey*[12] on the tour and it was very popular. I hope some lifeboatmen at the ready at the back of the hall weren't offended by the references to the 'Drunken Sailor'!

Some time ago I heard (unless I am mistaken) a transcription of yours of 'Love walked right in'.[13] Is this available? No music publisher over here knows anything about it. Where may I get a copy?

And now a modulation to a remote key. My book on Busoni grows under the pen. It is like a snail: if I cut it, it grows again. It is snail-slow too. It is taking longer than I envisaged, but I would have it take even longer if, by doing so, I could include a piece by you, similar to (tho' maybe not nearly so long) the one you did in 1950 for the reprint of the Heseltine monograph on Delius.[14] What remunerative arrangements would be agreeable to you for this?

I gather from the 'new' Grove[15] that you have been collaborating with Dom Anselm Hughes recently.[16] Under separate cover I am sending an article on plainsong by Dom Gregory Murray. Don't know if it interests you or if you would like to pass it on to Anselm Hughes.

Please send my typescript talk on Busoni. And if I get a letter so much the better. If not – well, I'll know that Mr. Kipling[17] is detaining you.

Hearty wishes to you and kind regards to your wife.

Yours,

Ronald Stevenson
23 VII 58

[12] *Cf.* note 8 on p. 77, above.

[13] The music for George Gershwin's 'Love Walked In' dates from 1930; Ira Gershwin's lyrics were added in 1937, and the song featured in the film *The Goldwyn Follies* in 1938. Grainger's transcription of the song for piano solo was made in 1945 and published by the Gershwin Publishing Corp. in 1946.

[14] Grainger contributed a reminiscence of his friendship with Delius to the Philip Heseltine (Peter Warlock) book *Frederick Delius* (London, Bodley Head, 1923) (it was reprinted by Oxford University Press with additions, annotations, and comments by Hubert Foss in 1952).

[15] The fifth edition of *Grove's Dictionary of Music and Musicians*, under the editorship of Eric Blom, had appeared from Macmillan, London, in 1954.

[16] In 1932 Grainger met the English musicologist Dom Anselm Hughes and commenced a collaboration which would result in seventeen editions of *English Gothic Music,* English works dating from around the year 1000 to the first half of the fifteenth century, the Gothic period in England. Hughes provided modern transcriptions of the works and Grainger prepared editions for practical performance.

[17] Stevenson is referring to the continuing work on Grainger's *Kipling 'Jungle Book' Cycle.*

Letter 4

July 27, 1958

Dear Mr. Stevenson,

Just back from Europe I find your kind letter of 23. VI 58, with its S.O.S. for your stunning radio talk on Busoni. I am happy to be able to send you the script today. This is lucky, as my correspondence is in terrible disorder, & mostly I can't find things at all. But your letter containing the Busoni script I took with me to Europe, & therefore knew just where to look for it. It is a very splendid talk, indeed – in my opinion.

I was interested to hear of your Arts Council Tour of Argyle & I am grateful that you played my *Strathspey & Reel.* Your alteration of the piano passages, towards the end, looks as if it might be a great improvement. For this also thanks.

I look forward very much to getting the article by Dom Gregory Murray on plainsong.

I wish I could do for your book on Busoni a recording of my memories of him. But it is beyond me, alas. I have so much musical work to do for pending concerts, & have no strength to do it with. I cannot collect my thoughts & this makes me so slow & feable at any task. Most of this is old age, no doubt. Whatever it is, I cannot master it.

My relation to Busoni is always a puzzle to me. He was so very nice to me to begin with & so very unpleasant later. Why I know not. But it is a matter I couldn't do justice to without a great deal of thought (perhaps a search for early letters, etc.?) & at present I do not have the strength to give to it.

I am most grateful to you for your idea of a Grainger Festival – in London or anywhere else. But I am not ready for it yet. I have so many compositions for *large chamber music* the parts of which are thoroly tried & well written but the scores of which are not clean-written as they should be. This clean-writing job should be done first.

I wish you all happy things with your Busoni book, & I hope we will meet as soon as possible.

Yours heartily,
Percy Grainger

Letter 5

Townfoot House/W. Linton/Peebleshire/Scotland
6 Aug. 58

Dear Mr. Grainger,

Many thanks for returning the script of my radio talk on Busoni so promptly, and many thanks for your kind words about it.

Since I last wrote, a new situation has arisen: I have decided to apply for the post of Lecturer in Pianoforte, Conservatorium of Music, Melbourne University.

May I ask you to give me a testimonial or may I include your name as a reference? You would send a testimonial to me, to accompany my application, but the reference would go to Melbourne when they contact you in Sept.–Oct. The closing date for application is Sept. 15th. A testimonial from you would need to reach me by the end of this month (August). Anything you may write would naturally be limited to an impression of my work in music, as distinct from personal character, etc.

You may recall that when I sent you the script of my radio talk last year, I told you I intended to send you a tape-recording of it. This recording has now been returned to me from Hamburg Radio and I have sent a copy of it on to you. This recording may also help you to form an opinion on my suitability for the Melbourne job. The recording of the talk is not very good, but the recording of a recent broadcast recital of mine (on the reverse of the tape) is much better. Please keep this tape-recording.

I am also sending you a composition of mine, which I have taken the liberty of dedicating to you.[18]

You speak with despair about the task of writing out clean scores of your compositions for 'large chamber music'. Could I not help you? If an untidy score had a list of errata I could make a clean copy, I feel sure. I do not offer this as repayment for any kindness you may do me apropos Melbourne: I offer it anyway. It would be a privilege for me. I could make the time. Money would not come into it at all. I would anyway regard such music-writing as an ordinary and necessary part of the preparations for a Grainger Festival.

[18] Stevenson'a piano-solo treatment of 'Sumer is icumen in' (*cf.* note 58, p. 65, above), the first of his *Two Eclogues*, is dedicated to Grainger.

Old Cherubini[19] copied out 18 volumes of music by others (some vols. more than 400 pages) – for the love of it, and of knowledge. So far, I have only copied out 30 vols. (and only 32 pp. per vol.) – but even that has taught me a great deal.

Send me a rough score. It is a job that needs doing. I will do it. Any tiny problems would be settled in correspondence.

For your information: I am 30; received my education at the Royal Manchester Coll. of Mus. (piano & comp.); had a symphonic composition played by Yorks Symph. Orch. Leeds Festival, June 1953;[20] was awarded Italian Government Scholarship for research on Busoni, 1955; lectured and gave concerts at the Summer School of Mus., Dartington Hall, S. Devon, 1956; have broadcast frequently and given Arts Council concerts throughout Scotland; have also contributed to various British music magazines. (I believe I sent you an article o mine from *The Musical Times*).[21] I am married and have two small children, a boy and a girl, Gordon and Gerda. It would mean a very great deal to me if I could secure the Australian post.

–And perhaps it would bring about our meeting.

Yours very heartily (and hopefully), Ronald Stevenson

Letter 6

August 10, 1958

Dear Mr. Stevenson

Please forgive these very short lines - but I am ill & not in a condition to attend to these things.

The business with Australia is very complicated. I know heaps of piano teachers there who are well fit to teach & lecture at the Conservatorium in Melbourne, but all the posts are filled by musicians from outside. How is Australia to develop its own lines of thought if

[19] The Italian-born composer Luigi Cherubini (1760–1842) was a dominant force in French opera, transforming the popular comic opera into a vehicle for psychological drama and contemporary statement, as well as being the composer of a large number of instrumental works, masses and other sacred works.

[20] This was Stevenson's *Berceuse Symphonique* of 1951, which was given its first performance by the Yorkshire Symphony Orchestra under Maurice Miles in Leeds Town Hall on 24 June 1953.

[21] Stevenson is possibly referring to his article 'Busoni: The Legend of a Prodigal' (*cf.* note 56, p. 62, above), which was enclosed in his first letter to Grainger (now missing from the collection) and mentioned by Grainger in his response to Stevenson dated August 22, 1957.

European ogres (such as Busoni, for instance) are always dangled in front of their eyes? Of course, if they send a reference to me (about you) I will fill it out nicely.

It is sweet of you to offer to write out scores & thanks & I am most grateful for your kind offer. But I *have* to write them all out myself – this is the way I work them up (you have lovely music-writing & letter-writing, by the way).

Percy Grainger

I am sorry I am so feable.

Letter 7

April 24, 1959

Dear Ronald Stevenson,

I am ashamed to be so slow in writing to you & acknowledging your piano setting of *Sumer is icumen in*, but I have been more or less ill since I wrote you last. I want to thank you most warmly for dedicating the setting to me – I appreciate it very much indeed. At the same time you must forgive my being bigotted & prejudiced where the piano is concerned. I simply hate the instrument & I regret deeply that I yielded in 1911 to my publisher's[22] request for piano versions of pieces such as Shepherd's Hey, Molly on the Shore, Mock Morris, Irish Tune from Co Derry etc. – all of them composed for non-pianistic mediums such as 7 strings, 10 strings & 2 horns, chamber orchestra & the like. I take a very narrow-minded view of music. For me music should be melody of one kind or another, & above all: music should *not* be florid. That is why I had no faith in Busoni as a composer – because he so easily lapsed into the florid. I do not say that my anti-florid view is a right one. I merely say that I can't help feeling that way. That is why I love Bach but hate Mozart. That is why I enjoy Schoenberg & *musique concrete.*[23] I would love to hear you play *Sumer is,* but I cannot get any impression from trying to play it myself. I read so badly – my eyes are weak. Do you want the MS back? If so, try & let me know (here) by May 4th. I am leaving for Europe, but with no settled address. All best wishes & greetings from

Percy Grainger

[22] Schott & Co. published piano versions of these works in 1911 and 1912. Most of Grainger's folk music settings were originally conceived for chamber ensemble ('Shepherd's Hey,' 'Molly on the Shore') or mixed chorus ('Irish Tune from County Derry') but became most well-known in their versions for piano solo.

[23] *Cf.* note 28 on p. 47, above.

Townfoot House, W. Linton, Peeblesshire, Scotland

6 Aug. 58

Dear Mr. Grainger,

Many thanks for returning the script of my radio talk on Busoni so promptly, and many thanks for your kind words about it.

Since I last wrote, a new situation has arisen: I have decided to apply for the post of Lecturer in Pianoforte, Conservatorium of Music, Melbourne University.

¶ May I ask you to give me a testimonial or may I include your name as a reference? You would send a testimonial to me, to accompany my application, but the reference would go to Melbourne when they contact you in Sept-Oct. The closing date for application is Sept. 15th. A testimonial from you would need to reach me by the end of this month (August). Anything you may write would naturally be limited to an impression of my work in music, as distinct from personal character, etc.

You may recall that, when I sent you the script of my radio talk last year, I told you I intended to send you a tape-recording of it. This recording has now been returned to me from Hamburg Radio and I have sent a copy of it on to you. This recording may also help you to form an opinion on my suitability for the Melbourne job. The recording of the talk is not very good, but the recording of a recent broadcast recital of mine (on the reverse of the tape) is much better.

Please keep this tape-recording.

Letter 5: Stevenson to Grainger on 6 August 1958

I am also sending you a composition of mine, which I have taken the liberty of dedicating to you.

You speak with despair about the task of writing out clean scores of your compositions for 'large chamber music'. Could I not help you? If an untidy score had a list of errata, I could make a clean copy, I feel sure. I do not offer this as repayment for any kindness you may do me apropos Melbourne: I offer it anyway. It would be a privilege for me. I could make the time. Money would not come into it at all. I would anyway regard such music-writing as an ordinary and necessary part of the preparations for a Grainger Festival.

Old Cherubini copied out 18 volumes of music by others (some vols. more than 400 pages) — for the love of it, and of knowledge. So far, I have only copied out 30 vols. (and only 32 pp. per vol.) — but even that has taught me a great deal.

Send me a rough score. It is a job that needs doing. I will do it. Any tiny problems could be settled in correspondence.

For your information: I am 30; received my education at the Royal Manchester Coll. of Mus. (piano & comp.); had a symphonic composition played by Yorks: Symph: Orch: 'Leeds Festival, June 1953; was awarded Italian Government Scholarship for research on Busoni, 1955; lectured and gave concerts at the Summer School of Mus., Dartington Hall, S. Devon, 1956; have broadcast frequently and given Arts Council concerts throughout Scotland; have also contributed to various British music magazines. (I believe I sent you an article of mine from The Musical Times).

I am married and have two small children, a boy and a girl, Gordon and Gerda. It would mean a very great deal to me if I could secure the Australian post.

—And perhaps it would bring about our meeting.

Yours very heartily (and hopefully). — Ronald Stevenson

Letter 8

April 27, 1959

Dear Ronald Stevenson

My wife has just found a tape recording, which you so kindly sent me.[24] I must have overlooked this somehow. Now the question is whether I can listen to the tape recordings before I sail for Europe. I do not have a tape-playing machine here, but I must try to find someone who has one. If I possibly can I will listen to it before leaving for Europe. If I cannot manage it I will listen to it on my return from Europe. The main thing is that the tape recording is safe & sound.

With apologies for overlooking the tape recording

Yours cordially

Percy Grainger

Letter 9

Townfoot House
West Linton
Peebleshire
Scotland
28 April 59

Dear Mr. Grainger,

Many thanks for your good letter dated 24 April.

I am very sorry to hear of your illness and hope your sojourn in Europe will renew your health. Should you think of coming to Scotland, my wife and I would be delighted to offer you hospitality and good wholesome vegetarian food. There would be strictly no celebrity-baiting. West Linton is in the country roughly 20 miles south of Edinburgh. If you omit Scotland but stay in London or the provinces, I should be happy to make the journey to visit you, even if only for a brief conversation. I have to pay London a visit soon and would make the journey coincide. Do let me know.

Your letter made me think. You say you hate the piano. When I remember your recording of Chopin's B minor Sonata, that confession seems unbelievable. But I do believe it. The piano has been, still is, a passion with me, though I am increasingly feeling that it is becoming

[24] Stevenson believes this to have been the tape of a broadcast for the BBC Scottish Home Service of three of his *Scottish Folk-Music Settings* and his *Chorale Prelude for Jean Sibelius.*

obsolete or entering a period of oblivion, a period which may see the diffusion of electronic music and the calm continuation of music for strings. (Surely melody is the soul of music and the violin its habitation.)

Your words on melody versus 'florid' music were of absorbing interest; and likewise your preference of Bach to Mozart. Is it not that you feel Bach, unlike Mozart, has no ornamentation as such, but that everything with him is essential and an organic part of the music?

I understand your criticism of Busoni. Most of the 'Busonians' (horrible idea!) that I know are very odd. Finding the disciples so, one wonders about the master. But, you know, the queer thing is that Busoni himself said, towards his end, that music's next development must embrace a recapture of melody. Just that. He planned a whole book on it: I have some of his notes.

It would be fine to talk with you one day. I hope it may be soon.

All good wishes – and to your dear wife.

Yours.

Ronald Stevenson

Letter 10

Townfoot House,
West Linton,
Peebleshire,
Scotland
30 IV 59

Dear Mr. Grainger,

To-day I received your second air-mail letter dated 29 IV and sent soon after your previous one. It was very kind of you to bother to reassure me about the safe-receiving of the tape-record I sent.

The fact that your latest letter arrived in 3 days gave me the idea of sending you some articles of mine,[25] in the hope that they might reach you before you set sail for Europe. Perhaps they would provide you with a little diversion while on board ship.

Have a good voyage and holiday and do please remember my invitation, if at all possible!

With many thoughts and good wishes from

Ronald Stevenson

[25] These articles appear to have included Stevenson's 'Maurice Emmanuel: A Belated Apologia', *Music & Letters,* Vol. 40 (April 1959), pp. 154–65, and his review of *A Personal Recollection of Arnold Dolmetsch* by Mabel Dolmetsch, in *The Chesterian,* Vol. XXXII, No. 194 (Spring 1958), pp. 121–23.

Letter 11

May 6, 1959

Dear Ronald Stevenson

I have found a friend who has a tape machine & last night we played your records[26] thru several times. What a delightful lecturer you are & what an exquisite pianist! Your tone-differentiation (bringing out middle melodies) is superb. I will write you again from the boat or from Sussex when we get there.

I think you wanted your tape back, so I am sending it to you today.

Best greetings

Percy Grainger

I am sorry my vitality is so low!

Letter 12

c/o Mrs. R. C. Bristow, Southolm, Pevensey Bay, Sussex, England
June 12, 1959

Dear Mr. Stevenson,

I have been reading your articles on music & admiring & enjoying them *very much indeed.* You are a magnificent worder & I consider very noble your championship of undervalued or overlooked talents, such as Busoni & Maurice Emmanuel.[27]

Thank you so much for your gift of the Emmanuel article.[28] I am very glad to have it.

I think I did return to you (from White Plains) your *Sumer is icumen in* piece, did I not? I believe you want the Stravinsky & Dolmetsch articles[29] back, so I enclose them in this letter. I think I enjoy the Dolmetsch article most of all.

Your complete articles (now or in a near future) ought to make an impressive collection. I would very much like to have them in

[26] Presumably a recording of the broadcast referred to in note 24, p. 86, above.

[27] The French composer Maurice Emmanuel (1862–1938) made a study of ancient Greek music, folk song, and plainchant, which made their mark in his music through its use of modality. His interest in Greek drama resulted in two operas based on the work of Aeschylus.

[28] *Cf.* note 25, p. 87, above.

[29] No particulars for the Stravinsky article have come to light. For Dolmetsch *cf.* note 25, p. 87, above.

Percy and Ella Grainger outside the Grainger Museum in Melbourne in 1956

my museum in Melbourne.[30] Could you spare copies? As you wrote articles I wish you would always send a copy to: Grainger Museum, The University of Melbourne, Carlton N.3, Melbourne, Vic., Australia.

I appreciate your & your wife's kind invitation to visit you in West Linton very much indeed. Unfortunately I am feeling very sick & will go on to Sweden, for a treatment there;[31] as soon as we can book a passage. If we return to England before going back to USA I will let you know.

For the moment: Warm thanks & greetings to you both

Percy Grainger

[30] The Grainger Museum was founded in 1935 on the grounds of the University of Melbourne as a repository for music manuscripts and memorabilia and a centre for the study of Nordic music and the music of the islands adjacent to Australia. Stevenson would eventually place copies of his correspondence with Grainger in the Grainger Museum (the originals are housed in the National Library of Scotland) as well as photocopies of his manuscripts and articles.

[31] Unfortunately, Grainger's leg and back became so painful that he returned to New York after a stay of only six weeks in England rather than going on to Sweden.

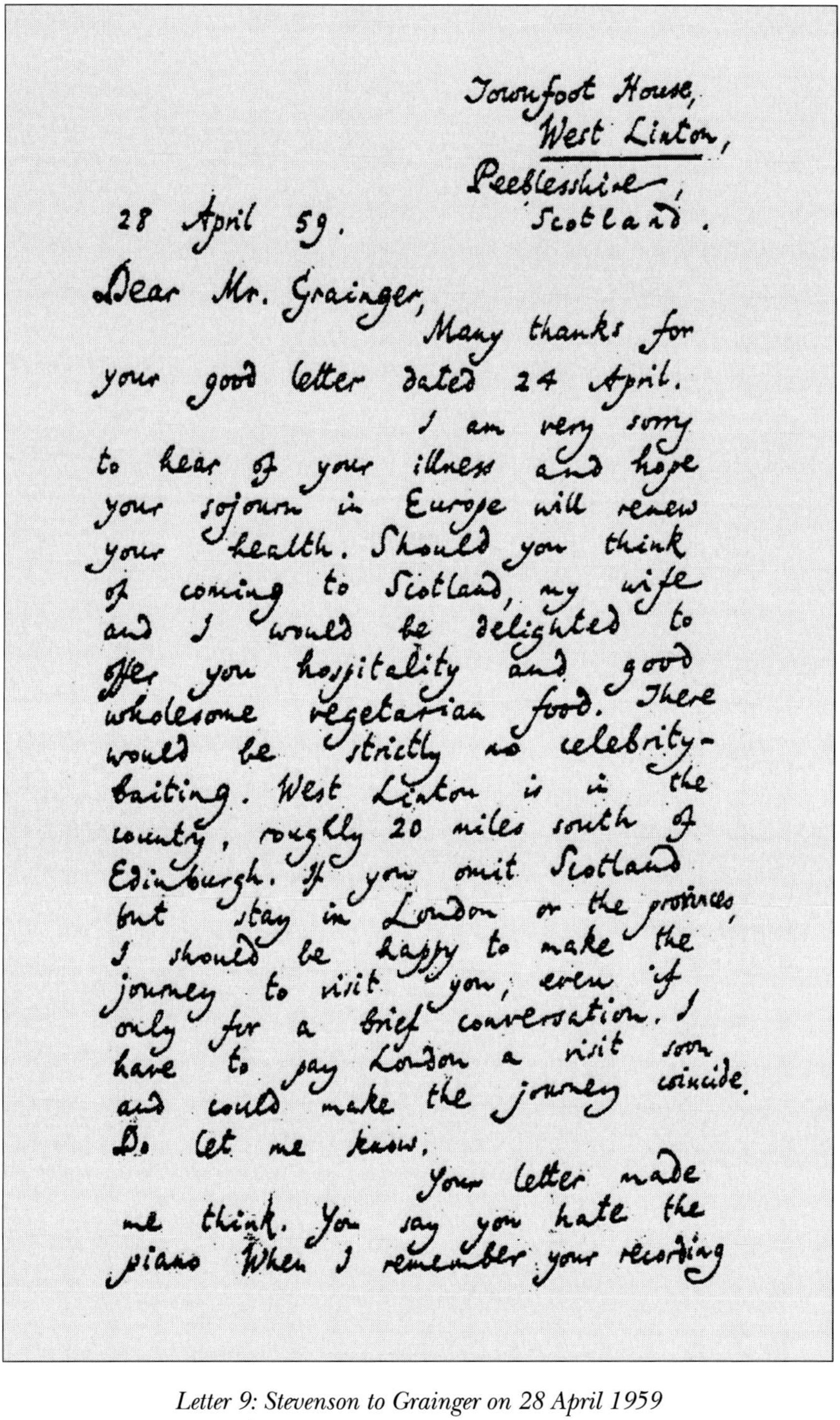

Townfoot House,
West Linton,
Peeblesshire,
Scotland.

28 April 59.

Dear Mr. Grainger,

Many thanks for your good letter dated 24 April.

I am very sorry to hear of your illness and hope your sojourn in Europe will renew your health. Should you think of coming to Scotland, my wife and I would be delighted to offer you hospitality and good wholesome vegetarian food. There would be strictly no celebrity-baiting. West Linton is in the country, roughly 20 miles south of Edinburgh. If you omit Scotland but stay in London or the provinces, I should be happy to make the journey to visit you, even if only for a brief conversation. I have to pay London a visit soon and could make the journey coincide. Do let me know.

Your letter made me think. You say you hate the piano When I remember your recording

Letter 9: Stevenson to Grainger on 28 April 1959

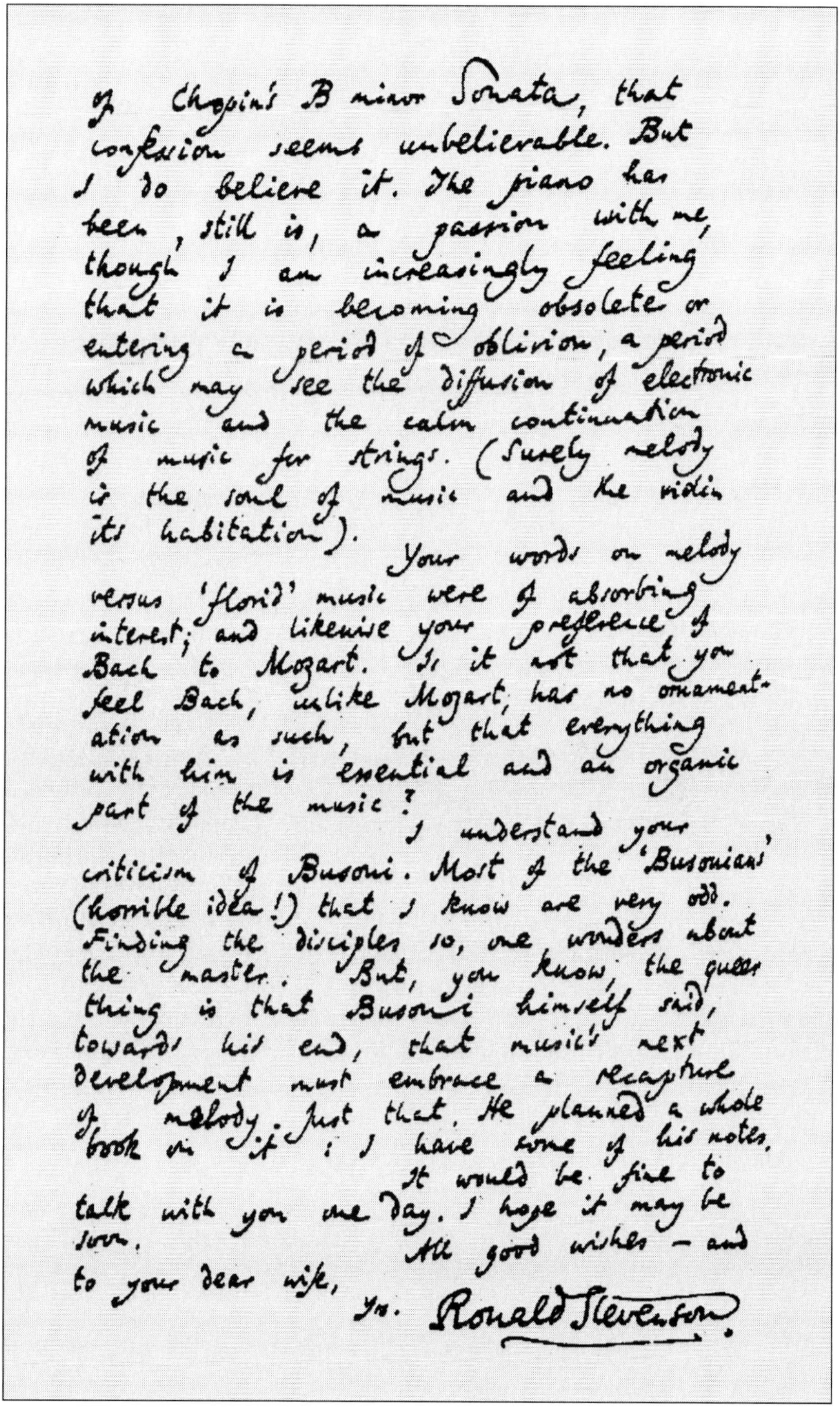

of Chopin's B minor Sonata, that confession seems unbelievable. But I do believe it. The piano has been, still is, a passion with me, though I am increasingly feeling that it is becoming obsolete or entering a period of oblivion, a period which may see the diffusion of electronic music and the calm continuation of music for strings. (Surely melody is the soul of music and the violin its habitation).

Your words on melody versus 'florid' music were of absorbing interest; and likewise your preference of Bach to Mozart. Is it not that you feel Bach, unlike Mozart, has no ornamentation as such, but that everything with him is essential and an organic part of the music?

I understand your criticism of Busoni. Most of the 'Busonians' (horrible idea!) that I know are very odd. Finding the disciples so, one wonders about the master. But, you know, the queer thing is that Busoni himself said, towards his end, that music's next development must embrace a recapture of melody. Just that. He planned a whole book on it: I have some of his notes.

It would be fine to talk with you one day. I hope it may be soon.

All good wishes — and to your dear wife,

Yrs. Ronald Stevenson.

Letter 13

Pevensey Bay, Sussex
June[32] 30, 1959

Dear Mr. Stevenson
Alas! My back got much worse, so we felt I must get back to White Plains as quickly as possible. We are embarking tomorrow (July 1st). If I feel up to it I will write you from the boat.

I would rejoice if you would write an article on me & I will be most happy to give you an interview when I am next in Europe.

Please thank your wife for her most hospitable invitation.

Regretting my inglorious retreat
Yours cordially
Percy Grainger

Letter 14

Southampton to N. York
Cunard Line
R.M.S. Queen Elizabeth
July 4, 1959

Dear Mr. Stevenson,
2 years ago we were in England, Denmark, Germany & Sweden.[33] I was slightly lame when we left America for that trip & the lameness grew so much worse in Sweden that I could only move inch-wise. However, I got radium treatment in Stockholm & by about 10 days a complete cure was effected. This year a pain in my left leg made it wellnigh impossible for me to lift my left leg – this was about 2 weeks (or 10 days) ago. So I thought it wisest to return at once to White Plains,[34] where my doctors understand my case. It is also very

[32]Misdated by Grainger as 30 July.

[33] In January 1957 the Graingers embarked on a voyage to England to visit with family and friends. In February they travelled to Denmark where Grainger gave a series of concerts, including a performance of the Grieg Piano Concerto with the Aarhus Symphony Orchestra (*cf.* note 15, p. 34, above). Following a brief visit to Frankfurt in March, Grainger underwent a series of treatments for his cancer in Stockholm and then returned to England for a BBC broadcast of his compositions from Birmingham in May.

[34] Grainger was in England in April of 1959 to deposit his collection of recorded folksong with the British Institute of Recorded Sound.

unpractical to be ill in a city like Stockholm at the height of the summer season, when it is hard to get hotel rooms.

So we have missed meeting each other, which I greatly regret. I hope we shall meet the next time my wife & I are in Great Britain.

In connection with your kind wish to write an article about me: Would you like to have copies of articles, statements, letters, etc. containing my own views of my own music & statements by me about the purposes of my music? If so, when I get to White Plains I will collect some material to send to you. My main view is this: that I am essentially an experimental composer, & that several of my innovations have been caught up into the body of 'modern music', things such as my discordant harmony (leading by way of Cyril Scott's to Schoenberg's atonalism), my irregular rhythms (leading by way of C. Scott's Sonata Op. 66 to Stravinsky's irregular rhythms in The Rite of Spring), my large chamber-music (Hill-songs I, etc.) leading to Vaughan Williams's, Schoenberg's, Stravinsky's, Hindemith's large chamber music. Should I send you such material as I have in mind it should be clearly understood between us that what I send is strictly 'one man's opinion only' & that I will not expect you to agree with me on any point. What I send should be regarded by me as evidence, but not proof. Personally I think a composer's opinions about his own music is always of interest. But these opinions need not be shared by others, of course. If you would prefer not to be bothered by my opinions about my own music I will respect your preference & will not send the proposed material.

I am very fond of argument & most of my musical friendships have grown out of arguments. It is in this spirit I say I do not agree with the statement, in one of yr splendid articles, that Bach was a beginning of things, while Wagner was an end of things. By that I mean that in Bach the music of several centuries before him survives. An example is the tail-piece of Antonio de Cabezon's 'Prelude in the Dorian mode'[35] (which I enclose in this letter) & the tail-piece of the D major Fugue in the 2nd book of the well tempered clavier. Examples of Wagner's copied-ness by his successors are Grieg's Norwegian Folksongs Op. 66, Grieg's 'Evening in the High Hills' (Lyric Pieces?), Delius's

[35] Spanish composer Antonio de Cabezón (1510–66) is known for his iconoclastic keyboard style, making use of chromaticism, dissonance and daring modulations over a hundred years before the birth of Bach in 1685. Grainger arranged his 'Prelude in the Dorian Mode' for three different instrumentations (wind band, saxophone choir and string ensemble) in his *Chosen Gems* series in 1941, 1943 and 1957, respectively.

'On hearing the 1st Cuckoo in Spring'. Wagner's English horn solo in Tristan led to Grieg's *Evening in the High Hills,* in my opinion, & also to the wonderful opening of *The Rite of Spring.*

Best greeting to your wife & yourself.

Percy

Letter 15

Townfoot House
West Linton
Peebleshire,
Scotland

25 July 1959

Dear Mr. Grainger,

Many, many thanks for your cordial letter of June 12th from Pevensey Bay and for the kind words about my writings. I would have written before but have been uncommonly busy – a reason which I dislike reading in other people's letters, because I think it sounds so petty, but a reason which in this case is true.

It is great good news that you are in England. When do you depart for Sweden?

I am writing an article on you and would dearly like to meet you for this reason (among others). Best of all would be your acceptance of our invitation to visit W. Linton, but if that be impossible, may I visit you in Sussex? If you would spare an hour it would be worth it. Or perhaps we could meet in London, if you intend to be there sometime soon.

Above all, I do not want to tire you and would rather postpone our meeting if that would be its effect at present. I am sorry to hear of your illness and wish you a good recovery.

Yrs.

Ronald Stevenson

Letter 16

September 7, 1959
Dear Ronald Stevenson,

I found your article on Busoni[36] very stimulating. It brought clarity into my thoughts about Busoni. When I first met him, in 1903, when he offered to give me piano lessons without payment, it was the originality of my sketches for *Scotch Strathspey & Reel*[37] that attracted him.

By 1907 he had soured on me, but when we played thru the 2-piano version of *Hill-Song No. 2*[38] his hostility melted & he said, quite wistfully: 'Das ist ein hübsches stück – das ist ein hübsches stück!' 108[39]

And of course I talked to him of the various innovations I had already tried-out (irregular rhythms, unresolved discords, large chamber-music, etc.) or intended to try-out in the future (close intervals, gliding tones, etc.). And while I am not denying that he may have got his 'music of the future' from all sorts of sources I do suggest that he got enough from me to account for his ideas of music to-come.

It was the same with Stravinsky & Schoenberg. Neither of these superb geniuses developed their iconoclastic innovations until my innovations, as incorporated in the Cyril Scott Piano Sonata Op. 66 (incorporated by C. Scott with full written permission by me) had been freely played & heard in Central Europe around 1908 – my 'unresolved discords' of 1898 leading to atonalism, my irregular rhythms of 1899 leading to irregular rhythms of 'Sacre du P.'[40] And when the 1st German War cut off compositional contact between Britain & Central Europe, what happens: These 2 geniuses *dropped* their British-rooted innovations & went back to less progressive stimulations. (Neither Cyril Scott or I have ever dropped our innovations.) Almost everything that European man does had an English-speaking origin: 5 o'clock tea, train, tram, steamer, flirt, bus, strike, lock-out, club, sandwich, lunch, golf, sport, skyscraper, chewing-gum, maxim-gun, revolver, etc. So why should it be otherwise in music? Is it not a fact that most musical innovations are English-speaking (according to the musicologists):

[36] 'Busoni: The Legend of a Prodigal': *cf.* note 56, p. 62, above.

[37] Grainger had been working on *Scotch Strathspey and Reel* since 1901 and completed an early setting for band with strings in 1902.

[38] Grainger worked on his *Hill Song No. 2* for large chamber ensemble from 1901 to 1907 with slight scoring revisions in 1911, 1940, 1942 and 1946. It was published by Leeds Music Co. in its completed form in 1950.

[39] 'That is a pretty piece! That is a pretty piece!'

[40] Stravinsky's *Le Sacre du Printemps* was first performed in 1913.

Frederick Fennell on a visit to Grainger at his White Plains home, late 1959

Foweles in the Frith,[41] Worcester Medieval harmony,[42] Dunstable,[43] William Lawes,[44] Jazz? So if an English-speaking composer happens to invent, or revise (for of course Claude Le Jeune[45] also had his

[41] 'Foweles in the Frith' is a two-part gymel (a form of improvisation in which the two parts begin and end in unison) dating from around 1270 which Grainger and Anselm Hughes edited as part of the series *English Gothic Music.*

[42] The Worcester Fragments from the late Middle Ages published by Dom Anselm Hughes in *Worcester Mediaeval Harmony* (Plainsong and Mediaeval Music Society, 1928) provided three selections, 'Beata Viscera', 'Puellare Gremium' and 'Worcester Sanctus' for the *English Gothic Music* series.

[43] The English composer John Dunstable (*c.* 1390–*c.* 1453) influenced composers on the Continent with his use of 'sweet' harmonies in thirds and sixths. Two of his works, 'O Rosa Bella' and 'Veni Sancte Spiritus', were edited by Grainger and Hughes for *English Gothic Music.*

[44] William Lawes (1602–45) was a prolific English composer whose music abounds with dissonance and unexpected turns. He developed the Fantasia into a complex, freely evolving form. Grainger edited and arranged his '6-Part Fantasy and Air, No. 1' (based on Arnold Dolmetsch's transcription from the original version for viols) for a variety of instruments from strings (*The Dolmetsch Collection of English Consorts* No. 3) to band (*Chosen Gems for Winds*).

[45] Claude Le Jeune (*c.* 1528–1600) was one of the most original and influential French composers of the late sixteenth century. Grainger arranged his 'La Bel Aronde' for a variety of small ensembles.

irregular rhythms), or transform some aspects of music, why should it seem so unthinkable that it cannot be mentioned?

I do not expect my 'serious' music to be liked or respected. But I *do* think I am a natural innovationist & I would like to see some day an acknowledgment of the changes that have come over music thru me. I think it is only fair to Australia.

I think I did send you some remarks & statements by me about my music, did I not? Do you have *Hill-Songs I & II* (arranged for 2 pianos)? If not, would you like to have them? *Hill-Song II* (for 21 single winds) has just been recorded by a superb wind ensemble.[46] When the disc appears, would you like a copy of it? Do you have Frederick Fennell's flawless recording of my *Lincolnshire Posy*[47] for band? If not, would you like me to send it?

I am getting stronger, I think. All the same, just writing a letter 'shivers my timbers'.

Yours heartily
Percy Grainger

Letter 17

Townfoot House,
West Linton,
Peebleshire,
Scotland

14 Sept. 59

Dear P.G.,

I am in the middle of writing a real letter to you, but present commitments have interrupted this; so I am sending these too few and unworthy lines to acknowledge receipt of that parcel of good things you sent me from N.Y. on August 20th (post-mark) and which I received on Sept. 8th; also to thank you for the wholesome and rich letter dated Sept. 7th, received on Sept. 11th.

On Oct. 12th I leave for Germany. I should be very happy if you would send, as you offer to do, to arrive before then by on-air mail:

[46] *Hill-Song No. 2* was recorded by Frederick Fennell and the Eastman Wind Ensemble on the album *Winds in Hi-Fi* on the Mercury label. *Cf.* also note 78, p. 113, below.

[47] Fennell's recording of *Lincolnshire Posy* with the Eastman Wind Ensemble remains one of the finest recordings of the work to this day.

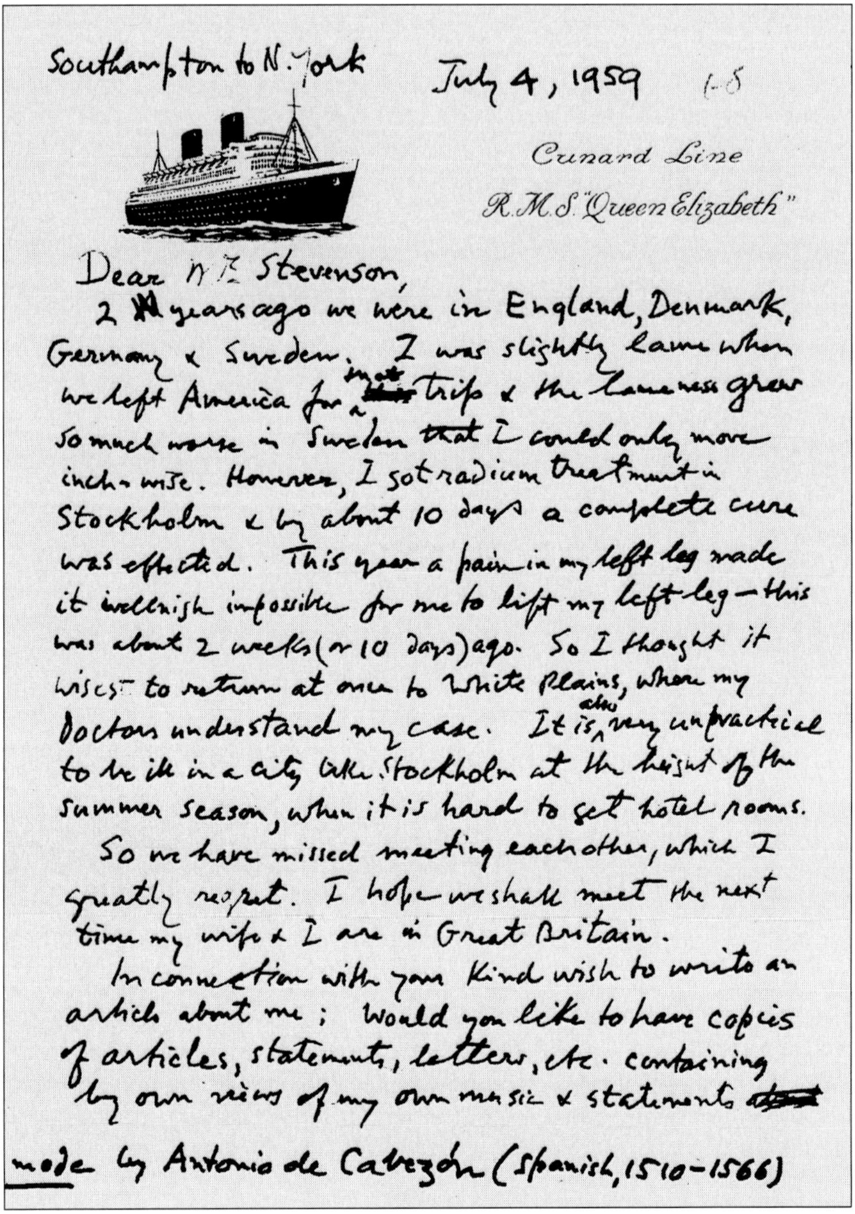

Southampton to N. York July 4, 1959

Cunard Line

R.M.S. "Queen Elizabeth"

Dear Mr Stevenson,

2 years ago we were in England, Denmark, Germany & Sweden. I was slightly lame when we left America for a mot trip & the lameness grew so much worse in Sweden that I could only move inch-wise. However, I got radium treatment in Stockholm & by about 10 days a complete cure was effected. This year a pain in my left leg made it wellnigh impossible for me to lift my left leg—this was about 2 weeks (or 10 days) ago. So I thought it wisest to return at once to White Plains, where my doctors understand my case. It is also very unpractical to be ill in a city like Stockholm at the height of the summer season, when it is hard to get hotel rooms.

So we have missed meeting each other, which I greatly regret. I hope we shall meet the next time my wife & I are in Great Britain.

In connection with your kind wish to write an article about me; Would you like to have copies of articles, statements, letters, etc. containing my own views of my own music & statements

mode by Antonio de Cabezón (Spanish, 1510–1566)

Two pages and the 'tail-piece' of Grainger's letter (Letter 14) to Stevenson of 4 July 1959

(3) (July 4, 1959)

Cunard Line

R.M.S. "Queen Elizabeth"

shared by others, of course. If you would prefer not to be bothered by my opinions about my own music I will respect your preference & will not send the proposed material.

I am very fond of argument & most of my musical friendships have ~~th~~ grown out of arguments. It is in this spirit ~~that~~ I say ~~that~~ I do not agree with the statement, in one of yr splendid articles, that Bach was a beginning of things, while Wagner was an end of things. By that I mean that in Bach the music of several centuries before him survives. An example is the tail-piece * Antonio de Cabeçon's "Prelude in the Dorian mode (which I enclose in this letter) & the tail-piece of the ~~De~~ D major Fugue in the 2nd book of the well tempered clavier. ~~A~~ Examples of Wagner's copied-ness by his successors are Grieg's Norwegian Folksongs op 66, ~~W~~ Grieg's "Evening in the High Hills" (Lyric Pieces?) Delius's

* Tail-piece of Prelude in the Dorian.

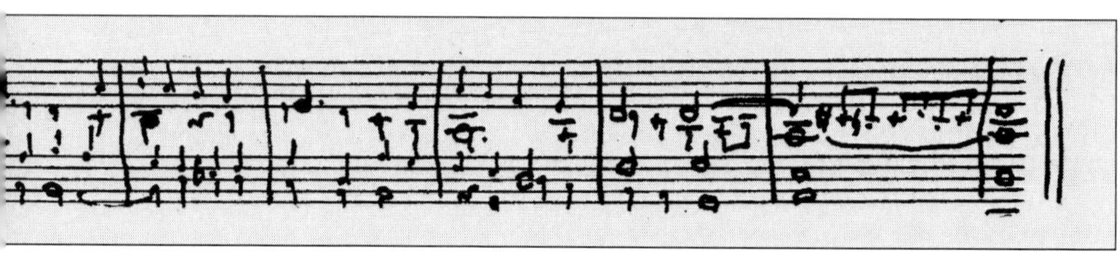

Hill Songs I & II (arr. for 2 pianos)
Lincolnshire Posy (for band)
– recorded by F. Fennell.

I shall also be happy to have a copy of the recent recording of *Hill-Song II*, when it is issued.

You have given me very much to think about and I thank you for providing me – merely by being yourself – with one of the best subjects I have ever had for an article. I believe I have already discovered some independent cases – one outstanding one* – of a salient contribution to 20th century art stemming from an English-speaking origin.

And I haven't forgotten our embryonic argument about Bach and Wagner, which I think will soon blow up an enjoyable gale and gust across the Atlantic!

So very glad you are getting stronger. I hope what I wrote on you will be a little of something to look forward to.[48]

Please excuse this very scrappy letter: I am jotting things down as they occur to me.

From Schotts (London) I have borrowed the compressed score of *The Warriors*[49] – a *tour de force* of a work. But they had not got the *Hill Songs*.

Many hearty greetings – and kind regards to your dear wife.

Yrs. With great expectations of myself for yourself,
Ronald Stevenson

*Edward Gordon Craig (son of Ellen Terry), great man-of-the-theatre, whose ideas were pirated by Max Reinhardt (see the *King Penguin* E.G.C.)

[48] 'Bach and Wagner: A Journey in Music (An Imaginary Conversation between Percy Grainger and the Author)' would eventually be published in The Grainger Society Journal, Vol. 3, No. 1, August 1980, pp. 10–13; *cf.* pp. 176–80, below.

[49] Grainger's magnum opus, *The Warriors* ('Music to an Imaginary Ballet'), for orchestra with three pianos and tuneful percussion ensemble was composed in 1913–16 and published by B. Schott's Sohne in 1926. Stevenson 's transcription of *The Warriors* for two pianos, dated 2 November 1989, bears the title *Warriors for Peace*, reflecting the universality of Grainger's vision of warriors from every time and place meeting in happy congress.

Letter 18

Sept. 22, 1959

Dear Ronald Stevenson,

I sent off the music to you a few days ago & hope it will reach you ere you leave. I also hope you have a nice trip to Germany.

Among the things are some that I would like back, if you are not wanting them particularly. For instance, I wanted you to see the full score of *Hill Song I*. But I think it is next-door to out of print, so I need all the copies I have of it. Likewise the *2-piano* version of *Hill Songs I & II*. If you can run them thru on 2 pianos, keep both copies. If you are not able to do this, please send 1 copy back.

My father was from Durham & I rejoice in Border or Scottish speech. With the exception of Kipling (who was born in India, & therefore to me something like an Australian. Also he was North English I think[50]) it has always been Scottish texts I have set to music.[51] I am sending you some samples of this.

I sent you my *Kipling 'Jungle Book' Cycles 8 va*.[52] This is the only copy of this that I have, so I want it back (these were prints printed for this world premiere in Sydney, Nov. 1960) when you have had a look at it.

I will send you Fennell's recording of *Hillsong II* as soon as it is released – I don't know when

With best greetings to you & your wife.

Percy Grainger

Letter 19

London, 11 Oct. 59

Dear Percy Grainger,

The German trip that I envisaged looks as though it will have to be postponed. But it seems that Britons wander just as much as

[50]Interestingly, the Kipling family actually had antecedents in Scotland.

[51] That is, 'Bonnie George Campbell', 'Drowned', 'Evan Banks' (Robert Burns), 'Fair Young Mary' ('Mhairi Bhan Og'), 'Leezie Lindsay', 'My Dark-Haired Maid' ('Mo Nighean Dhu'), 'My Faithful Fond One'('Mo Run Geal Dileas'), 'O'er the Moor', 'O Gin I Were Where Gowrie Rins', 'Skye Boat Song', 'This Is No My Plaid', 'Turn Ye to Me', 'Weaving Song', 'Willie's Gane to Melville Castle' and 'The Women Are A' Gane Wud'.

[52] Folio edition published by Schott & Co. in 1958.

Dutchmen do (no, they *fly*, don't they?) Anyway, here am I in London for a brief visit.

I am staying with friends who have Australian connections. In my bedroom here, there is a boomerang hung up on the wall. It reminded me of P.A.G. I had been thinking much of you, especially after having received – just before setting off for London – those two big parcels: one of your music, the other of your record. *Thank you* for sending these. I am sorry all this moving around has so far delayed my studying and learning these good things.

Yesterday – Saturday – I spent *most of the day* at the BBC, pre-recording another talk on Busoni for the Third Programme which they will transmit on Thursday Nov. 12th at 5:45 p.m. (The following evening, Friday the 13th there will be a broadcast concert performance of Busoni's *Doctor Faust.*[53] My talk will introduce it.)

And now after this gruelling experience is over, I am in my room again and the boomerang has made my thoughts boomerang back to you.

At home, in Scotland, on my desk an unfinished letter still awaits completion. It is to you.

One point that you might settle by a brief air-mail: I note that your setting of the Song of Solomon[54] is 'from the Vulgate'. May I – with all respect – ask if you are a Roman Catholic; and, if so, what part (if any) you consider your music has been influenced by your faith – or to what extent you think music is capable of being influenced by religion. This I need to know for my article on you.

Many hearty greetings to you and your wife.

Yours

Ronald Stevenson

[53] Busoni was still working on sketches for his grand opera *Doktor Faust* (begun in 1916) when he died in 1924. His student Philipp Jarnach completed the work based on these sketches, and it received its premiere in 1925. In 1985 the Busoni scholar Antony Beamont released a new version based on recently discovered sketches.

[54] Grainger's *Love Verses from 'The Song of Solomon'* (1899–1900, rescored 1931) for soloists with chorus or vocal and instrumental ensemble had as its inspiration the young composer's fascination with word rhythms and desire to mirror them in his music. It was published by G. Schirmer (Schott & Co., B. Schott's Sohne) in 1931.

Letter 20

Oct. 29, 1959

Dear Ronald

No, I am not a Catholic, nor have I ever been associated with any church. I happened to know a lady in Frankfurt (Englishwoman) who had the Catholic bible & she lent it to me, around 1899, when I was examining the irregular rhythms of prose speech, which investigations led to my musical irregular rhythms, the first examples of which were *Love Verses, Train Music, Hill Song I,* etc. I used to ask Roger Quilter,[55] & other English friends to read aloud things like the Psalms, Song of Solomon, etc.

How very nice that you recorded a talk about Busoni's music, in connection with his *Doktor Faust,* you, who have given so much thought to Busoni. I wish I could have heard both your introduction & the Doktor Faust music.

Thanking for your kind inquiry re catholicism

Percy

No one in my family, on either side, was religious, as far as I know. I was anxious that my work was not limited to any sectarian belief.

Letter 21

Townfoot House,
West Linton,
Peebleshire,
Scotland
10 XI 59

Dear Percy,

A long letter to you lay on my desk for weeks. It became longer and longer. It became unmanageable. So I decided to recast it in the

[55] Roger Quilter (1877–1953), who achieved early fame as a composer of songs, was a fellow student with Grainger at the Hoch Conservatory in Frankfurt-am-Main. Along with Grainger, Cyril Scott, Balfour Gardiner, and Norman O'Neill, he was a member of the so-called 'Frankfurt Group' and remained a close life-long friend of Grainger. As a composer he is best known for his songs and light-orchestral music.

form of an imaginary conversation between the two of us. I enclose the result.[56]

It tries to develop an incipient argument on Bach and Wagner which I find in your letter to me written on board R.M.S. 'Queen Elizabeth' on July 4th.[57] To achieve 'authenticity,' I have used quotations from that letter and other letters and articles of yours. I am sure you will be able to trace the sources. Using those passages as ground-work, I have endeavoured to fill-in by ascribing other ideas to you which I think may be consistent with your approach to music.

Roger Quilter with Grainger, late 1920s

My purpose has been twofold: to develop the Bach-Wagner argument; to try and think myself into your ideas, as preparation for writing an extended article on your work.

If you would kindly go through the typescript, commenting in the margin or in between lines wherever you feel I have done you an injustice, and if you would at your convenience, return the typescript with emendations, I should be deeply grateful and should be well-prepared to begin the larger task (which will also be a great pleasure as well as a task).

Many thanks for your 'air-mail' of Oct. 29th in answer to my question re Catholicism. I gave a whoopee to read: 'No, I am not a Catholic' – because I could not believe Catholicism to have any reference to your world of ideas. But three things had puzzled me:

1. The Catholic Bible was utilized in your *Love Verses.*

2. The new Grove Dictionary asserts that you are collaborating with Dom Anselm Hughes.[58]

[56] *Cf.* p. 17, above, and pp. 176–80, below.

[57] 4 July 1959.

[58] *Cf.* pp. 12–13, above.

3. I wondered if your studies in speech rhythms were inspired by those of the Jesuit, Gerard Manley Hopkins.[59]

So perhaps you can excuse the irrelevancy.

No, I could not really think of the Icelandic Sagas as having any relation to the Roman Church! Incidentally, I should like to do some reading in the sagas as I know they are some of your favourite reading. Which would be a good one to start with, do you think?

I am making a detailed study of your scores. Please let me know the date by which you may need any of them back.

Some years ago, I remember seeing a monogram on you (with two photos, I think – one with Byronic collar, the other in U.S. Army uniform with saxophone in hand).[60] Where is this little book obtainable?

I hope your leg is better by now and that you are enjoying good health. Kind regards also to your wife.

Yrs.

Ronald

P.S. I suppose you know that Beecham has published a book on Delius this month?[61]

Letter 22

Townfoot House,
West Linton,
Peebleshire,
Scotland
14 May '60

Dear Percy,

I do hope that your silence of these last few months does not mean that you have been seriously ill. I know that you were unwell last year – you wrote in some detail of your illness; and I know that you are easily tired these days. But I am still hoping for a few words from you, however brief.

[59] Gerard Manley Hopkins (1844–89) was a Victorian poet and Jesuit (from 1868) whose work was little-known during his lifetime but exerted a major influence on twentieth-century poetry, especially through his attempts to approximate everyday speech (sprung rhythm).

[60] D. C. Parker, *Percy Aldridge Grainger: A Study*, Schirmer, New York, 1918. *Cf.* p. 150 for the photograph Stevenson mentions.

[61] Sir Thomas Beecham. *Frederick Delius*, Hutchinson, London, 1959.

Did you ever receive the typescript of my imaginary conversation with you that I sent just before Christmas '59? I wonder what you thought of it. Do you think with some cleaning-up it may be print-worthy? I didn't think of this when I wrote it: it was in the nature of a literary improvisation (and not too 'literary' either) – something thrown off. I didn't keep a copy of it, even. So if you do think it may warrant publication, please return it. Otherwise, wastepaper-basket it.

Not that this was the article I intended to write – not by any means. That I am still writing. I am immersing myself in the music you sent, with increasing admiration of your intentions *and* of your achievements.

Enclosed is a recent review by me of Beecham's new book on Delius.[62] In inserting a paragraph about your music I intended to drive a wedge in. It is strange that a composer of your years should still provide an article writer with something new to say. Stranger still when one reflects that some of the music that is 'newest' was written 60 years ago! (I am thinking of your *Hill Song I*[63]). But if it is strange, it is also inspiring, for it means that your music still presents a challenge.

Three weeks ago, our mutual friend John Amis[64] presented the recording of your *Lincolnshire Posy*.[65] When I saw the broadcast announced in 'The Radio Times', I experienced a moment of apprehension, for, much as I like the very likeable Amis, I reflected that he is at the crux of London musical (?) *haute couture.* But dear John introduced your item admirably and admiringly. (I met Amis at the Summer School of Music, Dartington Hall, Devon,[66] 1956: he was secretary, I was lecturing there.) Maybe he has told you he hopes to

[62] *The Chesterian*, Vol. XXXIV, No. 202, Spring 1960, pp. 132–35.

[63] *Cf.* note 63, p. 69, above.

[64] Writer, critic, broadcaster and musician (b. 1923), best-known for the popular BBC radio show *My Music.*

[65] British Folk-Music Settings No. 34, *Lincolnshire Posy,* composed by Grainger in 1937 for the annual American Bandmasters Association convention, was based on five folk-songs collected by Grainger in 1905–6 and one collected by Miss Lucy Broadwood. Published by Schott & Co. and G. Schirmer in 1940, it is considered to be his masterpiece of band scoring. Grainger was probably the first composer to exploit the sonorities of the wind band systematically, balancing the upper and lower reaches of the winds and brass and using relatively uncommon instruments to achieve balance within families; he was also the first composer of the twentieth century to create a substantial body of band literature.

[66] *Cf.* note 54, p. 61 above.

embark on a new career as singer – see enclosed cutting.[67] I'd like to hear him in your *Dedication*.[68]

All the best, dear Percy.

Yr. Ronald Stevenson

P.S. Any likelihood of your coming over here this year?

P.P.S. Likelihood – aren't words funny things?

Letter 23

May 18, 1960

Dear Ronald,

I consider your book review of Beecham's 'Delius'[69] a masterpiece of justice, insight & superbly fine writing. I have enjoyed reading it very much indeed & feel very grateful for your remarks about the influences of my music upon Delius. I also enjoyed reading the Imaginary Conversations & look forward to reading it again carefully before returning it to you. Indeed, my impression was that I had returned it to you. But my long bout of half-illness made my memory very unreliable. As to the print-worthiness of the Imaginary Conversation: After reading several articles, etc., by you my conviction is that anything & everything written by you is certain to be print-worthy in the extreme. Through half a year or more of half-illness I have got my correspondence into a hopeless muddle, so cannot lay

[67] This cutting from *Radio Times*, 6 May 1960, under the title 'The Biter Bit!', was preserved with the letter:

> The name of John Amis, who is at present introducing *Your Concert Choice* on Sunday mornings (Home), has appeared frequently in radio times, both as broadcaster and contributor. This burly, genial and gifted man is London music critic of *The Scotsman*, secretary of the Dartington Summer School of Music, and secretary of the Apollo Society, which promotes the performance of verse and music.
>
> But John is now, at the age of thirty-seven, setting out on a new career – as a singer. 'It all started last year at Dartington,' he told us, 'when I attended Frederick Husler's singing class just for fun because he was complaining that he had only women to teach. I thought he was pulling my leg when he told me I had the makings of a *heldentenor* (heroic tenor), and asked me to go to Germany to study with him.
>
> 'He was so pressing that I agreed to a trial period, and as that seemed to go pretty well I have decided to begin studying seriously in the autumn.'

[68] *Cf.* note 66, p. 70, above.

[69] *Cf.* note 63, p. 69, above.

my hands on the Imaginary Conversation at this moment. But I do not doubt I will find it soon. Then I shall send it to you with grateful comments.

Yes, I have been more or less ill for a long time. After the operations I have had they like to examine one now & then, to see how one is getting along. Some of these examinations are very painful & leave one knocked out for a long time. Quite apart from that is arthritis or bursitis or something of that sort that I stupidly bring on myself by walking too far, carrying something too heavy. That is dealt with by Rontgen Ray Treatment,[70] which makes one feel seasick for a while. Mixed up with all these are concerts, lectures, long journeys – which, however, I am now giving up, thank goodness. During this bodily-miserable period (a year, or more?) my gramophonic life has been magnificent – for the first time in my life. There are 2 young American conductors[71] who are inexplicably keen about my music & have, between them recorded: 11 orchestral pieces; Children's March & Lads of Wamphray March, Hillsong No. 2, Lincolnshire Posy. These records I shall be sending to you, probably in 2 separate parcels.

Yes, my wife & I hope to come to England, if I am not too lame & if we can get a boat.

I consider it a piece of extraordinary good luck to have Hill Song No. 2 recorded[72] (& so well recorded.)

In the meantime, congratulations on your magnificent Delius book review.

Warmest greetings to you & your wife, in which my wife joins.

Percy

[70] Grainger underwent Roentgen Ray therapy a number of times during the last decade of his life.

[71] Grainger is undoubtedly referring to Richard Franko Goldman (1910–80) and Frederick Fennell (1914–2004). Goldman, director of the famous Goldman Band, often programmed Grainger's works for wind band on his concerts and recorded *Children's March* (with Grainger at the piano) and *The Lads of Wamphray*. Fennell, founder of the Eastman Wind Ensemble, made a number of recordings of Grainger's works for wind band with that ensemble, including *Hill-Song No. 2* and *Lincolnshire Posy*, as well as with the Eastman Rochester 'Pops' Orchestra, including the LP *Country Gardens and Other Favorites by Percy Grainger*, in the late 1950s.

[72] *Cf.* also p. 97, above.

Letter 24

May 24, 1960

Dear Ronald,

I found your *Imaginary Interview* typescript yesterday & sent it off, so you have it as soon as possible.

This *I.I.* is splendid, like all that you write. If there is anything to criticize in it (from my standpoint) it may be that you make me appear too learned. I am extremely ignorant, not only musically, but in all sorts of ways.

My wife & I hope to arrive in England late July that is, if we can get a boat sailing. I am far from well & my doctor is against long or longish train trips, such as London to Scotland. But I think we ought to meet. Is there any likelihood of your being in London for a day or so, let us say early in August?

I was to have played & conducted in Kentucky last Sunday. But I had to cancel the engagement – I was too feeble. Best greetings.

Percy

Letter 25

May 25, 1960

Dear Ronald

I see in the announcements of *Contemporary Music in London* that you are down for *A 20th Century Music Diary*[73] on June 26.

Is this a talk? Will it printed & procurable? If so, I would like to have 2 or 3 copies.

Heartily

Percy

[73] A collection of sixteen piano pieces composed between 1956 and 1959, Stevenson's *A 20th-Century Music Diary* is a series of studies in the possibilities of twentieth-century music incorporating triadic and quartal harmony, canonic techniques, counterpoint, inversion, modal scales, polytonality and chromaticism (*cf.* Ates, Orga, 'The Piano Music' in Scott-Sutherland (ed.), *Ronald Stevenson: The Man and his Music, op. cit.*, pp. 50–60).

Letter 26

31 May 60

Dear Percy,

Many thanks for safe return of typescript of my 'Imaginary Interview with P.A.G.' – and more especially for your illuminating comments. In the light of these I shall revise it and think about publishing it.

Thanks, too, for your air mail letters – two received on the same day (yesterday).

It is great good news that you hope to visit these shores this summer. I shall certainly come to London in early August and look forward *hugely* to our meeting. I hope your health improves. Though I understand your doctor's concern about long train journey, I can't help but feel regret at a lost opportunity of offering you and your wife a little hospitality in Scotland. But the possibility of meeting *anywhere* is wonderful. Our London meeting – the idea of it – already suggests a composition to me: *Grainger in the Strand.* Maybe I'll do it!

How on earth did you find out about my *20th Century Music Diary*? – and that it is to appear in London on June 26th? No, it is not a talk or article but a piece of music! Thanks for your kind interest. I shall send one or two copies of the programme, nearer the date.

Listen! I have a little birthday present for you. Just *what* it is will remain a secret. But do you intend to spend your birthday in White Plains or afloat? *Please let me know.*

Bless you.

With all my heart.

Ronald

P.S. Where may I obtain music and poetry by your wife?[74]

R.S.

[74] Ella Grainger was an accomplished poet as well as artist. Her published work includes *The Pavement Artist and Other Poems* (1939) and *The Wayward Girl* (1941). She had a gift for melody which Percy immortalised in his harmonisation and scoring of eight of her tunes, including 'Love at First Sight' for soprano solo and mixed chorus published by G. Schirmer in 1946. In Ella's hand on the back of the envelope of letter 25 is written: 'Sent my 2 poem books June 9, 1960. 2 Poem Books & 1 Love at First Sight'.

Letter 27

July 4, 1960

Some records I sent to England were broken in transit & some English friends had to pay £3-0-0 duty on a parcel of 3 (2-sided) records I sent. Did you have any similar experience with records I sent you! If so, I will reimburse you for the duty money!

My doctors say I must not travel to either England or Australia this year – perhaps in 1961.

Best greetings

Percy

Letter 28

West Linton, 5 July 60

Dear Percy,

Yesterday I posted to you my setting for solo piano of your *Hill-Song I.*[75] I intend it as a tribute to you on your 78th birthday. May it be a happy day for you and may the next year bring joy and better health for you – and strength to the cause of your music!

My setting of *Hill-Song* was made by way of preparation for the essay on your music which I am now beginning to write. But it was also made because I wanted to hear as often as I like this music which I love and admire. As far as I know, no version for piano solo exists. So I made one.

I should love to play this music in Grieg's house at one of the lunch-hour recitals given during the annual Grieg Festival. Would you object to my pursuing that project? What would the situation be about copy-right? Would there be any point in approaching Schirmer or Schott with a view to publication? I had two photostats made. You have one; I have the other.

I have worked at my transcription, knowing all the time that you don't like the piano and that the piano cannot do more than *suggest* the sonorities of your orchestra. But you yourself made a 2-piano version: I took heart from that thought.

Another reason for heart-searching: I have been bold (or foolish?)

[75] Stevenson's transcription for piano solo of Grainger's *Hill-Song No. 1* (*cf.* note 6, p. 11, above) was performed in the 1966 Aldeburgh Festival's 'Tribute to Grainger' and later recorded by Stevenson in *Percy Grainger: Salute to Scotland* (*cf.* pp. 255–56, below).

enough to add to the *Hill-Song* a quotation of your Kipling *Dedication*[76] for the following reasons:

1) I felt the need to make my setting a *comment* on your work, not merely a pale replica of it;

2) *Dedication* and *Hill-Song I* have a common tonality (and were composed about the same time);

3) there exist strong connections between them; the cadence in bar 1 of *Dedication*

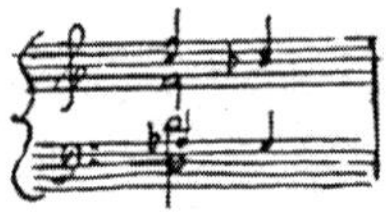

is also found in *Hill-Song I* at 7, 385, 388, 390 and 393;

4) the gapped melody of *Dedication*

also features in *Hill-Song I* at 280;

5) *Dedication* itself, with its first line 'If I were hanged on the highest hill' is also a hill-song;

6) the repetition of *Dedication* – I know you believe repetition to be contrary to the unfolding nature of music – I would seek to justify by reference to your own repetition between bars 249 and 258 of *Hill-Song I.*

I think of my quotation of the Kipling song as a cairn on the hill, in honour of you.

You will be frank, if you disapprove of the licence I have taken. In any case, it is easy to indicate a cut of the quotation.

At the end of my setting of *Hill-Song I,* realizing that your final chord is that of your *Willow, Willow,*[77] I used the 'harped' form as it appears in that song; it allows a more finely graded diminishing of tone than a plain chord would.

Dear friend, I have yet to thank you for the bounteous gift of the

[76] *Cf.* note 66, p. 70, above.

[77] 'Willow, Willow' from William Chappell's *Old English Popular Music* was set by Grainger for voice and piano and for voice and strings between 1902 and 1911. In 1960 he prepared a version for unison male chorus, harp or piano and strings.

five *superb* records.[78] They give great pleasure. I enjoy *Hill-Song II* best of them. The *Children's March* 'Over the Hills and Far Away' (with your good self at the piano) is a good runner-up. *Lincolnshire Posy* also is very fine. All of them are. Bless you.

Will you please thank the good Ella for her dear letter of June 9th? It was kind of her to think of sending me her poems. I look forward to receiving them.

Hoping we shall all meet this summer.

Yrs.

Ronald

Letter 29

Sunday, 10 July 60

Dear friends,

I was thinking much of you on July 8th and felt even nearer to you in thought when the mail brought the two books of poems[79] and an air-mail letter from Percy.

The poem-books must have just missed one ship and had to wait for another for I see from the stamp-mark that they were posted in White Plains on June 9th. So far, I have only had time to savour a few of the verses. I particularly like 'The Old Woman and the Apple Tree' and 'The Beach-comber'. I know that some of the rhymes were written for pleasant reading. Why not? But, if I may shyly say so, others seem to have often a colloquial freedom from style which I also know from Edgar Lee Masters and Robert Frost: sometimes a delicate strangeness that flits in and out of the lines (and between them) with a girlish ghost of Emily Dickinson; and always the words – and the pictures too, which I like – have a childlike ingenuousness which owes nothing to anybody but is its own. And now, through your goodness of heart, it is mine also.

Percy, it was good to get your letter on your birthday. I hope you got mine on the same day (and the music). Bless you for bothering about whether your records sent to me got through the customs without

[78] Stevenson is most probably referring to the recordings made by Frederick Fennell on the Mercury Label, *Country Gardens and Other Favorites by Percy Grainger* (Eastman Rochester Pops), *Winds in Hi-Fi* (including *Hill Song No. 2*) (Eastman Wind Ensemble), and *Lincolnshire Posy* (Eastman Wind Ensemble), and Richard Franko Goldman's *The Sound of the Goldman Band,* which included 'The Lads of Wamphray', and *Band Masterpieces Played by the Goldman Band,* featuring 'Children's March', for Decca.

[79] *Cf.* note 74, p. 110, above.

West Linton, 5 July 60.

Dear Percy,

Yesterday I posted to you my setting for solo piano of your Hill-Song I. I intend it as a tribute to you on your 78th. birthday. May it be a happy day for you and may the next year bring joy and better health for you — and strength to the cause of your music!

My setting of Hill-Song was made by way of preparation for the essay on your music which I am now beginning to write. But it was also made because I wanted to hear as often as I like this music which I love and admire. As far as I know, no version for piano solo exists. So I made one.

I should love to play this music in Grieg's house at one of the lunch-hour recitals given during the annual Grieg Festival. Would you object to my pursuing that project?

What would the situation be about copyright? Would there be any point in approaching Schirmer or Schott with a view to publication? I had two photostats made. You have one; I have the other.

I have worked at my transcription, knowing all the time that you don't like the piano and that the piano cannot do more than suggest the sonorities of your orchestra. But you yourself made a 2-piano version: I took heart from that thought.

Letter 27: Stevenson to Grainger on 5 July 1960

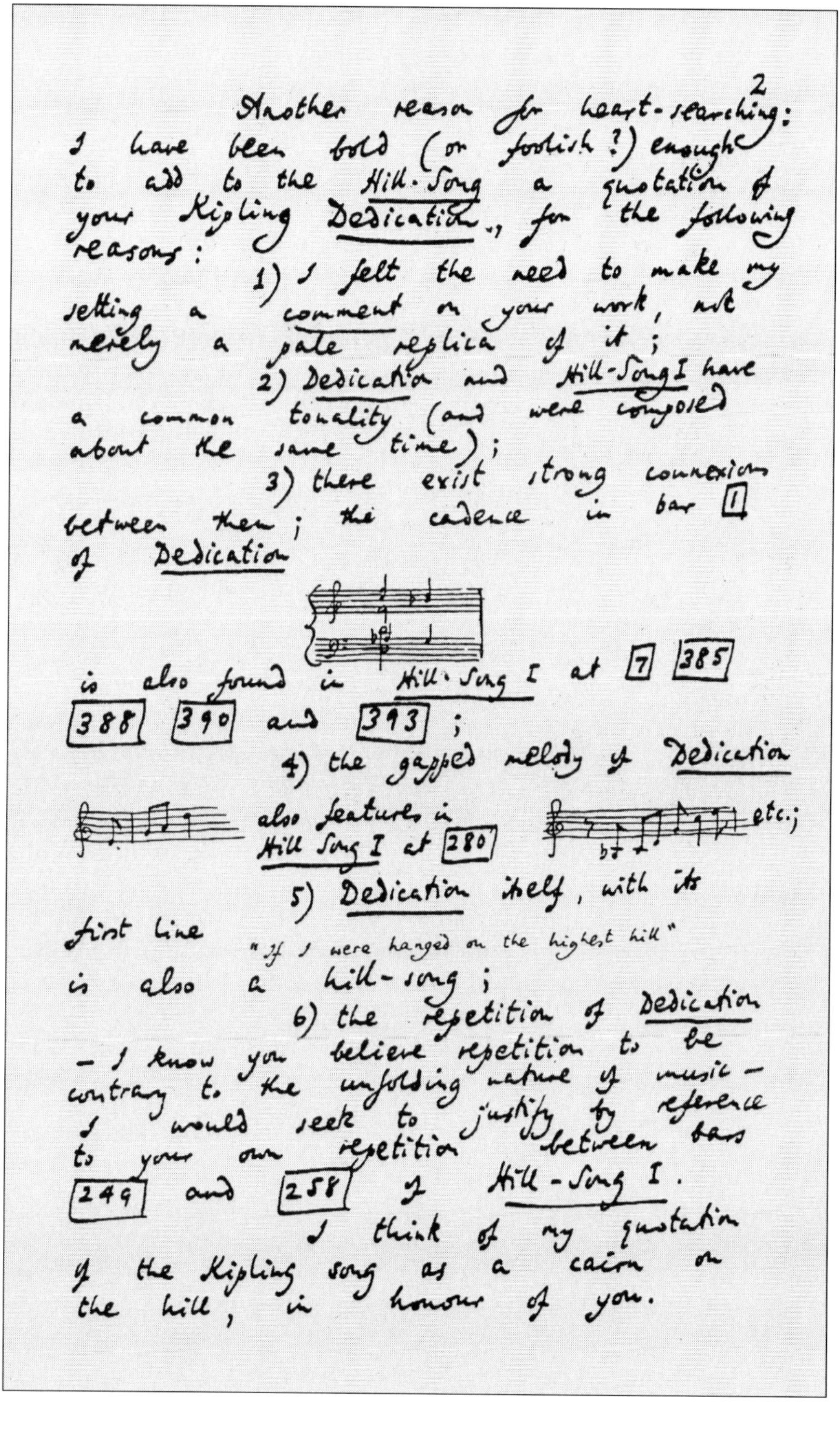

2

Another reason for heart-searching: I have been bold (or foolish?) enough to add to the Hill-Song a quotation of your Kipling Dedication, for the following reasons:

1) I felt the need to make my setting a comment on your work, not merely a pale replica of it;

2) Dedication and Hill-Song I have a common tonality (and were composed about the same time);

3) there exist strong connexions between them; the cadence in bar 1 of Dedication is also found in Hill-Song I at 7 385 388 390 and 393;

4) the gapped melody of Dedication also features in Hill Song I at 280 etc.;

5) Dedication itself, with its first line "If I were hanged on the highest hill" is also a hill-song;

6) the repetition of Dedication – I know you believe repetition to be contrary to the unfolding nature of music – I would seek to justify by reference to your own repetition between bars 249 and 258 of Hill-Song I.

I think of my quotation of the Kipling song as a cairn on the hill, in honour of you.

breakage or fuss or payment. They did. And if I had had to pay a tax on them, I would have paid without demur: my gratitude for such a splendid present would not have been diminished one iota.
Love.

I am really sorry that you can't visit England this year. I hope we may meet next year. Take care of yourself.
In spite of disappointment – all gladness and greetings.
–Ronald

P.S. An *important* P.S. – not just an afterthought – a P.S. that might have become a new letter, but I see I have an inch or two left over. For my article on you, Percy, what is your attitude to *opera*? Can find no mention of that in any previous article on you. But don't bother to reply quickly if you are not well. – R.S.

Letter 30

July 20, 1960

Dear Ronald,
I was looking at your piano solo transcription of my *Hillsong No. 1* this morning & admiring it. You are a splendid craftsman, indeed. It is a fine way to get to know a piece of music – to transcribe it, or orchestrate it, or otherwise creep inside its texture. I feel *greatly* honored that you should wish to investigate my music so thoroughly, & I congratulate you on your mastery of graceful details – in wording, in your handwriting, in your transcribing. I will write again about the transcription as such. I need more than one session with it, as my eyes are slow. I would *love* you to play your transcription in Grieg's house, as you suggest. Your remarks about affinities between *Dedication*[80] & *Hillsong I* are very clever & deep. But under no circumstances would I sanction the publication of a piano solo transcription of *Hillsong I.* If it were published musicians would be faced with the following facts: 1) I am a pianist, therefore likely to write for the piano. 2) My most important work (Hillsong I) is published for piano solo & also 2 pianos. 3) It would seem obvious that the work was pianistically conceived. I had the 2 Hillsongs published when I did because it then (1920?) seemed unlikely that any publisher would want to publish them in their original form (about 24 single instruments). But Delius

[80] *Cf.* note 66, p. 70, above.

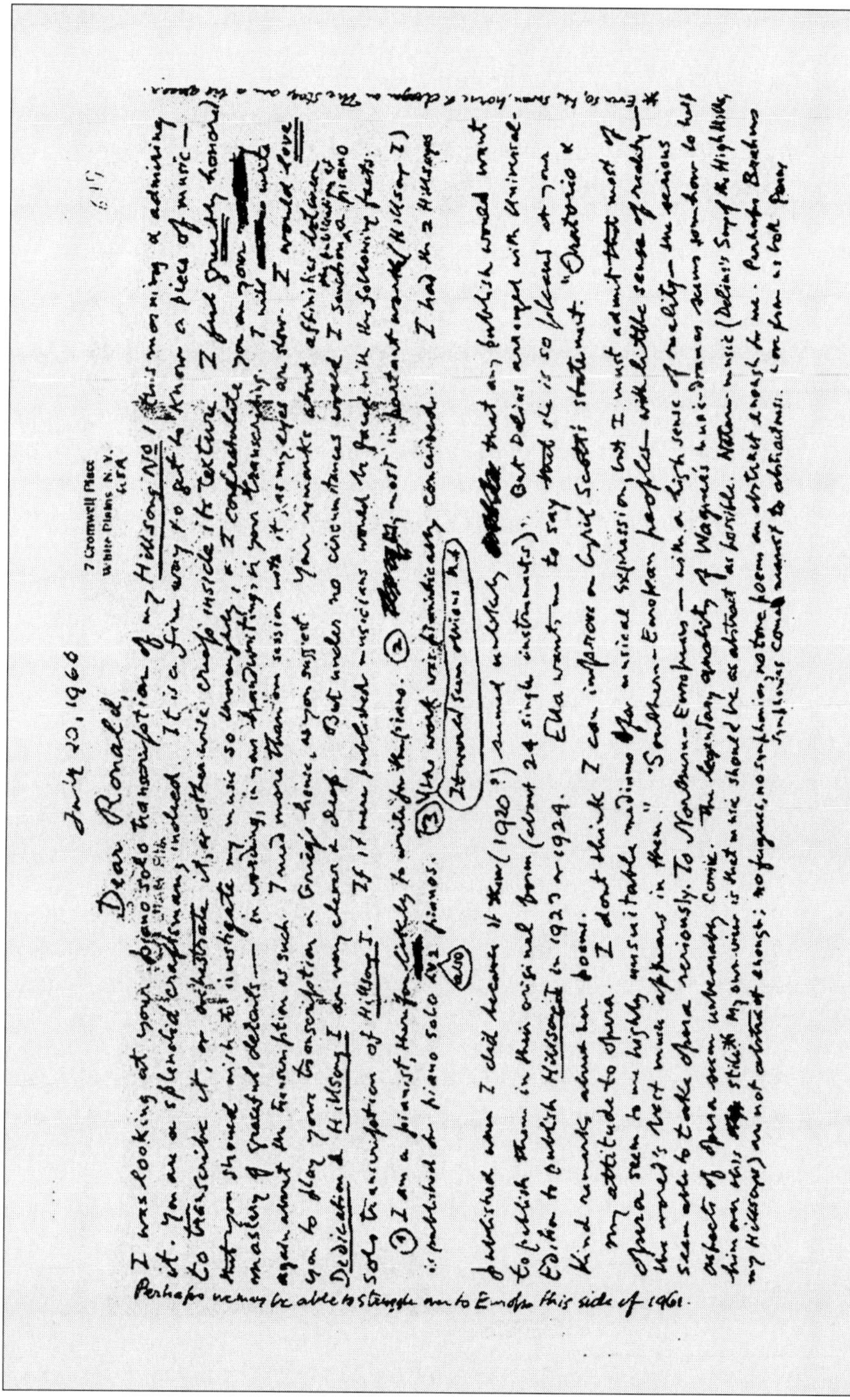

619

July 20, 1960

7 Cromwell Place
White Plains N.Y.
USA

Dear Ronald,

I was looking at your piano solo transcription of my Hillsong No 1 this morning & admiring it. You are a splendid craftsman, indeed. It is a fine way to get to know a piece of music— to transcribe it, or orchestrate it, or otherwise creep inside its texture. I feel greatly honored that you showed wish to investigate my music so thoroughly, & I congratulate you on your mastery of graceful details— in wording, in your handwriting, in your transcribing. I will write again about the transcription as such. I need more than one session with it, as my eyes are slow. I would love you to play your transcription in Grieg's house, as you suggest. Your remarks about affinities between Dedication & Hillsong I are very clever & deep. But under no circumstances would I sanction the publication of a piano solo transcription of Hillsong I. If it were published musicians would be faced with the following facts:

(1) I am a pianist, therefore likely to write for the piano. (2) my most important work (Hillsong I) is published for piano solo (also 2 pianos). (3) the work was pianistically conceived. It would seem obvious that. I had the 2 Hillsongs published when I did because it then (1920?) seemed unlikely that any publisher would want to publish them in their original form (about 24 single instruments). But Delius arranged with Universal-Edition to publish Hillsong I in 1923 or 1924. Ella wants me to say that she is so pleased at your kind remarks about her poems.

My attitude to opera. I dont think I can improve on Cyril Scott's statement. "Oratorio & opera seem to me highly unsuitable mediums for musical expression, but I must admit that most of the world's best music appears in them." Southern-European peoples— with little sense of reality— seem able to take opera seriously. To Northern-Europeans— with a high sense of reality— the serious aspects of opera seem unbearably comic. The legendary quality of Wagner's music-dramas seems somehow to help him over this still.* My own view is that music should be as abstract as possible. Nature-music (Delius's Song of the High Hills, my Hillsongs) are not abstract enough; no fugues, no symphonies, no tone poems are abstract enough for me. Perhaps Brahms symphonies come nearest to abstractness. Love from us both Percy

* Even so, the swan, horse & dragon in The Ring are a bit queer.

Perhaps we may be able to struggle on to Europe this side of 1961.

Letter 29: Grainger to Stevenson on 20 July 1960

arranged with Universal-Edition to publish *Hillsong I* in 1923 or 1924. Ella wants me to say that she is so pleased at your kind remarks about her poems.

My attitude to opera. I don't think I can improve on Cyril Scott's statement: 'Oratorio & opera seem to me highly unsuitable mediums for musical expression, but I must admit that most of the world's best music appears in them'.[81] Southern-European peoples – with little sense of reality – seem able to take opera seriously. To Northern-Europeans – with a high sense of reality – the serious aspects of opera seem unbearably comic. The legendary quality of Wagner's music-dramas seems somehow to help him over this stile.* My own view is that music should be as abstract as possible. Nature-music (Delius's Song of the High Hills, my Hillsongs) are not abstract enough; no fugues, no symphonies, no tone poems are abstract enough for me. Perhaps Brahms symphonies come nearest to abstractness. Love from us both

Percy

Perhaps we may be able to struggle over to Europe this side of 1961.

*Evenso, the swan, horse & dragon on the stage are a bit queer.

Letter 31

Oct. 18, 1960

Dear Ronald,

You must not take it amiss that I do not write you in detail about your remarkablc transcription of *Hill Song I* for piano solo. To begin with, my eyes are too poor at present to be able to read any kind of complicated music with the care & speed needful to get an artistic impression at all. That does not mean that I might not get a most vivid impress if it were played to me by somebody else – preferably you.

In the meantime, please do not feel that I am unresponsive to the hard work & insight with which you have tackled the task.

I am having a bad time – pains in most parts of my body & extreme exhaustion.

Hearty greetings from us both

[Letter unsigned]

[81]This quotation does not seem to appear in either of Scott's books (*My Years of Indiscretion,* Mills and Boon, London, 1924; *Music: Its Secret Influence Throughout the Ages,* Rider, London, 1958) and so may have originated in his correspondence with Grainger.

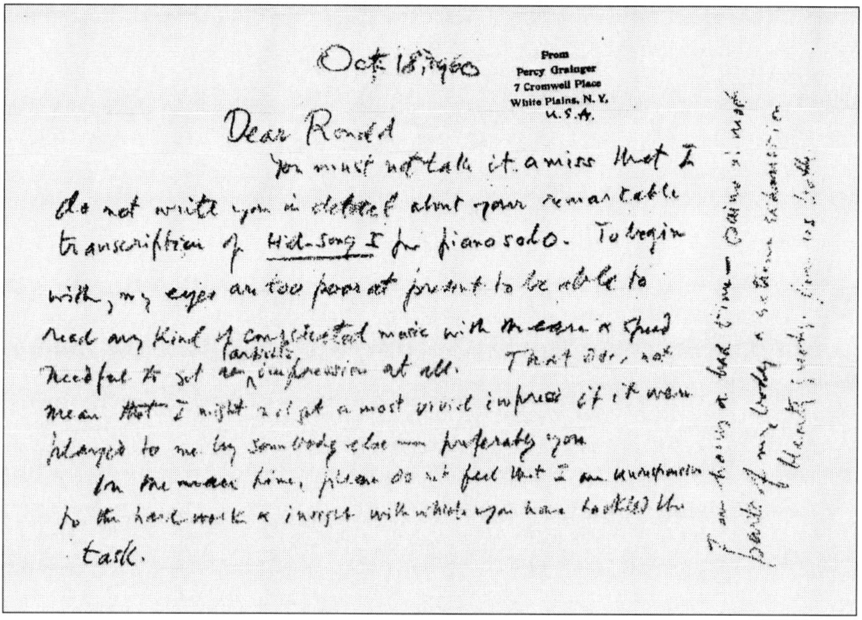

Oct 18, 1960

From
Percy Grainger
7 Cromwell Place
White Plains, N.Y.
U.S.A.

Dear Ronald

You must not take it amiss that I do not write you in detail about your remarkable transcription of Hill-Song I for piano solo. To begin with, my eyes are too poor at present to be able to read any kind of complicated music with the ease & speed needful to get any fantastic impression at all. That does not mean that I might not get a most vivid impress if it were played to me by somebody else — preferably you.

In the meantime, please do not feel that I am unimpressed by the hard work & insight with which you have tackled the task.

Letter 30: Grainger to Stevenson on 18 October 1960

Letter 32

Postcard from Ella and Percy Grainger to Ronald Stevenson, Christmas 1960

Picture of Ella and Percy at American-Swedish Institute, Minneapolis, 31 January 1960 inscribed by Ella 'To Ronald Stevenson with warm greetings from Ella & Percy Grainger. Xmas 1960'.

Letter 33

7 II 61

Dear Percy, dear Ella, dear friends,

Bless you and thank you for that splendid photo of you both, which arrived with your Christmas card; for which also Many thanks. And special thanks, Ella, for your kind inscription.

Curse me and forgive me for my ungracious dilatoriness in acknowledging this present.

I have been engulfed and deluged with work on all sides, and, in the middle – no in the *vortex* – of it all – I have been (and still am) embroiled in the best creative period of my 33 years. Within the past months, namely, since Christmas Eve, I have composed a *passacaglia* for piano on

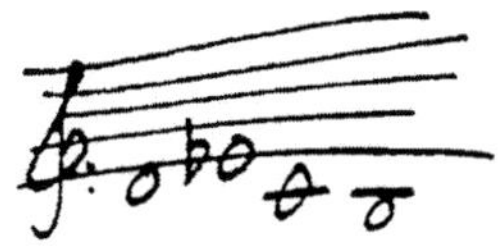

(Dedicated to D. Schostakovich).[82] When I tell you that it lasts *one* hour, you will realize the work involved; you, dear Percy, who have put so many little black symbols on paper in your time. I have also, in the same period, composed two songs, settings of words by Rabindranath Tagore,[83] from his *Gitanjali.*[84]

Work on my essay on you has been interrupted by a commission to write a monograph on that legendary Parsi composer Kaikhosru Shapurji-Sorabji.[85] Quilter[86] knew and admired him. Did you? Hugh

[82] Stevenson's *Passacaglia on DSCH* was begun on Christmas Eve 1960 and completed in final form in December 1963 for the world premiere in Cape Town. Based on the musical signature of Russian composer Dimitri SCHostakovich in the German nomenclature, D, E flat, C, B, this main theme is repeated as a continuous ground under a series of free variations, the traditional form of the passacaglia (a repeated harmonic formula used as a foundation for melodic variations). Stevenson expands the structure of the passacaglia to include many tonalities and changes of mood. Described by Stevenson's biographer Malcolm MacDonald as 'quite simply one of the supreme summits of 20th-century piano literature' (*op. cit.*, p. 46), the *Passacaglia on DSCH* is possibly the longest continuous movement in piano literature, lasting around 80 minutes in performance, and encompassing, almost literally, a world of ideas. *Cf.* Orga, *loc. cit.*, pp. 81–98.

[83] The Bengali poet Rabindranath Tagore (1861–1941) won the Nobel Peace Prize for his *Gitangali* ('Song Offerings') of 1910. It was this work, first published in 1912, that brought him to the attention of western literary circles.

[84] Stevenson's *Two Tagore Songs* – 'The Source' and 'When and Why' – have been published by The Ronald Stevenson Society under the title *Diptych.*

[85] Sorabji (1892–1988) was an English pianist, composer and writer of Parsi, Sicilian and Spanish extraction. His best-known composition – of almost five hours' duration – is the *Opus clavicembalisticum* (1930). His writings include *Mi contra fa: The Immoralisings of a Machiavellian Musician* (The Porcupine Press, London, 1947). The phenomenal difficulty of his works and his self-chosen isolation led to many myths concerning the man and his music. In the 1980s there was a resurgence of interest in his works, with recordings by a number of fine pianists, including Ronald Stevenson. The monograph Stevenson refers to (it is still unpublished) began life in January 1961 as an all-night discussion between himself, the Scottish poet Hugh MacDiarmid (*cf.* note 87, opposite) and English pianist John Ogdon (1937–89). This discussion is reproduced in

McDiarmid,[87] the *doyen* Scottish poet, will be the co-author.

Best wishes, Percy! My work on your music is growing out of hand and can now only assume the form of a book. *This I shall certainly do.* You recall my transcription of your *Hill Song I*: well, I am making a comparable study of your *Warriors*.[88] (I am convinced of the *rightness* of your claims as the first innovator of the 20th century and shall seek to attest to them. I am making enquires about some financial scheme which might bring me to White Plains.)

I do hope you are recovering, dear friend. Look after yourself. From my childhood your vital, joyous music has been like a second sun in my life. –

Ronald

MacDiarmid's autobiography *The Company I've Kept* (Hutchinson, London, 1966, pp. 38–70). Stevenson devotes a page to Sorabji in his book *Western Music: An Introduction, loc. cit.*, p. 203

[86] *Cf.* note 55, p. 103, above.

[87] Hugh MacDiarmid was the pen name of Christopher Grieve (1892–1978), Scottish poet and critic, co-founder of the Scottish Nationalist Party, a radical socialist, and passionate devotee of Scottish language and culture. He is credited with reviving Scots as a modern literary language.

[88] *Cf.* note 49, p. 100, above.

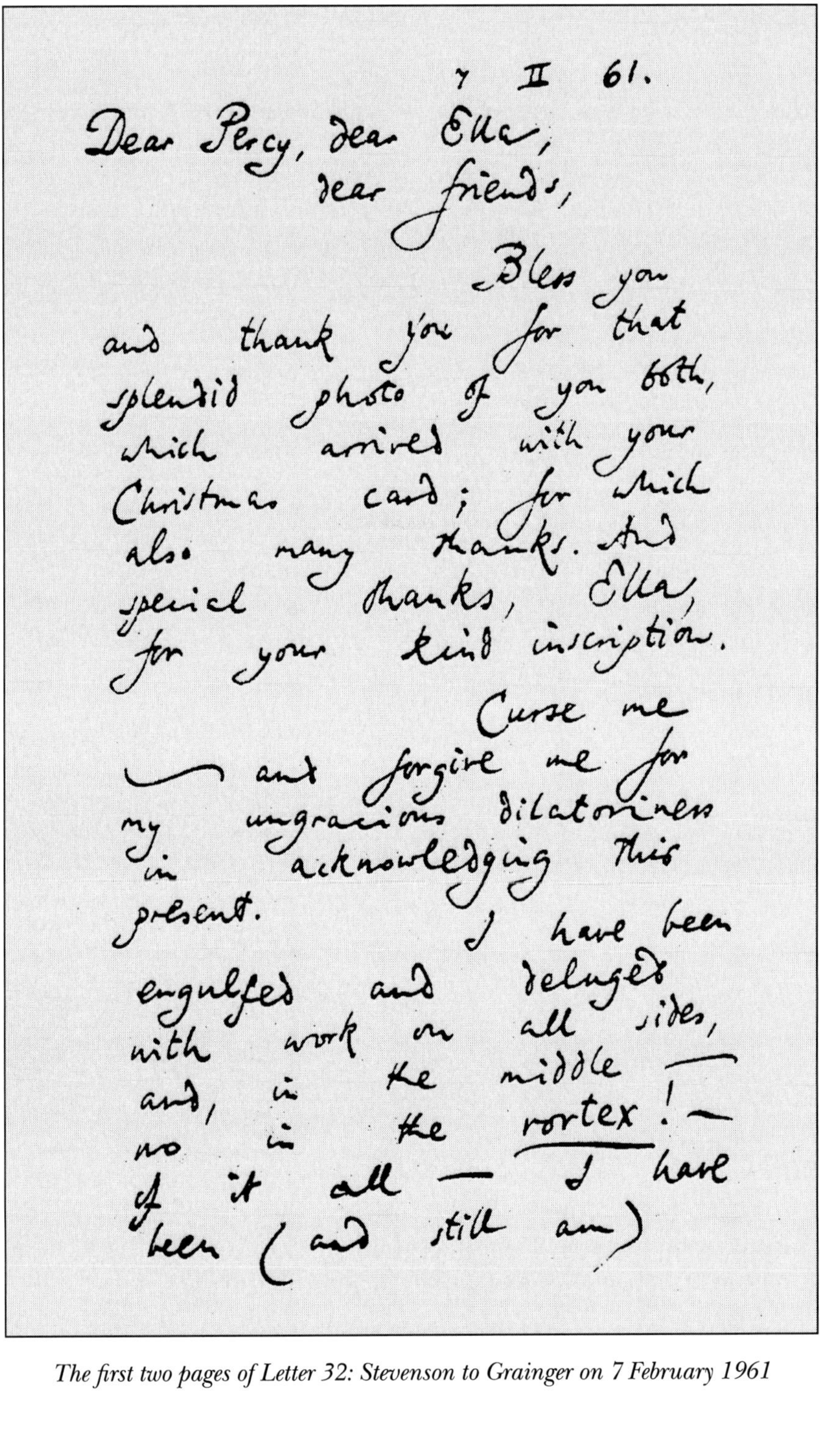

7 II 61.

Dear Percy, dear Ella,
dear friends,

Bless you and thank you for that splendid photo of you both, which arrived with your Christmas card; for which also many thanks. And special thanks, Ella, for your kind inscription.

Curse me — and forgive me for my ungracious dilatoriness in acknowledging this present.

I have been engulfed and deluged with work on all sides, and, in the middle — no in the <u>vortex</u>! — of it all — I have been (and still am)

The first two pages of Letter 32: Stevenson to Grainger on 7 February 1961

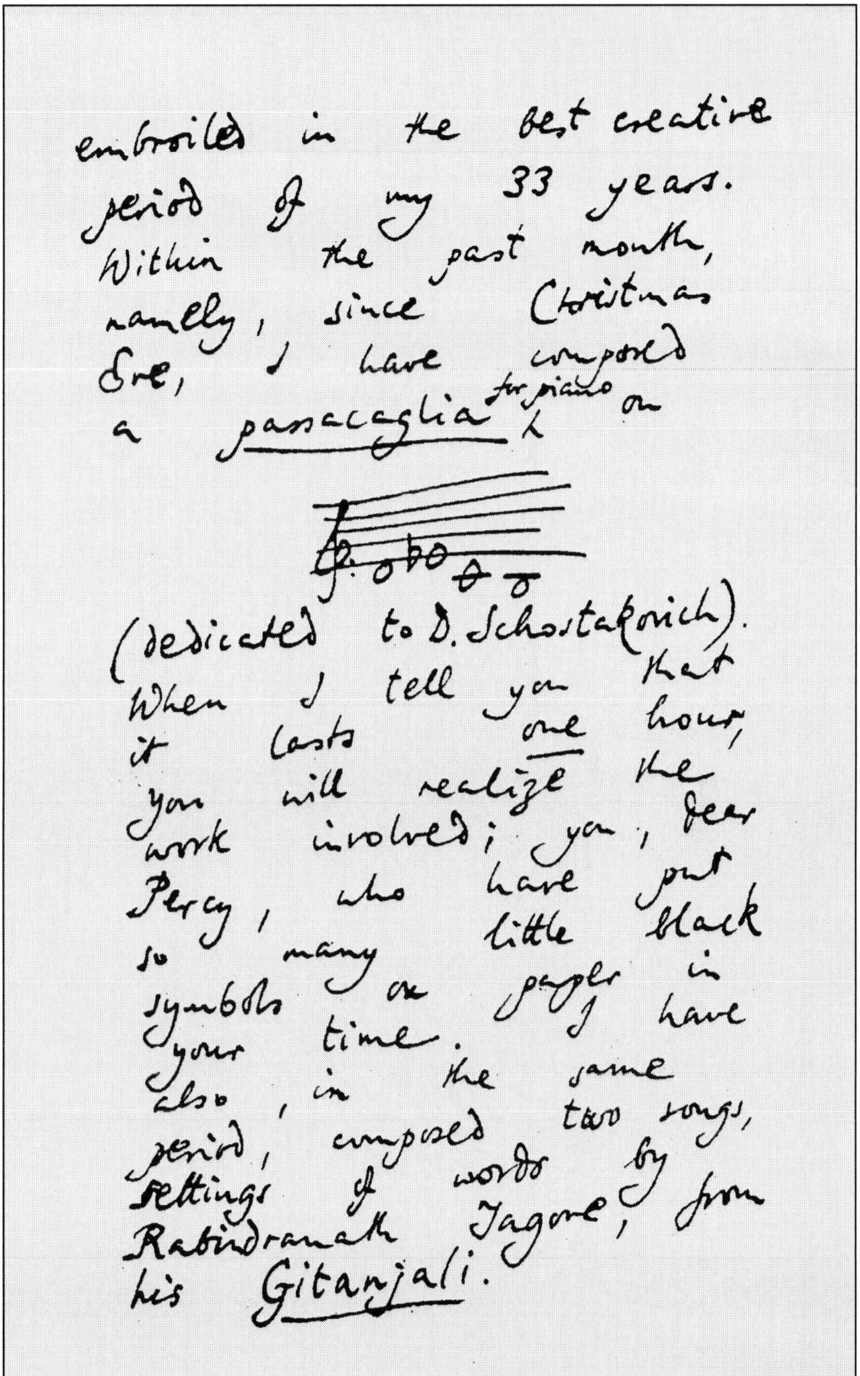

embroiled in the best creative
period of my 33 years.
Within the past month,
namely, since Christmas
Eve, I have composed
a *passacaglia* for piano on

(dedicated to D. Schostakovich).
When I tell you that
it lasts *one* hour,
you will realize the
work involved; you, dear
Percy, who have put
so many little black
symbols on paper in
your time. I have
also, in the same
period, composed two songs,
settings of words by
Rabindranath Tagore, from
his *Gitanjali*.

Grainger two weeks before his death, on 20 February 1961: Stevenson's last letter to him must have been in the post when this photograph was taken

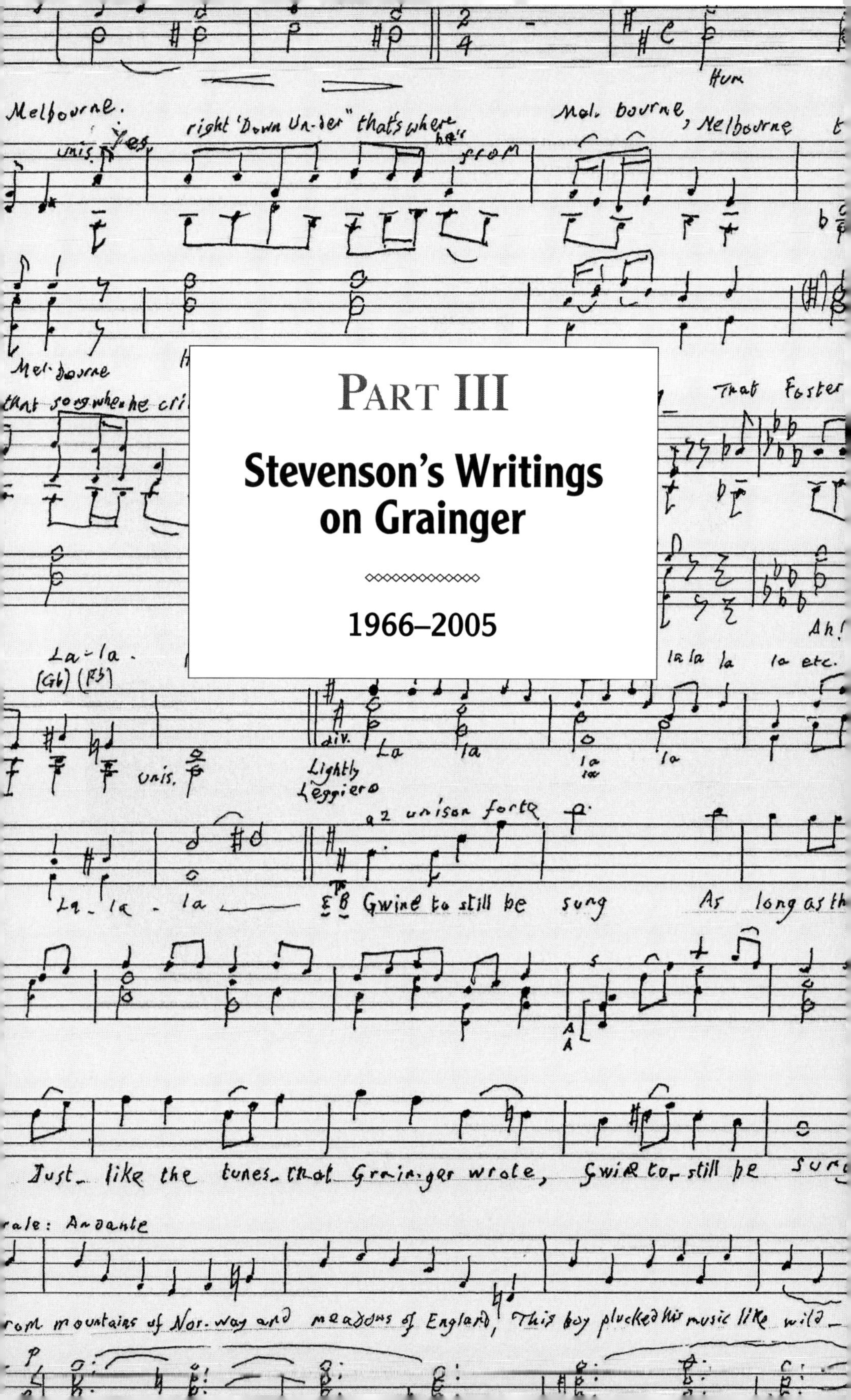

Part III

Stevenson's Writings on Grainger

1966–2005

The twelve essays, articles and lectures which follow were written by Stevenson over a period of 38 years in homage to the man who had meant so much to him as mentor, colleague and friend. Two were introductions to published editions he made of Grainger works. Five articles appeared in various periodicals and books. Stevenson also prepared a number of lecture-recitals and broadcasts on Grainger's music, several of which have been preserved on tape or in typescript and appear here. Of course, there were many more spontaneous discussions of Grainger's life and art during the course of a career filled with performances of Grainger's music, such as those given at The University of Western Australia, the White Plains Public Library, and the Aldeburgh Festival, to name only a few of many venues.

This section is presented in chronological order, beginning with Stevenson's 1966 introductory essay for *The Young Pianist's Grainger* (published in 1967) and concluding with his more recent thoughts on two men who have much influenced his creative life: Walt Whitman and Percy Grainger.

Stevenson's insight into Grainger's music and thought is profound. There is hardly another person living who has reached as deeply as he has beneath the sometimes perplexing and contradictory exterior of one of music's most original geniuses. Sifting aside the unessential, he presents an insightful portrait of a man who felt duty-bound to bring humanity to an understanding of the moral uses of an art which he saw as being too often trivialised and de-humanised. In this understanding, Stevenson and Grainger stand as one.

Preface
to *The Young Pianist's Grainger*

Stevenson composed this introduction to *The Young Pianist's Grainger* (Schott & Co, London, 1967), which he edited, on what would have been Grainger's 84th birthday.

Introductory Note

This album consists of fifteen pieces by Percy Grainger. The melodic material of six of the pieces (No. 4, 6, 8, 9, 10 and 14) is Grainger's own, with no 'borrowings' from folk-music sources. There are five re-prints, collected in one volume for the first time, including three folk-music settings, an arrangement from Bach and another from Dowland. Then there are three previously unpublished easy arrangements which Percy Grainger made of his own folk-music settings.[1] Finally, there are also seven easy arrangements by the editor of Grainger pieces which, until now, have been published only in more difficult versions.

Moderately difficult – and sometimes really difficult – versions of all the pieces in this album are also published by Schott.[2] So, when the young pianist can play all the pieces in this book, he can then try his hand at the more difficult versions. In this way, the material for a progressive course of piano-playing is available.

About Percy Grainger

Percy Grainger was born on 8 July 1882 in Brighton, a suburb of Melbourne, Australia.

From his sixth year, his mother, a piano teacher, sat by him for two hours a day, while he practised the piano. He gave his first concert when he was ten. By the time he was twelve, his concerts had made

[1] With acknowledgments to the National Library of Scotland. –RS

[2] With the single exception of No. 5, which is taken from an unpublished Grainger manuscript. –RS

enough money for his mother to take him to Germany. In Frankfurt he studied at Dr. Hoch's Conservatorium.

Even as a young boy, Percy imagined what he called 'free music': music not divided into regular rhythmic patterns, but with a free, wayward rhythm, like that of ocean waves; music with a melody not divided into separate pin-pointed notes, but with a melody that swooped from the heights to the depths and up again, like the flight of a bird; harmonies that melted into each other like sunset colours; and many different tunes – polyphony – all shining together like stars and planets.

In comparison with this dream, the music of his German professors sounded stiff and conventional to him.

When he was twelve, he made his mother a birthday gift of his first compositions, presented in a satchel which he had made from cardboard, patchwork, kitchen curtains, an old stocking, and small silver-paper stars. For the rest of his mother's life, he presented her with new compositions for every birthday and Christmas.

He dreamed of the Chinese and Japanese music he had heard from the Asiatic communities in Australia, during his childhood. When he was fifteen, his piano professor advised him to enter for the famous Mendelssohn Scholarship. Percy wondered whether, if he won it, he would be allowed to use the prize-money to go to China and study Chinese music. The professor answered curtly, 'Certainly not! The Mendelssohn Scholarship is not awarded to idiots!' He didn't win the scholarship and he never went to China, but later he studied Chinese music and made at least one arrangement of an old Chinese folksong.

He took piano lessons from Professor James Kwast and a few composition lessons from Professor Ivan Knorr, who was also teaching the British composers Balfour Gardiner, Norman O'Neill, Cyril Scott and Roger Quilter at that time. They were known as the 'Frankfurt Gang'. Percy was the youngest of them – and the most rebellious! He reacted against many things which he considered to be stupid conventions. Among these were Italian and German speed indications on printed music published in English-speaking countries. On his own music he always used English terms, even using slangy expressions. He did this because he wanted more people to feel at home with his music, and not to think it was a 'high falutin' thing far above them. Instead of *crescendo molto* he would write 'louden lots' and instead of *staccatissimo* he would write 'chippingly'. Of course, people thought this was funny, but Grainger himself was earnest and serious about this idea of his.

In 1900 the Graingers moved to London. In England Percy began collecting folk music from old villagers who remembered the old

The cover of The Young Pianist's Grainger

songs. He did this in between concert tours, for he was now earning his living as a concert pianist.

In 1903 he took some lessons from the great Italian composer-pianist Busoni.

During Grieg's last visit to London, Percy was introduced to him. They quickly became friends. In 1907 Percy visited Scandinavia for the first time and was Grieg's guest in Bergen, Norway. Grieg wrote in his diary: 'As a pianist, I don't know with whom of the masters I can compare him. He has realised my ideals of piano-playing. If I had his technique, my ideas about piano-playing would be just the same as his. When he plays, we hear a true human being, a fine and great man'. They discussed the Grieg Concerto, which Percy was to play in the Leeds Festival of 1907, with Grieg conducting. But Grieg died in September 1907, before the concert, and only a month after Percy Grainger had visited him. Grainger loved the Grieg Concerto so deeply that he made it his mission to play it in many countries. His performance of it was considered the most authentic.

Percy also collected Scandinavian and Icelandic folk-music. The Icelandic sagas (those long, heroic poems of ancient deeds of bravery) were among his favourite reading. He was also very fond of Kipling's 'Jungle Book' and made many songs out of its poems. His favourite poet of all was the American, Walt Whitman, to whom he dedicated his 'Marching Song of Democracy'.

It was the Balfour Gardiner Concerts of New British Music, financed by Percy's friend from the Frankfurt student days (who was a benefactor of many British composers) that really established Grainger's fame. They were held in London in 1911 to 1914.

In September 1914, Percy and his mother emigrated to America. In 1918 Percy became an American citizen and joined the U.S. Army as a bandsman. He played the oboe and the saxophone and composed much music for his band.

In 1917 his father died in England, and in 1922 his mother died in America.

He married a Swedish girl, Ella Viola Strom, in 1928. They lived in White Plains, New York, though they often travelled to many countries.

In 1930 he lectured in the University of New York and surprised everybody by bringing the jazz musician Duke Ellington to illustrate his lecture.

Percy Grainger probably had a wider range of interest in music than any other musician of his time: from Early English Gothic music (dating back to 1200)[3] to the popular songs of George Gershwin.[4] In his piano recitals, he played his favourite classical composer, Bach, side by side with sea-shanties and folk-songs. His favourite modern

[3] *English Gothic Music*, ed. Percy Grainger and Dom Anselm Hughes (Schott). –RS

[4] *Love Walked In* by George Gershwin, concert transcription for piano solo by Percy Grainger. –RS

composer was his friend, Frederick Delius. Grainger performed a good deal of 16th and 17th century music, often in collaboration with his friend, Arnold Dolmetsch; and he included much modern music in his programmes, particularly by British, American and Scandinavian composers and by men whose work was formerly neglected, such as Hindemith and Schoenberg.

In 1933–34 Grainger toured Australia. He gave all the money he earned on this tour to the University of Melbourne, to found the Grainger Museum (in memory of his mother). He designed the building himself. It houses many manuscripts of famous composers, old phonograph recordings (the phonograph was the early gramophone), souvenirs of musicians, photographs, paintings, books and even inventions!

Percy Grainger was always inventing gadgets. He invented a sheet-music-roller for the piano, when his memory began to fail as he grew older. He pasted his music to big sheets of brown paper which moved round a roller-mechanism, and on to the piano stand, when the pianist's left foot operated a roller-skate! This automatically placed the music on the side of the reading desk, a section at a time, and got over the problem of turning the pages.

He also invented an electronic machine for making the 'free music' he had dreamed of as a boy. Nowadays, many young composers are interested in electronic music. They play – almost like children with new toys – with the machines made by scientists and engineers. They see what strange new sounds they can produce. With Percy Grainger it was the other way round: he had imagined the strange new sounds as a boy and then made the machine to produce them. His wife and a young American scientist, Burnett Cross, helped him to construct it.

Percy Grainger died on 20 February 1961, nearly seventy-nine years old.

He was as different from the conventional picture of a musician as may be imagined. He was a great open-air enthusiast, loved to go for long hikes, liked to dress very 'casually' – preferably in old clothes, and was very skilled in athletics, being able to leap over gates and fences and to turn one perfect 'cartwheel' after another. He was a vegetarian and never drank alcohol or smoked. With his golden curly hair, merry blue eyes and ruddy complexion, he was the picture of health. And the music he wrote was a reflection of the nature he so passionately loved: wild, free and as open as the road over the moors.

Ronald Stevenson
8 July 1966

Music's Mowgli

Published in the magazine *Books and Bookmen*,
Vol. 22, No. 6, March 1977, pp. 18–19.

Last Spring, for a fortnight, I was the guest of Ella Grainger, Percy Grainger's widow, in their home in White Plains, New York. Whilst I was there, proofs of John Bird's new book on Grainger[5] arrived. I sat up late alone, reading them every night. It was the perfect setting for reading this book. I could hardly get nearer to Grainger than to be living in his home, surrounded by souvenirs and his wife's colourful paintings of him in various guises – in Eskimo clothes and hiking gear and so on. And between that atmosphere and John Bird's book there was perfect consonance: I also felt I couldn't get nearer to Grainger than in these pages. I was reminded of Whitman's words about his *Leaves of Grass*: 'Camerado, this is no book: who touches this touches a man'.

Bird has not written hagiography but real biography. His subject is a complex genius. He has written with compassion, love, understanding and sound sense. If you think of Grainger as a light-music composer of such popular trifles as *Country Gardens*, you're in for a surprise. That was only a small part of his musical map. He travelled much further. The legend of Grainger the aesthetic athlete – Apollo and Mercury in one – the man of natural social charm and gentle affability – is true; but it's only half a picture. There's another side which may shock some sensibilities. Here's the background, briefly.

Grainger was born in Melbourne in 1882, son of a big, burly, architect father and a diminutive music-loving mother who came from a farming and horse-raising family. Grainger's father was a syphilitic alcoholic and a wife-beater. The mother defended herself with a horsewhip. The child Grainger witnessed terrible scenes. He became himself a secret, life-long flagellant. If he could have lived with some tribe who practised stoic, masochistic rites, he would have been happy. But he lived in a civilisation and urbanisation he loathed and observed the *mores* so that even his friends knew nothing of his secret life. Grainger could never have married while his mother lived:

[5] *Cf.* note 23, p. 42, above

Ronald Stevenson at Grainger's piano in the White Plains house, 1987

she exercised such power over her only son, after the separation from her husband. Her own syphilis plus false, malicious gossip drove her to suicide by throwing herself from the eighteenth floor of a New York skyscraper. Grainger was forty at the time and away on concert tour. He contemplated suicide himself but overcame it and eventually married and declared his marriage the best thing he'd ever done. It is a story of considerable human courage.

Though Grainger consorted with seeming ease among his colleagues the composers and virtuosos, he despised the snobbism and socialising surrounding the world of symphony concerts and operas, and only really felt at home with folk singers. As is well known, he was a pioneer folklorist. It was his initiative that succeeded in getting the first commercial recording made of a folk singer. This was in 1908 and the folk singer was Joseph Taylor of Brigg, Lincolnshire. Thirty years after recording Lincolnshire folk singers, Grainger, a man of sterling loyalty, dedicated to their memory his *Lincolnshire Posy* for windband.

An open-air spirit blows through this suite and it even contains the ornamentations of the folk song style of singing.

John Bird's book is full of unexpected insights. For example, we learn that H. G. Wells once accompanied Grainger on a folk song expedition and declared to him: 'Percy, you are trying to do a more difficult thing than record folk song: you are trying to record *life*'. This was apropos Grainger's concern to document not only folk song but the folk singer's family, economic and ecological background. Bird quotes a wonderful letter of the young Grainger's written to a fellow composer, which shows how well Grainger understood his own creative process:

> There are hundreds of other ways of developing composition techniques beside actual writing: the chief thing is constant observation and thought. When you play music, observe it always from the composer standpoint, note modes of construction, develop a sharp criticism for musical *inventiveness* – the seat of all musical strength. When you see forms and beauty in nature, apply it in your mind to the forms and types in music. When you feel fine emotions, or sweet noble impressions, or think strong thoughts, *straight away* translate them into your musical language, at least in thought. Think out *exactly* how a composition should be, to express those lovely things in their fullness. If you think in this way, you will find life full of the *need* of musical expression: all emotions will require to become compositions. So it is with me. I have already *done* my thinking (the elementary part of it).[6]

It was this certainty that made Grainger an unruly pupil of Ivan Knorr in Frankfurt, where his fellow students included Cyril Scott, Roger Quilter and Balfour Gardiner, who became his life-long friends. It was also this brimming creative confidence which impressed Grieg. After Grainger studied piano with Busoni, the Italian master presented the young Australian with a portrait inscribed: 'To dear Percy Grainger, as dear as he will surely be great'. The second part of that inscription came true, though the warmth between the two men cooled with time. Grainger became a fierce critic of Busoni. In commenting on Grainger's relish for argument, John Bird puts it in a nutshell where he says that Grainger could 'cap or capsize any argument'. Another target for Grainger's criticism was the gentle Fritz Kreisler, whose cardinal sin was to make a transcription of a Grainger piece, giving the fiddle the tune all the time (which was contrary to Grainger's democratic idea of each musician getting his fair share of the tunes).

[6] *Op. cit.*, p. 67; Stevenson's quotation omits some of Grainger's original text and regularises his spelling and syntax.

Busoni and Kreisler will survive, though these arguments make engrossing reading.

This new biography is studded with a galaxy of musicians who make entrances (and sometimes exits) in Grainger's life: Debussy, Delius, Schoenberg, Bartok, Stravinsky, Arnold Dolmetsch and Duke Ellington – and oh so many. He plays to Fauré who declares 'He has plenty of flame – a supreme energy. It's as if the total population was dancing'. And Grainger, in characteristic self criticism, comments in relating the incident: 'So Fauré fished the true typical impression out of my rotten hammering'.[7] Anyone who has heard the finale of Grainger's historic 1925 recording of the Chopin B minor Sonata will see – or rather, hear – the flame spurting and dancing as Fauré heard it.

About Grainger's performance of the Grieg Concerto, recorded in 1957, when he was seventy-five, I agree completely with John Bird's assessment: 'the noblest interpretation ever recorded'. And Bird adds,

> Yet a generation of pianistic typists have attuned the ears of most critics and audiences to expect faultless performances these days, and Grainger's performance (which, let it be admitted, is liberally sprinkled with lapses and avalanches of wrong notes) would doubtless be treated with scorn and derision were it made generally available.[8]

Bravo, John Bird! Splendidly said! Those interpretations of Chopin and Grieg epitomise the dual character of Grainger: the public virtuoso in the 1925 recording; and the fierce, ecstatic flagellant of the keyboard in the 1957 recording

This book is to be read for what it tells of Grainger's life, rather than for enlightenment about his music. Indeed, some of its comments on the music are gauche. To find Webernesque economy in Grainger's music, as Mr. Bird does, is wide of the mark: in fact (to use Scott Fitzgerald's comparison of his own novels with those of Thomas Wolfe) Webern is a 'leaver-out' – Grainger a 'putter-in'. Again, when Mr. Bird finds Grainger's experimental electronic music of the 1950's suggests a fusion of classical music, jazz and popular music and even invokes a comparison with the currently fashionable (or yesterday's fashionable) 'Pink Floyd' group, it is a purely fanciful description, unrelated to the swooping, siren-like sounds Grainger's machines made in the private recordings I've heard (which are *all* the recordings of them in existence). In the many fine photos in John Bird's book, we see Grainger Savile Row tailored and Grainger in open-neck shirt,

[7] *Ibid.*, p. 125; quotation as in Stevenson's original text.

[8] *Ibid.*, p. 247. *Cf.* also p. 34, above.

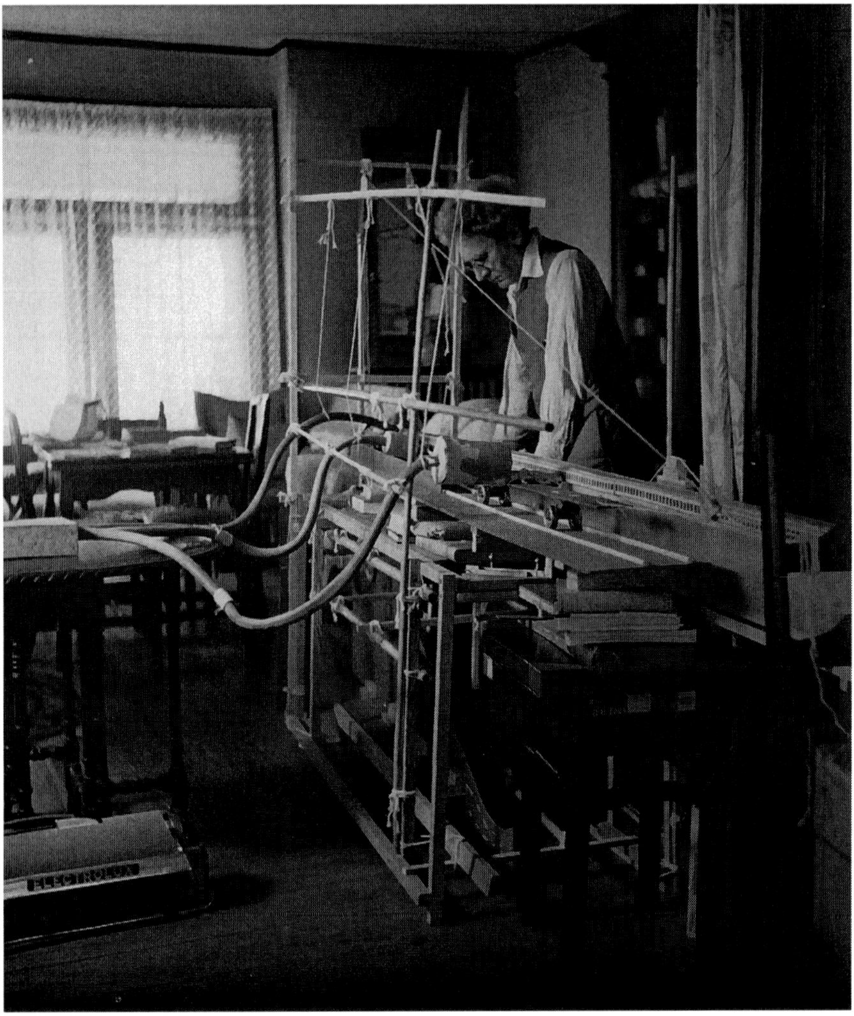

Grainger with his 'Free Music Machine', 1950s

horse riding or scaling up to the crow's nest on board ship.

One of the chapters is entitled 'Saint and Sinner'. I don't believe Grainger was either. For me, he was music's Mowgli. This wild voice is heard in his composition for voices and gamelan-like orchestra entitled *The Lonely Desert Man Sees the Tents of the Happy Tribes,* which has recently been issued on a recording available in the UK.

Towards the end of Grainger's life he built a Heath Robinson-like machine for the realisation of what he called his 'Free Music'; that is, music free from rhythmic beats or scales, and without harmony, either traditional or 'atonal'. This machine synchronised eight oscillators. I brought back from America last Spring a private recording of Grainger's 'Free Music'. In Canada I heard the music of a wolf pack. There exists a commercial recording of the musical language of the wolves, issued in Canada. It reminds me forcibly of Grainger's 'Free Music'.

The work which best reveals the hitherto unknown Mowgli-aspect of Grainger in his Kipling *Jungle Book* choral cycle. In the song *Red Dog* Grainger puts the baying of the wolves into music. In Grainger there was always the boy who felt kinship with the wolves. Could fear of wolves be *not* for what they are but for what we *imagine* them to be; and could it be a fear of something in ourselves? Grainger's music not only expresses the winsome charm of the country garden, but the strange lure of the wilderness.

Random Relics of Percy Grainger

by one of his pen-pals

Published in *The Grainger Journal*,
Vol. 1, No. 2, December 1978, pp. 12–13

I've been re-reading my file of letters from Percy to me, written during his last decade. I leaf through the pages (always hand-writ in blue ink, with no letter-heading but the address printed with an unpretentious rubber-stamp): I linger to mull over a few choice thoughts:[9]

April 1951: The snobs and prigs have always ruled music with an iron hand.

24 April 1959: For me music should be melody: it should not be florid.

29 October 1959: Almost everything that European man does had an English-speaking origin: five o'clock tea, train, tram, steamer, bus, strike, lock-out, club, sandwich, lunch, golf, sport, skyscraper, chewing-gum, maxim gun, revolver, etc. So why should it be otherwise in music? If an English-speaking composer happens to invent or revise or transform some aspects of music, why should it seem so unthinkable that it cannot be mentioned? I *do* think I am a natural innovator and would like to see some day an acknowledgment of the changes that have come about in music through me. I think it is only fair to Australia.

I could go on quoting from Percy's words, but last year Kay Dreyfus (Archivist of the Grainger Museum, Melbourne University) visited me and took photocopies of this correspondence back to Australia with her; I understand all of it, or part of it, may be published.

The range of thought covered by these letters indicates Percy's huge relish for life. The range of his own music activities (as composer,

[9] In fact, the first and third of these 'few choice thoughts' were voiced by Grainger on a number of occasions, such as in 'English-Speaking Music and the War Effort' (broadcast for the Australian Broadcasting Commission on 21 October 1943), and the second is presented in Stevenson's paraphrase.

arranger, editor and pianist) exceeds that of any other musician whose work is known to me. This range included: Aboriginal and Asiatic musics from Grainger's native Australia; London music-hall songs: English morris dance; Scottish bagpipe and fiddle music; film music (this may surprise, but I refer to his two-piano version of 'The Warsaw Concerto' – academics, beware of a heart attack!); electronic music (his 'Free Music' of his last years); and folk music from the five continents. Look at the range of composers he transcribed for piano: Bach and Dowland – others have made similar transcriptions; but also Fauré, Gershwin and Richard Strauss – a rare assortment. The Strauss transcription of the Love Duet from *Der Rosenkavalier* is demonstrably the most minutely detailed notation of piano writing in virtuoso piano literature. On top of all that, he collaborated with Arnold Dolmetsch and Dom Anselm Hughes on editions of 'ye olde musick' and with Duke Ellington in a New York lecture-recital on jazz.

He employed abundant, extreme, unresolved discords before anybody else; irregular rhythms 14 years before Stravinsky; and scored for large chamber groups 6 years before Schoenberg's first Chamber Symphony.

All that may (or may not) impress musicologists and critics. They may still dismiss Grainger as the composer of jiggy ditties. But more than his innovations, it's his *character* – his social character (for, of course he had his private life, with more than its share of problems) – it's *this* that interests me. What was this character, as it comes over in his letters and in countless anecdotes told to me by other friends of his? He was true, open, direct, bold, comradely, affectionate, garrulous, argumentative, inconsistent, abrasive, athletic, fearless, berserk. He was Australian by birth, American by choice, nomad by nature. His only eccentricity was his uninhibited social naturalness.

My son (a young man now), when he was in his teens, had, like countless other adolescents, an amateur folk group: fiddle, concertina, guitar and so on. He didn't *study* music: he made it. To him, and to those countless other youths, Percy Grainger has become part of folklore. They play the tunes he collected without even knowing that he was responsible for their preservation. This reminds me of a line by the American tramp-poet, Vachel Lindsay (who, incidentally, was a friend of Percy's):[10]

> To live in mankind is far, far more than to live in name.

[10] *Cf.* note 8, p. 32, above.

Kicking into Space: A Portrait of Percy Grainger

This undated typescript of a lecture-recital is held in the archives of the Ronald Stevenson Society.

RONALD STEVENSON (opening with *Country Gardens* at the piano):

Percy Grainger was born in Australia; the right place for kicking out into space. From there he had 10,000 miles to kick out into. What he was kicking against was European and specifically English good taste.

This antagonism was manifested in Grainger's *Colonial Song*. Sir Thomas Beecham, that embodiment of English good taste (with the right tincture of eccentricity), thought this music 'the worst piece of modern times'. Grainger thought it one of his best. For Beecham, the aristocrat, Grainger's *Colonial Song* was vulgar; for Grainger, the democrat, it was vulgar in the true sense – 'of the people'.

Let's hear what Grainger himself has to say of this music:

ACTOR: No traditional tunes of any kind are made use of in this piece, in which I have wished to express feelings aroused by thoughts of the scenery and people of my native land (Australia), and also to voice a certain type of emotion that seems to me not untypical of native-born Colonials in general.

Perhaps it is not unnatural that people living more or less lonelily in vast virgin countries and struggling against natural and climatic hardships (rather than against the more actively and dramatically exciting counter wills of their fellow men, as in more thickly populated lands) should run largely to that patiently yearning, inactive sentimental wistfulness that we find so touchingly expressed in much American art: for instance, Mark Twain's 'Huckleberry Finn' and in Stephen Foster's adorable songs 'My Old Kentucky Home', 'Old Folks at Home', and so on.

I have also noticed curious almost Italian-like musical tendencies in brass band performances and ways of singing in Australia (such as a preference for richness and intensity of tone and soulful breadth of phrasing over more subtly and sensitively varied delicacies of expression) which are also reflected here.'

STEVENSON: Melba Anecdote, Red Cross Concert, World War I.[11]

PIANO: *Colonial Song*

That piece, like most of Grainger's, was dedicated to his Mother, Rose Grainger. When she was in middle life, Percy asked her to write down some of her memories.

ACTRESS (ROSE GRAINGER): I was born in a block of buildings in Adelaide called 'White's Rooms'. My Father used to engage celebrated artists to appear at concerts at these rooms. I was the eighth child, the third girl and the 'baby' for 8 years, when another brother was born. I can remember running after street bands and organs and trying to play the Jew's harp and making little musical instruments out of wood and elastic bands and playing on combs with soft paper over them which tickled my lips. My Father often used to sing popular songs such as *Tom Bowling, My Pretty Jane, Hearts of Oak* and others, and as children we were accustomed to hear the American tunes and jokes.

All boyish games and sport gave me pleasure and I was often called 'Tom boy' and was very happy wearing a little tweed skirt, jacket and cap, thinking it was very like my brother Charlie's clothes.

STEVENSON: Rose Grainger's Mother, Sarah Jane Aldridge, was a mixture of gentleness and hardiness and her grandson Percy bore a strong resemblance to her. Once on an outward voyage from England to Australia she insisted on being lashed to the ship's mast to witness the ferocity of a storm at sea.

Percy Grainger was born on July 8th, 1882, in Melbourne. His father was an architect. His Mother had a small piano-teaching practice. From his sixth year she supervised his daily piano practice: two hours a day, a purgatory for a five-year-old. He gave his first public concert at ten.

Rowing on Melbourne's Albert Lagoon as a boy, he wondered why music couldn't be as free as the lapping waves or the hill contours. Even then he imagined what he later called 'Free Music': music not divided by regular beats, but with an *irregular* wave-like rhythm; music not divided into pin-pointed notes, but with a melody that glided and swooped like a bird's flight; harmonies that melted like the sunset; and many different tunes – polyphony – all shining together like stars and planets.

[11]The next portion of the text is lost.

ACTRESS: When he was twelve he made me, his Mother, a birthday gift of his first compositions, presented in a satchel which he'd made from cardboard, patchwork, kitchen curtains, an old stocking and small silver-paper stars. For the rest of my life he presented me with new compositions for each birthday and Christmas – which he always called 'Yule'.

STEVENSON: Grainger's father was big and burly; his mother, tiny. She came from a farming and horse-raising family. Percy's father was a syphilitic, alcoholic wife-beater. The mother defended herself with a horsewhip. The child witnessed terrible scenes. He became a secret flagellant. If he could have lived with some tribe who practised stoic, masochistic rites, he would have found his place. But he lived in a civilisation and urbanisation he loathed and observed its social mores. He could never have married while his mother lived; such was the power she exercised over her only son, both protective and possessive, after the early separation from her husband. But Rose Grainger never allowed all these problems to interfere with her total belief in her son's great gift. Though gifted, he was up to all the usual boy's pranks.

ACTOR: When there was a concert coming up that I had to give as a child, I always made a bargain with my Mother that I should be allowed to do what I liked afterwards, and my favourite amusement was to get on to one of the street tram-cars and climb up on to the roof. In this forbidden position I'd thoroughly enjoy my ride. I say 'forbidden' because there are no roof seats on Melbourne trams and all passengers are supposed to travel inside the cars. After a bit I got friendly with some of the conductors, who would beckon me to mount their trams and discreetly look the other way while I clambered up on top.

STEVENSON: Percy only had three months' official schooling in his life. He refused to go back to school after witnessing some schoolmates stoning chickens. His mother was his only private tutor.

ACTRESS: We read together: Hans Christian Anderson, The Arabian Nights, Homer, Greek mythology, Byron, Goethe, Shakespeare, Heine, Tennyson, Zola, Balzac, Thomas Hardy and Robert Louis Stevenson.

The music we shared includes old English songs, Stephen Foster (Percy's lullaby was *De Camptown Races*), Grieg, Schumann, Beethoven, piano selections from Verdi, Gounod and Mozart operas, Schubert's songs. We heard Wagner at orchestral concerts and Sir Charles Halle's piano recitals.

We enthused together about the natural beauties of the Blue Mountains in New South Wales; we went 'mushrooming' together; and we acted in amateur Shakespeare productions in Melbourne.

STEVENSON: A public subscription in Melbourne financed the twelve-year-old Percy's further music education in Frankfurt, Germany. Rose supported them by giving private lessons in English. Percy attended the Hoch Conservatorium. He rebelled against composition lessons which he abandoned after only a few weeks. He became friendly with an amateur musician, Karl Klimsch, whom he acknowledged as his only composition teacher. He got on very well with his piano professor, James Kwast, and made rapid progress. When he was fifteen, one of his professors advised him to enter for the Mendelssohn Scholarship. Percy wondered whether, if he won it, he might be allowed to use the prize money to go to China to study Chinese folk-music. The Teutonic professor rounded on him: 'Certainly not! The Mendelssohn Scholarship is not awarded to idiots!' Percy didn't win the scholarship; he never went to China, but he *did* pursue his interest in folk-music of all peoples.

His fellow students included the young British composers Balfour Gardiner, Norman O'Neill, Roger Quilter and Cyril Scott. They became life-long friends and were known as 'The Frankfurt Gang'. Percy was the youngest of them – and the most rebellious. He reacted against what he considered stupid conventions, such as Italian terms for music. He preferred English expressions, even slangy idioms. He thought all those *allegros* and *andantes* made people think music was 'high falutin'. For *crescendo molto* he wrote 'louden lots'; instead of *staccato* he wrote 'chippingly'; for *stringendo* he wrote 'give it more pep!'

On completion of his course in Frankfurt, Karl Klimsch presented Percy with a volume of Scottish folksongs and paid for him and his mother (whose health was failing – she had contracted syphillis from her husband) to have a holiday in the Scottish Highlands.

Here's a *Walking Tune* Percy composed in that summer of 1900, based on a scrap of a tune he made on a three-days' walk in Argyll as a hummed accompaniment to his tramping feet.

PIANO: *Walking Tune*

That same summer he conceived a *Hill Song* for wind band. He loved wind instruments because they sound in the open air. The open air was what he wanted to get into his music – great gusts of it.

ACTOR: My *Hill Song* arose out of thoughts about and longings for, the wildness, the freshness, the purity of hill countries, hill-peoples and hill-musics – the Scottish Highlands and their clansmen, the Himalayas and their hill-men, the Scottish and Asiatic bagpipes and their like.

RECORDING: *Hill Song* No. 2 (University of Illinois Band)

STEVENSON: From Scotland Percy and his Mother went to London and settled there. He supported them by activity as a concert pianist.

He was the first *jogger*! He used to jog daily in London in shorts. Imagine him running in and out of the crowded thoroughfares, past the startled City gentry in toppers and frock-coats! In London he met the great Italian composer-pianist Busoni. In 1903 Percy had gratis lessons with him in Berlin.

Grainger was one of the superlative virtuoso pianists of the early twentieth century. Among his many innovations is his recording of Chopin's B minor Sonata: made in 1925, it was the first electrical recording of piano-playing to be made. His scale-playing is like tearing a perforated strip of paper. His rhythm is indomitable. Here is Percy Grainger *himself* in Chopin's B minor Sonata. We hear the finale:

RECORDING: Chopin B minor Sonata Finale

In 1906 he met Grieg in London. In 1907 Grieg invited Grainger to study the Grieg concerto with him in Bergen. Before breakfast, Percy swam in the fjord. Each afternoon he jogged to the local railway station to collect the post.

In his diary, Grieg wrote of Grainger:

ACTOR: What an artist, what a man! What a lofty idealist, what a child and, at the same time, what a broad and mature outlook he has on life. A future socialist of the purest water. As a pianist I don't know to whom among the greatest I should compare him. Grainger is himself. He has realised my ideals of piano playing.

STEVENSON: In a letter to Grainger, Grieg wrote:

ACTOR: Let me say at once: I like you. I like your fresh healthy outlook on art, I like your unspoiled nature which not even 'High Life' has been able to corrupt, and then I like your deep feeling for folksong.

STEVENSON: In 1908 Grainger went on a folksong-collecting expedition in Lincolnshire. H. G. Wells went with him. He told Percy: 'Grainger, you're not only documenting folksong: you are trying to document the *whole of life*!' Percy had a way with him: his charm could elicit even private information from folksingers: he wanted to document their wages, their diet, their habits (smoker or non-smoker, drinker or non-drinker – Percy himself was tee-total and vegetarian and never smoked).

Here is Grainger's pen-portrait of one of his folksingers, Joseph Taylor:

ACTOR: [Mr. Taylor] was bailiff on a big estate, having formerly been woodman and carpenter. Though his age was seventy-five (in 1908) his looks were those of middle-age, while his flowing, ringing tenor voice was well nigh as fresh as that of his son, who repeatedly won the first prize for tenor solo at the North Lincolnshire musical competitions. He sang in the choir of Saxby-All-Saints Church from the age of thirty. He was a courteous, genial, typical English countryman, and a perfect artist in the purest possible style of folk-song singing. Though his memory for words was not uncommonly good his mind was a seemingly unlimited storehouse of melodies, which he swiftly recalled at the merest mention of their titles; and his versions are generally distinguished by the beauty of their melodic curves and the symmetry of their construction. He relied more on purely vocal effect than almost any folk-singer I have come across. His dialect and his treatment of narrative points were not so exceptional; but his effortless high notes, sturdy rhythms, clean unmistakable intervals, and his twiddles and 'bleatin' ornaments (invariably executed with unfailing grace and neatness) are irresistible. He most intelligently realised just what sort of songs collectors were after, distinguished surprisingly between genuine traditional tunes and other ditties, and was, in every way, a marvel of helpfulness and kindliness. Nothing could be more refreshing than his hale countrified looks and the happy lilt of his cheery voice.

STEVENSON: Grainger recorded the Lincolnshire folksingers on an Edison phonograph. In 1908 he successfully negotiated for the Gramophone Company (the precursor of HMV) to dub his recordings on to disc. This was historic: *the first commercial recording of genuine folksong*. We are going to hear Joseph Taylor sing, on this

1908 recording, *Rufford Park Poachers.*

This is the text Grainger wrote in his log-book:

ACTOR:

They say that forty gallant poachers
they was in a mess;
They'd often been attack-ed
when the number it was less.
So poacher bold as I unfold
keep up your gallant heart,
And think about those poachers bold
that night in Rufford Park.

ACTRESS:

A buck or doe, believe it so,
a pheasant or a hare
Was sent on earth for everyone
quite equal for to share.

ACTOR:

The keepers they begun to fight
with stones and their flails,
But when the poachers started,
why, they quickly turned their tails.

ACTRESS:

So poacher bold, as I unfold,
keep up your gallant heart
And think about those poachers bold
that night in Rufford Park.

RECORD: *Unto Brigg Fair: Rufford Park Poachers*

STEVENSON: Now let's hear what Grainger made of that in his *Lincolnshire Suite*[12] for wind band, composed in the 1930s.

RECORDING: *Winds in Hi-Fi: Rufford Park Poachers*

Up to 1914 Grainger toured the world as concert pianist – Europe, Australasia, Africa. In 1914 he and his mother settled in New York. His success was a thunderstorm compounded by an explosion of

[12] *Lincolnshire Posy*, composed between 1905 and 1937.

the sun. Western Union telegrams dropped like hail on his agent's desk.

ACTRESS: Grainger in triple capacity of pianist conductor composer had tremendous success in Minneapolis and St Paul concerts with Minneapolis Symphony. Innumerable recalls. Forced to play several encores after Tschaikowsky Concerto. Conducted his Children's March and Colonial Song. Oberhoffer playing piano part. The two artists changing places for Gum Suckers March. Repeated recalls rewarded their performance. Shepherd's Hey given for encore had to be repeated. Happier audiences never left the auditoriums. Grainger's playing composition and personality a rejuvenating influence.[13]

ACTOR: Percy Grainger's success last night colossal audience. Biggest of all piano recitals this season and enthusiastically demanded eight encores. Papers today carry sensational praise. Want him again soon as possible.[14]

STEVENSON: During the First World War Grainger became an American citizen and joined the US Army playing saxophone and oboe in the Band of the Coast Artillery Corps. He felt himself to be a pacifist in uniform. After the war, he resumed his concert career. He and his Mother moved from New York City to White Plains, New York State. He bought her a roomy old frame house.

In 1922 Grainger was away from his Mother for the most extended period of his life: he had a two-month concert tour of the Southern States. After a concert in California, he received a telegram. His mother had died suddenly. She had thrown herself from the eighteenth floor of a skyscraper in New York.

One of his first transcriptions in memory of his Mother was a free fantasy on the last duet from Richard Strauss' opera *Der Rosenkavalier* (*The Knight of the Rose*). His mother's name, Rose, was enshrined in the title. Perhaps it was a reminiscence of their opera evenings in Germany in the 'nineties. Grainger didn't call this piece a 'fantasia' but a 'ramble': he was a rambler both in nature and in music. So – Grainger's *Rosenkavalier Ramble.*

[13] Carlo Fisher in a telegram to Antonia Sawyer dated 28 February 1920, Minneapolis, Minnesota. –RS

[14] Selby Oppenheimer in a telegram to Antonia Sawyer dated 1 May 1920, San Francisco, California. –RS

Grainger as saxophonist in the US army, 1917

PIANO: *Ramble on Love*

ACTOR: Karl Klimsch said: 'While the grandeurs of mountain scenery appeal to the rougher and more dramatic side of man it is the gentler and more subjective nature of the plains and prairies that create the dreamer and the introspective thinker. The softer shadings of emotion are enticed forth by the great empty spaces, whose vague horizons exert a rare stimulus to the more subtle chambers of our imagination, whereas in the mountains our musings are cut short by the hard but magnificent faces of rocky walls'.

ACTRESS: This explains why it is that such specially poetic and dreamy artists as Hans Christian Andersen, J. P. Jacobsen, Chopin, Walt Whitman, Edgar Lee Masters are practically without exception the products of flat countries and the great plains.

For the musician, the desert is teeming in music, for singing birds abound on all hands. In passing I should like to remark that the Australian magpie seems to me the most prolific and exquisite singer I have ever encountered anywhere – so infinitely varied in his cadences, so wide is his intervalic range.

By what strange irony did it happen that the early British settlers termed the native Australian birds 'songless' when, actually, they are so much more melodious and diversified than anything Europe can offer along these lines?

ACTOR: When a boy of sixteen or seventeen, I began a chamber music work entitled *Bush-music*, expressive of the impressions I had received from the South Australia sandy desert and in the near future I hope to complete this work. Another piece emanating from similar origins is my *Colonial Song*.

The sandy nature of much of the soil and the weight of my pack naturally made my pace slow. I found the country traversed ideal for such a lone jaunt, and the sunny days and bright moonlit nights of winter perfect beyond description. I shall always count those three days as one of the most golden experiences of my life.

STEVENSON: We have all that set to music, as it were, in Grainger's piece for 2 voices and tuneful percussion and strings, *The Lonely Desert Man Sees the Tents of the Happy Tribes.*

RECORDING: *The Lonely Desert Man Sees the Tents of the Happy Tribes* (Sydney Symphony Orchestra, John Hopkins conductor, EMI)

STEVENSON: Grainger was music's Mowgli, Kipling's boy brought up by wolves. Kipling was another of his favourite poets and he set poems from *The Jungle Book* – but not the *Imperialist* Kipling. How did this 'Mowgli' cope with civilisation? We glimpse something of this in an interview Grainger gave to a journalist in Paris in 1926.

ACTRESS: The journalist wrote: 'I sat in the lobby of the Hotel Palais d'Orsay when a sight at which even the jaded eyes of the weariest liver of life might snap in lively interest and blink in astonishment presented itself before me to contradict my musings upon the ingratiating propensities of Paris sophistication.

It was Percy Grainger! The aesthetic-looking pianist, arguing with the dynamic force of an Australian pioneer to be allowed to carry his own luggage from the taxi into the hotel and on to the lift. That he was followed by a gesticulating, frantically explosive French porter, only intensified his strength of muscle, will and determination.

ACTOR: Why shouldn't I carry my own luggage if I want to?

ACTRESS: Why should you when you have two wrists, two palms and ten fingers to keep limber and relaxed for the piano?

ACTOR: *Nonsense!* It doesn't hurt them! It makes them stronger; my hands are never free from calluses. People are too afraid of work. Did you ever hear of a pianist with gout?'

ACTRESS: In front of the Hotel on the Quai d'Orsay sped limousines, Citroëns and madly manœuvred taxis warning other chauffeurs by tooting the nerve-rasping French horn (which doesn't belong to any orchestra).

ACTOR: The way people drive is an affront to nature! Any person who runs wild like this is asking for death.

ACTRESS: And would you have the ladies walk?

ACTOR: More than that, I'd have them plough the fields and dig. Oh, yes! Women have been put on the shelf. You don't know how ghastl[il]y women are being treated. If they were given an equal chance at gaining strength, all this prejudice against them would be eliminated. Look at the proof of it. In Norway, where women plough and cultivate the fields along with the men, what do you find? The National Theatre run by a woman – *the only National Theatre in the world where the Director is a woman!* And the greatest woman writer of today – Selma Lagerlof – is the first woman winner of the Nobel Prize. Yes! Physical hardiness means spiritual achievement! Jog-trotting ten miles every day does more to accelerate the progress of mankind than any course of study offered by an university.

STEVENSON: In that same year, 1926, Grainger met Ella Viola Strom, a

Swedish poet, painter and music-lover. They fell in love on board the steamer *Aorangi* returning from Australia to the States. In January 1928 a press announcement was issued from the New York office of Grainger's concert agent.

ACTRESS: New Grainger Work as Part of Wedding Ceremony
Just before Ella Viola Strom and Percy Grainger are united in marriage by a brief ceremony at the Hollywood Bowl[15] on August 9th (at the conclusion of the second symphony concert he is to conduct there) the composer will present his latest orchestral work, specially written to figure as part of the marriage ceremony. Entitled *To a Nordic Princess*, its inspiration and purport are thus set forth by Grainger in his program-note:

ACTOR: Now and then in Scandinavia may be met a Nordic type of womanhood, half-boyish yet wholly womanly, whose soft flawless loveliness is like that of a fairy-tale princess; whose wondrous radiance makes real for us the sun-goddesses of the nature-myths; whose broad shoulders, amazon limbs, fearless glance and freedom of deed and bearing recall the viking chieftainesses of the sagas; whose cornfield hair and cornflower eyes awake thoughts of the silent fruitfulness of the soil and of the lowly lives of land-tillers; whose graceful ease in riming, painting, singing, dancing, swimming is the all-life-embracing giftedness of an unspoiled nature-race.

Such an uncrowned princess may be found in castle or cottage, in town or country-side, amongst high-born or low-born alike; for hers is bedrock aristocraticness of race, not mere top-layer aristocraticness of class, culture and breeding.

To meet her is to have all one's boyhood fairy-dreams and hero-dreams come true.

Such a one is my sweet wife-to-be – Ella Viola Strom – and to her this bridal song is fondly honor-tokened in pride of race and personal love.[16]

[15] Ella Grainger told Ronald Stevenson that 'she had no idea what the Hollywood Bowl was; she thought it was a little grotto! Evidently Percy didn't explain. I think he had agreed to his American agent's publicity plan' (e-mail from Marjorie Stevenson to Martin Anderson, 26 November 2008).

[16] Grainger's programme note for a performance of *To a Nordic Princess* for piano solo, given at Coatesville, Pennsylvania, on 16 January 1928 (and published by G. Schirmer, New York, the following year).

The Graingers' wedding ceremony at the Hollywood Bowl, 9 August 1928

STEVENSON: Percy and Ella lived in his mother's old house in White Plains, though they lived as a couple of globe-trotters. Ella often played the tubular bells in Percy's concerts.

He welcomed American jazz. In the Thirties he lectured on it in New York University. His guest artist was Duke Ellington.

He also made transcriptions from George Gershwin. Here's one of them: *Love Walked In.*

PIANO: *Love Walked In* (Gershwin-Grainger)

STEVENSON: In the late Thirties, Percy and Ella spent a long time in Australia. Grainger used proceeds from an extended concert tour to build – and he was there as a brick-layer off the 5 a.m. tram helping to build it with his own hands – a museum, gifted to Melbourne University in memory of his mother. Grainger wrote a statement of 'The Aims of the Grainger Museum.'

ACTOR: The contents of the Grainger Museum have been assembled with the main intention of throwing light upon the processes of musical composition (as distinct from performances) during the period in which Australia has been prominent in music – say from about 1880 on.

Through the generosity of friends and music-lovers in Melbourne my mother was enabled to take me, at the age of twelve, to Frankfurt-on-Main to continue there the musical studies begun in Melbourne about six years earlier.

While studying music at the Hoch Conservatorium in Frankfurt from 1895 to 1899 I was struck by the fact that the most gifted composition-students were all from the English-speaking and Scandinavian countries. I foresaw that a period of English-speaking and Scandinavian leadership in musical originality and experimentation lay just ahead – a fluorescence comparable to the iconoclastic innovations of the Worcester composers of the 13th century, of Dunstable of the 15th century, of the pre-Bach English string fancies of the 17th century.

So I began to collect manuscripts, musical sketches, letters, articles, mementos, portraits, photographs, etc., by and of those English-speaking and Scandinavian composers that seemed to me the most gifted and progressive – always with the intention of some day putting this collection on permanent display in Melbourne.

The contents of this Museum are thus the product of one man's taste and criticism – my own – and are limited accordingly: my taste in music, having been molded by early familiarity with the conventionally-known German and Austrian 'masters' of the 18th and 19th centuries.

The composers represented in the Museum appear for the most part in the chronological order of my contact with them, or in the order of their artistic importance in my eyes, and not in accordance with their year of birth. My collection cannot pretend to present all important progressive English-speaking and Scandinavian composers of the last seventy years, nor all significant works by such composers as are represented. As a rule, extremely well-known works (such as Elgar's 'Enigma Variations') are omitted altogether, my preference being to concentrate on unknown or less-known works of genius.

I have tried to limit all statements about composers and their works to things and happenings, personally witnessed by me, or communicated by the composers in letters and conversations.

Believing that great achievements in musical composition are seldom the result of a purely individualistic effort on the part of

For their honeymoon Grainger took his wife on a hiking tour in Glacier National Park, Washington State

a composer, but are oftener the outcome of a coming-together of several propitious circumstances or fructifying personalities, I have tried in this Museum to trace as best I can the aesthetic indebtedness of composers to each other (the borrowing of musical themes or novel compositional techniques) and to the culturizing influence of parents, relatives, wives, husbands and friends. [...]

I feel very strongly that musical culture in all parts of the world suffers from the lack of cosmopolitan and universalist outlook on music. In the last fifty years a vast mass of significant and beautiful folk music, primitive music, and Asian and African art-musics has been collected by means of the phonograph and gramophone. But very little of this vast treasure trove has been transcribed into musical notation. And such transcriptions as exist suffer for the most part from misleading simplification, so that the transcriptions sound un-life-like and ineffective in performance.

Perhaps the most world-changing musical discoveries of the last half-century have been those of the musicologists, notably in the domain of early English music – say 1200 to 1700. It has been said [...] that the now-available pre-Bach music of Europe exceeds in quantity, and certainly rivals in quality, all post-Bach music. But the reclamations of the musicologists still go for the most part unexamined and un-performed, as do likewise the larger and more exacting masterpieces of 20th century 'Nordic' composers (British, Irish, American, Canadian, Australasian, Dutch, and Scandinavian).

I have tried to equip this Museum with publications, manuscripts, gramophone records and other material conducive to the study of the above-mentioned neglected musics. This material includes journals of the various folk-song and musicological societies; English, American, Scandinavian, Dutch and Frisian language and dialect dictionaries, useful in dealing with folk-song texts; Bibles in native languages and dictionaries in native languages, useful in dealing with texts of primitive musics.

It would seem only natural for Australia to become a centre for the study of musics of the islands adjacent to Australia – Indonesia no less than the South Seas. Some of the world's most exquisite music is found in this area.

Yet none of these exotic musics, however charmful, should draw Australian musicians away from intense participation in the all-important developments of experimental music in the white man's world. [...]

It would be a wonderful thing if Australia should be the first country to live up to the axiom: 'Music is a universal language'.[17]

STEVENSON: Grainger spent most nights of World War II travelling on trains in the States, never taking a 'sleeper', sleeping sitting up, going from one concert to another; playing all over America, bringing music to people in a time of stress.

In 1945 he completed a work begun during his own army years in the First World War, conceived when he witnessed the sickening experience of bayonet-charge practice. He called this piece *The*

[17] 'The Aims of the Grainger Museum,' October 1955 –RS; reprinted in *A Guide to the Grainger Museum*, University of Melbourne Press, Melbourne, 1975, and in Balough (ed.), *op. cit.*, pp. 133–34.

Grainger with the builder Frank Hansen on the roof as an extension is built onto the Grainger Museum, 8 November 1938

Power of Rome and the Christian Heart. He called it his 'conscientious objector' piece. It has a special message for a world threatened by nuclear mushroom clouds.

ACTOR: This work is a protest against the Roman Empire concept of life – a privileged few catered to by a host of slaves – which spread from Rome to France, from France to England and from England to America. The composition is the unfoldment of musical feelings started by thoughts of the agony of individual souls in conflict with the Powers-That-Be – as when the Early Christians found themselves at strife with the Power of Ancient Rome.

PIANO: *The Power of Rome and the Christian Heart.*

STEVENSON: In the last decade of his life I corresponded with Percy. I leaf through the pages. They were always written by hand in blue-ink with no letter heading but his address printed with an unpretentious rubber stamp. I linger to mull over a few of his choice thoughts:

ACTOR: The snobs and prigs have always ruled music with an iron hand.

STEVENSON: 'For me music should be melody: it should not be florid'.

ACTOR: I have never been associated with any Church. I wanted my music to sound as 'heathen' as possible.

Grainger and the Interaction of Australian and Scottish Cultures

Stevenson gave this 'Percy Grainger Lecture' at the University of Western Australia on 3 June 1980.

RECORDING: *Kintra Gairdens* for bagpipe – Grainger-Stevenson

I couldn't bring a Scottish piper with me, so I've brought him on cassette to pipe-in my lecture recital, my celebration of Percy Grainger – for all the world like the piping-in of the haggis at a Burns supper. Percy, who prized folk-musicians even more highly than concert-hall musicians, would not have grudged the appropriation of his *Country Gardens* by a fourteen-year-old Scottish piper laddie, Stuart Campbell, from my village of West Linton in the Scottish Border Region.

You'll have noticed that the Highland bagpipe speaks a different dialect – accent – plays a different scale from 'standard English', or the major scale. In the Scottish 'Kintra Gairdens', thistles grow as well as roses. This is by way of clarifying at the start that my subject is Scotland – not a province of England, but a country of independent culture (if without autonomy) – Scotland – and Australia.

It was in Frankfurt in 1898 that the sixteen-year-old Percy Grainger's attention was drawn to Scottish folk-music by Karl Klimsch.[18] Grainger later (in September 1951) wrote a memorandum on Klimsch: he described him as 'a gifted and highly-conscienced musical amateur [...] his furious criticisms of my compositions, when I was about 15, were the only really helpful lessons in composition I ever had'.[19]

In 1900 Percy's mother Rose experienced a serious breakdown of health. Karl Klimsch paid for her and Percy to have a summer holiday in Argyll in the Scottish West Highlands. As a parting gesture he loaned Percy two volumes of *Songs of the North* gathered together from the Highlands and Lowlands of Scotland, edited by A. C. MacLeod and Harold Boulton; the music arranged by Malcolm Lawson; published by Cramer of London – no date but late nineteenth century. (In 1923 Klimsch presented Grainger with these two volumes.)

[18] *Cf.* note 20, p. 40, above.

[19] Grainger, 'Karl Klimsch', manuscript dated September 1951, housed in the Grainger Museum, Melbourne, Australia.

June 1900 found Rose and Percy Grainger in Argyll. In September 1949, in Grainger's remarks about his *Hill-Song No. 1,* he remembered what he described as the 'soul-shaking hill-scapes' he saw on a three-day tramp in western Argyllshire. During that trip, Grainger composed a little tune as a whistling accompaniment to his tramping feet. In 1904 he extended this tune for wind 5-some and in 1911 'dished it up' for piano solo, calling it *Walking Tune.*

PIANO SOLO: *Walking Tune*

In 1939 Grainger made an easy piano duet version of this piece. In his notes to this duet he wrote: 'At that time – I had just turned 18' – he means in June 1900 in Argyll: he was actually 17 years 11 months old – 'I was deeply in love with thoughts of the Celtic world. I had already made settings of several Scottish, Irish and Welsh folksongs. So I was delighted to find that most of the older folk in the glens of Western Argyll spoke only or mainly Gaelic – the most of the children spoke both Gaelic and English. It was in this pro-Celtic mood that I worked up my walking tune [...].'

In a letter from Grainger to his Danish friend Karen Holten (18 February 1909) he writes of his own efforts at learning Scots Gaelic.

Grainger's *Walking Tune* is very like the Irish tune *The Minstrel Boy* from Moore's *Irish Melodies.*

PIANO SOLO: *The Minstrel Boy*

This, far from plagiarism, is of the very essence of the continuing variation process of folksong's oral tradition. And there's something deeper behind this kinship of tunes: Scottish culture came, as did the Ur-Scots, from Ireland; so Grainger's tune-making with a Scots accent, related to an *Irish* tune, is only a latter-day echo or recapitulation of a historic cultural process.

In that same summer of 1900, the seventeen-year-old Percy made twelve settings of Scottish folksongs, culled from *Songs of the North,* and two more for chorus. These settings show at a glance how, in one swoop, his genius as folklorist was manifest – especially if we compare his settings to the versions in *Songs of the North.*

Take *Leezie Lindsay.* Malcolm Lawson, in *Songs of the North,* treats it as a Viennese waltz with a gratuitous German military fanfare as peroration.

PIANO SOLO: *Leezie Lindsay* (Lawson)

Now let's hear Grainger's treatment of the tune.

PIANO SOLO: *Leezie Lindsay* (Grainger)

Again, take the *Skye Boat-Song*. Lawson's version is compounded of Victorian music platitudes corseted in close harmony.

PIANO SOLO: *Skye Boat-Song* (Lawson)

Grainger's setting is set in *open* harmony – as open as the seas round the Isle of Skye, or as the skies above the seas. And it suggests the possibility of terror – never far removed from the sea – in dissonances that appear in no Victorian harmony textbook. Incidentally, this harmonisation is uncannily more Delian than anything Delius was writing in 1900.

Grainger holds aloft his Danish girlfriend Karen Holten, Slettestrand, North Jutland, Denmark, 1909

PIANO SOLO: *Sky Boat-Song* (Grainger)

The best exposé I've read about how to set a folksong is in a poem by the contemporary English poet Keith Bosley, from his poetry collection *The Possibility of Angels*,[20] in a poem entitled 'Setting a folksong'.

You discover her naked
naked
and taking her
you will want to
show her off to your friends.

First you will clothe her
for clothing is proof
of possession.

Do not overdress her
lest she think you

[20] MacMillan, London, 1969, p. 32.

wish to disguise her
or (worse) patronise her.

And do not
underdress her either:
a peasant girl
she has no need
of foundation garments.

But study her shape
and set it
sweetly against itself
as your fancy directs
be rich or plain
but never modest.

And remember always
that she is best naked:
let this be an understanding
between you.

Perhaps it wasn't only essentiality in folksong-setting that Grainger discovered in Scotland but also other basics to his later way of thinking, to his view of life. Certainly, one of Scotland's staple diets – oatmeal – was one of his elected affinities in his regimen. Also his interests in colourful traditional costume and in athletics would both be satisfied by seeing the wearing of the kilt, not only as everyday garb but in the Highland Games. Grainger's own predilection was for callisthenics more than sport. The Scottish national game of golf was something he became initiated into much later, by his Swedish wife, on holiday on the south coast of England in the late Twenties. Scottish country dancing, like all folk-dance, was something that certainly appealed to him: we may be sure that he thought of it as related to the virile folk-dances of the Faroe Isles. His *Scotch Strathspey and Reel* is one of his better-known compositions in one of its scorings for orchestra and chorus, in the recording conducted by Benjamin Britten. Here's his 1939 version of it for piano.

PIANO SOLO: *Scotch Strathspey and Reel*

It was the snarling, skirling, double-reed, 'open-air' sound of the bagpipe that appealed to Grainger most of all in Scottish music: the wild cry of it. This he sought to put into his *Hill-Song* for 23 solo instruments, composed at nineteen, directly under the influence of his first visit to Scotland. I've made a piano version of this extended work. In the middle of it I've added a transcription of *another* hill-song of his, his setting of Kipling's *Dedication,* which opens

> If I were hanged
> on the highest hill,
> Mother o' mine, mother o' mine,
> I know whose love
> would follow me still [...].[21]

I intended this as my stone added to the memorial cairn of his *Hill-Song*. In a letter to Percy,[22] I pointed out similarities between the melodic material of his *Hill-Song* and his *Dedication-Song* and reasoned that this justified its addition as a central climax. Critically, I felt his piece suffered from a Wagnerian plethora of climaxes and the big transcription of the *Dedication-Song* made one big summit of a climax. In his reply,[23] he accepted my suggestion very openly. I'll play you this addition of mine to his *Hill-Song*, which he approved.

PIANO SOLO: *Dedication* transcribed by Ronald Stevenson

Australians don't need any 'Pommie' to tell them that, among the first Europeans to settle Australia, the most songful were not London pickpockets, nor Midlands poachers but Irish rick-burners. Risking flogging or hanging for treasonable singing of rebel songs, the Irish still sang. *Van Dieman's Land* was probably sung by Irish convicts in Australia before it was sung in Erin.

But it wasn't only in *folk* music that the Irish – and Scots – flourished in adversity in Australia. They also contributed significantly to Australia's concert-hall and music and opera, by the mid-nineteenth century. Two Irish-born composers whose music was widely performed in Australia were William Vincent Wallace, an Irishman of Scottish parentage (1814–65), and Michael William Balfe (1808–70), a Dubliner. Wallace's famous opera was *Maritana*; Balfe's was *The Bohemian Girl.*

Vincent Wallace was possibly an even *more* colourful figure than Percy Grainger. He married young and emigrated to Australia, sheep-farming. Musical life in Sydney rekindled his creative spark. He separated from his wife and became a romantic rover in Australia, the South Seas, India and South America. He returned to London as a concert pianist. He was nearly blown up in a steamboat in 1850

[21] *Cf.* p. 70, above.

[22] Letter 28, p. 111, above.

[23] Letter 30, p. 116, above.

and became bankrupt by the financial failure of a New York piano-factory, but he rallied and became solvent by concertising. He had a miraculous escape during a tiger hunt in India: a tiger sprang upon his horse and felled him, overleaping him. As it was about to spring again, he shot it dead. Wallace's operas were in demand in the opera houses of Vienna and Paris. His eyesight failed and he became poor. He sold the rights of his last opera (at Covent Garden) for ten shillings which he gave to the widow of a stage carpenter whilst the management netted £50,000 from the deal. Grainger would certainly have heard Wallace's music.

I'll play you a transcription I've made for piano left hand solo of Wallace's 'Scenes that are brightest' from his opera *Maritana*.

PIANO SOLO: 'Scenes that are brightest' by Vincent Wallace transcribed by Ronald Stevenson

In Wallace's last years, a baby girl was born in Burnley on Melbourne's Tarra Braes in 1861. You've guessed: Nellie Melba. She was the daughter of a Scottish contractor, David Mitchell. During World War I Melba sang Grainger's *Colonial Song* in a Red Cross concert in Melbourne from her seat among the audience, as a symbol of the music's welling-up from the nation. Australia's greatest gift to the world of music was certainly Percy Grainger. But Australian sopranos – Melba, Joan Hammond and Joan Sutherland (notice the prevalence of Scottish names, for Melba was the daughter of a Scot and married a Scot) – these too have contributed saliently to the international music scene. The great achievement of these Australian women is to have convinced the traditionally opera-hating Britishers that they, too, can enjoy opera. Scotland has only established its national opera in the last decade.[24]

In the world of Australian visual arts, Norman Lindsay – another Scottish name – is the artist nearest to Grainger. Lindsay's work with its teeming Rubens-like female forms is a gigantic affront to Scottish Presbyterian prudery. Lindsay is sumptuous in his art as Grainger was in his harmonies. Both offend good taste.

The Scottish strain in nineteenth-century Australian *poetry* is very strong: its pantheon is full of Scottish names – Adam Lindsay Gordon, Andrew Barton Paterson, and Will H. Ogilvie, who was born a Scottish Borderer and became a poet in the Lallans (or Lowlands) Scots tongue, who later wrote bush ballads in Australia. Henry Lawson, Australia's leading folk-poet, was of Norwegian descent; though it

[24] Scottish Opera was founded by Alexander Gibson in 1962.

is yet another indication of Scottish influence in Australia that his family name was not Anglicised but 'Scotticised' from the original Norwegian.

The sixteen-year-old Percy Grainger set Adam Lindsay Gordon's poem *A Song of Autumn* to one of his first original melodies. Gordon's suicide at only 37 in 1870 had a Scottish background: he was deeply depressed by his failure to substantiate his claim to property in Scotland and this drove him to desperation.

But Scots in Scotland were driven to desperation and exile long before that. The barbarous English victory over Jacobite Scotland at the battle of Culloden in 1746 bore such a bloody aftermath that one Scot in every twenty was hanged and all Scotland was exploited financially, to the extent that many tradesmen emigrated. One such was the Aberdonian boat-builder Alexander Greig. He went to Bergen, became Norwegian in 1779 and changed his name to Grieg. His son John took over the business and became British Consul in Bergen. Of their lineage was Edvard Grieg, the great friend of Percy Grainger's youth.

There was much trade between Scotland and Bergen between 1500 and 1800. The Scots were timber-merchants. Many place-names in Western Norway are Scottish. When Lord Maxwell was murdered in 1613 (an event commemorated in a Grainger song-setting), some noble Scottish families found new homes in Norway. The oldest Bergen registers disclose that from 1550 to 1750 nearly 400 Scots became citizens of Bergen. In the early and mid-sixteenth century an annual average of 146 ships sailed from Scotland to Bergen to fetch timber. Many of the Scots stayed in Bergen, so that it became known as 'skottebyen' (Scotstown).

The Scots were made welcome. They brought their bagpipes and dances, customs and costumes. They also brought the viola d'amore, a fiddle with resonance-strings, a kind of droning 'bagpipe-fiddle'. Some musicologists think this may have been the origin of the hardanger fiddle. Grieg's music was considerably influenced by Scottish folksong. Here are two examples.

PIANO SOLO: *Bonnie Buckhaven* (Scots folksong) – *In the Hall of the Mountain King*
Whaur hae ye been all the day (Scots folksong) – *Solveig's Song*

During his Frankfurt student years, Percy heard concerts by two major Scottish-born Liszt pupils: Eugen d'Albert and Frederick Lamond. In a later essay on pianism (quoted in John Bird's Grainger biography, p. 30), Percy recalled the overwhelming impact of D'Albert's playing:

> When I saw D'Albert swash around over the piano with the wrong notes flying to the left and right and the whole thing a welter of recklessness, I said to myself, 'That's the way I must play'. I'm afraid I learnt his propensity for wrong notes all too thoroughly.

He was rather less impressed by Lamond, though struck by his kindness personally. The memoirs of Grainger's concert agent, Antonia Sawyer (*Songs at Twilight,* Devon Adair Co., N.Y., p. 187) include her recollection of a meeting between Lamond and Grainger in the agent's New York office (this may have been in the Twenties): 'One morning they met in my office and it was a sight. Lamond placed his arms around Grainger as though he were his long lost son'.

But the major pianistic influence on Grainger was Busoni, from whom he had a short course of lessons in the summer of 1903. Busoni, one of the great Bach scholars, instructed Percy in Bach-playing. In the appendix to the Busoni edition of the '48', there is an innovatory section on the use of the middle or 'sostenuto' pedal of the Steinway grand piano, as used in the Bach-Busoni transcriptions. Percy applied this in all his piano writing – even in song accompaniments. But Busoni also was at one with Grainger in interest in the music of ancient, tribal cultures, and particularly in that of the American Indians.

On 28 March 1915 *The Public Ledger* of Philadelphia printed a news item:

> Percy Grainger, who was a pupil of Busoni, went with him last Saturday to hear the first American performance of his (Busoni's) 'Indian Fantasy' by the Philadelphia Orchestra, under Stokowski. After hearing it, Grainger wrote to a friend: '... The work pulsates with real nature (and, it seems to me, real prairie) feeling. The Indian themes in themselves are very striking, and Busoni has used them in a very unconventional way, producing great natural flow of form and introducing many shimmering, sensitive and subtle colour effects and polyphonic treatments.[25]

This, incidentally, is a corrective to the misleading and only partially accurate account of the relationship between Busoni and Grainger in John Bird's Grainger biography.

But you may be wondering what this has to do with interaction between Australian and *Scottish* cultures. Well, there *is* a connection between these things and American Indian culture. During the American Revolution, the Scots Gaelic language was used as a secret

[25] It seems odd that *The Public Ledger* should be quoting a letter from Grainger so soon after the concert, but this is the quotation as it appears.

code between the revolutionaries and their Amerindian guides. Some American Indians had indeed intermarried with émigré Highland Scots. The well-known Amerindian word 'mocassin', to give only one example, derives from the Scots Gaelic for 'my feet'. Also, it is possible that some of the pentatony of Amerindian folk-music was of Scottish origin. 'The Song of the Bluebird' in Busoni's *Indian Fantasy* is very like a Hebridean folksong, both in its pentatony and in its characteristic 'Scots snap' rhythm. These Indian folk-tunes were collected by Busoni's pupil (and Grainger's friend) the American Natalie Curtis Burlin (see her collection *The Indian's Book* (New York: Dover)). Later, Grainger was to arrange material from the same collection.

What interests me about Grainger's 'free music' is not the Heath Robinson-like machine that made it, but its *expressive content.* Burnett Cross, the American physicist who assisted Grainger in building his 'free music' machines, when I put this to him two years ago in New York, hadn't thought of this music's *expression.* He had been so concerned with building the machines to make it possible. Let's hear Grainger's *Free Music No. 1* synthesised at Melbourne University.

RECORDING: *Free Music No. 1*

Now listen to this:

RECORDING: *Wolf Music*

That was a wolfpack in Canada which I heard in 1976.

I think of Percy Grainger as 'Music's Mowgli' – remember Kipling's boy brought up by wolves: music's outrageously natural man. What do the wolves cry? And what does Mowgli cry with them? Surely messages to the pack – the wolf-pack or the people-pack. Messages of warning, about mankind and its threat to survival. Warnings and deep Freudian fears. And loneliness and wildness and longing for freedom. This is what I hear in the 'Free Music'. It is a mood that tallies with that of the skirling Scottish bagpipe and the majesty and solitude of the Scottish Highlands and the wilderness of the Australian bush.

Percy Grainger and his Circle

These two programmes for The Australian Broadcasting Commission were recorded on 7 June 1980.

Programme 1: Grainger, Australia and Britain

Percy Grainger, composer/pianist, folklorist, arguably the first ethnomusicologist, and a pioneer of electronic music, was born in Melbourne in 1882. His mother took him to Germany as a boy, to continue his piano studies. As a young man he studied piano with Busoni. Grainger made London his base as touring virtuoso. In 1909 he revisited Melbourne and heard the first phonograph recordings ever made of Australian Aboriginal music. Grainger made the first music-notations of these melodies. He planned to write a piece called *Bush Music,* to voice the Australian wilderness, but he only left a fragment of it. I'll play it for you and join on to it the first Aboriginal tune Grainger notated: a musical evocation of the emergence of the Aborigine from his environment. This is the premiere.

PIANO: *Bush Music* by Percy Grainger and *Aboriginal Tune*

In his *Colonial Song* Grainger wanted to write for Australia a similar kind of popular music to that which Stephen Foster had given America. During World War I Melba sang a vocal version of this piece at a Melbourne Red Cross concert, from her seat among the audience; as a symbol of the music's welling up from the Australian nation.

PIANO: *Colonial Song* by Percy Grainger

As a child in Australia, Grainger heard Asiatic music. He remembered this in two pieces: *Eastern Intermezzo* and *Arrival Platform Humlet.*

PIANO: *Eastern Intermezzo and Arrival Platform Humlet* by Percy Grainger

Grainger's greatest friend among British composers was Frederick Delius. He particularly admired Delius's large-scale orchestral and

Grainger with Delius in the Domplatz in Frankfurt on 5 April 1923

choral works, but he also admired his aquarelle-like miniatures. Here are three of them: the three piano Preludes Delius composed in 1922–23, during a period when Grainger – after the death of his mother – went to live with Delius and Delius's wife in Frankfurt: a nostalgic re-visit for Grainger to the city of his student years. Maybe these Delius piano pieces were suggested by his hearing Grainger play the piano daily at that time. They are reminiscent of water-music and birdsong.

PIANO: *Three Preludes* by Frederick Delius

In his student-years in Germany Grainger's fellow-students numbered four British musicians. With Grainger they became known as the 'Frankfurt Gang'.[26] They remained life-long friends and all became distinguished composers. Together they represent a cross-section of Edwardian and Georgian music: a time which produced music of great

[26] *Cf.* pp. 130 and 145, above.

charm and fragrance, which still lingered even after the barbarism of the First World War. The most experimental of these composers, apart from Grainger, was Cyril Scott, who, as exquisite pianist himself, wrote much piano music. Debussy admired him. Scott's music owns affinity to Debussy and also to the Russian Skryabin, as we hear in his *Rainbow Trout*, dedicated to Percy Grainger.

PIANO: *Rainbow Trout* by Cyril Scott.

Roger Quilter was one of the same group of composers. He is best known for his songs. His piano music is also lyrical. Here's an exquisite miniature by Quilter, 'Will o' the Wisp'.

PIANO: 'Will o' the Wisp' by Roger Quilter[27]

Norman O'Neill was an Anglo-Irish member of the 'Frankfurt Gang'. He was mainly a composer of theatre music. Here's the piano-solo version of his *Prelude* No. 3 to J. M. Barrie's play *Mary Rose.*

PIANO: *Prelude* No. 3 by Norman O'Neill

The benefactor of the 'Frankfurt Gang' was Balfour Gardiner, who financed London concerts of music by his fellow-composers just before World War I and helped to put them on the map. Gardiner composed little himself. Later he abandoned composing and interested himself in tree-planting. Here's a Gavotte by Balfour Gardiner which is very near to the ebullient spirit of his friend Percy Grainger.

PIANO: Gavotte by Balfour Gardiner[28]

Percy Grainger was the *enfant terrible* of the 'Frankfurt Gang'. They had *specialised* interests: one in theatre music, one in songs, one in piano music; but Grainger was interested in *everything.* And basic to all his interests was *folk music.* In 1900 on holiday in Scotland – he was not yet eighteen – he made his first folksong settings: a group of Scottish songs.[29] They bring the open air into the concert hall.

[27] 'Will o' the Wisp' was originally composed as part of Quilter's incidental music to Clifford Mills' and John Ramsey's children's play *Where the Rainbow Ends,* first performed on 21 December 1911; it was published the following year in two different selections of music from the play.

[28] The Gavotte is the last of Balfour Gardiner's *Five Pieces* published in 1911.

[29] *Cf.* in particular p. 40, above.

The Graingers with Balfour Gardiner, 1927

As an old man, living in New York State, he made a *piano* version of three of these Scots songs. Their fearless, sumptuous harmonies and outrageous energy show that Grainger remained an *enfant terrible.* The titles are: *Will ye gang to the Hielans, Leezie Lindsay?* which is a courting song; *My dark-haired Maiden,* a Highland love-song; and *O gin I were where Gowrie rins,* a tramping song.

PIANO: *3 Scottish Folksongs* by Percy Grainger

Programme 2: Grainger, Scandinavia and America

It was one of Percy Grainger's fellow-students in Frankfurt, the Danish composer and cellist Herman Sandby,[30] who first aroused Grainger's interest in Scandinavian folk-music, which was to remain a life-long passion. In the Twenties Grainger went on folksong-collecting expeditions in Denmark with the veteran Danish folklorist Tang Kristensen. In 1949 Grainger arranged two of these Danish folksongs

[30] *Cf.* also p. 174, below.

The Graingers with the Danish composer Herman Sandby and his wife Alfhild, c. 1940

for piano, linking them into one composition: *The Nightingale and the Two Sisters,* dedicated to Herman Sandby. This is the premiere.

PIANO: Percy Grainger's setting of two interlinked Danish folksongs: *The Nightingale and the Two Sisters*[31]

Herman Sandby introduced Grainger to Grieg in 1906. The following year – only weeks before Grieg's death – Grainger spent some time in Grieg's Bergen home, discussing their music. Grieg admired Grainger's performance of the Grieg *Slåtter.* This Norwegian word refers to the virile bowing-style of Hardanger fiddle-tunes. The Hardanger fiddle is a folk-violin with four sympathetic strings which vibrate like a bagpipe-drone when the upper strings are played. An old Norwegian folk-fiddler prevailed upon Grieg to perpetuate his

[31] No. 10 of Grainger's *Danish Folk-Music Settings,* composed 1923–30 and published by Schirmer in 1931.

Grainger with the Danish folklorist Evald Tang Kristensen, 1922

Slåtter before they died with him.[32] Grieg did this in 1902, composing a set of seventeen pieces. They are therefore twentieth-century music. Indeed, in their rhythmic quirks and daring dissonance they pre-vision Bartók. I'll play three of these *Slåtter*: Nos. 4, 14 and 16 from Grieg's Op. 72. The first is a Halling, a Norwegian fling. The second is a bridal procession of gnomes led by a troll-fiddler. The third is entitled 'The Three Maidens of Kirle Valley'. These three maids were pagans. For blowing their cowhorns down the valley during Sunday morning mass, the priest turned them into stone; yet in Kirle Valley in Norway you may still see these three maidens playing their cowhorns – as mountain formations! But first the Norwegian Fling and the Gnomes' Bridal Procession. Three *Slåtter* by Grieg.

PIANO: three *Slåtter*, Op. 72, Nos. 4, 14, 16 by Edvard Grieg

In 1940 Herman Sandby published a piano piece, *Autumn Mood at the*

[32] The old fiddler in question was Knut Dahle (1834–1921) who had learned his craft directly from legendary players like Myllarguten ('The Miller's Boy') and Håvar Gibøen. It was Grieg's fellow composer Johan Halvorsen – himself a violinist – who transcribed Dahle's playing, with Grieg working from Svendsen's transcriptions.

Coast. It is full of wind and wave-sounds and of autumnal nostalgia, expressed in a harmonic language that shows kinship with Grainger. *Autumn Mood at the Coast* by Herman Sandby.

PIANO: *Autumn Mood at the Coast* by Herman Sandby

In the late Twenties, Grainger, on a visit to Norway, encountered the music of Sparre Olsen and, soon after, they became friends. Olsen was born in 1903 and is still alive.[33] In 1963 he published a Norwegian biography of Grainger.[34] Percy Grainger considered Olsen 'the direct successor of Grieg in his rare gift of concentrated miniature musical utterance' – Grainger's own words. Here's Olsen's 'Leitom'n Halling', a Highland Fling from the Norwegian Alps.

PIANO: 'Leitom'n Halling' by Sparre Olsen[35]

In 1928 Percy Grainger married a Swedish poet and painter, Ella Viola Strom. They lived in White Plains, New York State, but were inveterate globe-trotters – and they supervised the building of the Grainger Museum in Melbourne in 1935. Infected by Percy's enthusiasm for all things musical, Ella composed a handful of her own songs, writing both poem and melody. One of them, *Love at First Sight*, was published in a choral version by Percy Grainger in 1946. In 1976 I made a piano transcription of this song and played it in a New York recital for Ella Grainger's birthday. This is the broadcast premiere.

PIANO: *Love at First Sight* by Ella Grainger transcribed by Ronald Stevenson

In 1944 Percy Grainger published a concert arrangement of Gershwin's song *The Man I Love.* In his foreword to it, Grainger claims it ranks with the great songs of all time.

PIANO: *The Man I Love* by George Gershwin transcribed for piano by Percy Grainger

One of Grainger's colleagues in the States was the Irish-American composer Henry Cowell, who was born in 1897 and died in 1964.

[33] He died on 8 November 1984.

[34] *Cf.* note 31, p. 49, above.

[35] 'Leitom'n Halling' is the sixth number of Olsen's *Leitom Suite*, Op. 33, from 1952.

Grainger played much of Cowell's music. Cowell was an innovator in cluster-chords and in playing in direct contact with the piano strings. His *Aeolian Harp* is played *entirely* on the piano strings, either 'brushed' or plucked, while chords are held silently on the keyboard. It suggests the Aeolian harp's mythological origin: a small harp suspended in an open window and resonating in response to breezes.

PIANO: *Aeolian Harp* by Henry Cowell

Another of Grainger's friends was the Canadian-born black composer Nathaniel Dett, whose dates are 1882–1943. He was the first North American black composer to graduate with a music degree. One of the most popular items in Grainger's repertoire was Dett's 'Juba Dance'.

PIANO: 'Juba Dance' by Nathaniel Dett[36]

Yet another of Grainger's American friends was the ethnomusicologist and composer Natalie Curtis-Burlin. She was born in New York in 1875 and died in a traffic accident in Paris in 1921; so she was a friend of Grainger's early American years. She was a pioneer researcher in Black American and in Amerindian folk music. Here is her piano piece based on an Indian flagellation-song, sung in an Easter procession in Santa Fe, New Mexico: *Sangre de Christo (Blood of Christ).* This is the Australian premiere.

PIANO: *Blood of Christ* by Natalie Curtis-Burlin[37]

In 1922, on a rail-journey in the Rockies, Percy Grainger wrote his *Spoon River,* based on an American folk-fiddle dance. He dedicated it to the American poet Edgar Lee Masters who wrote a *Spoon River* anthology. With this breezy reel, the open-air spirit of Percy Grainger bids us a merry farewell to these two programmes.

PIANO: *Spoon River* by Percy Grainger

[36] 'Juba Dance' is the fifth and final number in Dett's piano suite *In the Bottoms* of 1913.

[37] 'Sangre de Christo', an Indian-Spanish Lenten hymn from New Mexico collected and arranged by Natalie Curtis-Burlin was orchestrated by Grainger from her scoring sketches in 1925.

Bach and Wagner:
A Journey in Music
An Imaginary Conversation
between Percy Grainger and the Author

Published in *The Grainger Journal,* Vol. 3, No. 1, August 1980, pp. 10–13. Stevenson prefaced the text with a brief explanation: 'N.B. This article was written whilst Percy Grainger was still alive.[38] The conversation was imagined by Ronald Stevenson, based on his correspondence with Grainger. The footnotes denoted P.G. are Grainger's original comments on the manuscript when it was sent to him for comment. R.S.'

R.S. It's pleasant to be travelling with you, Percy. The beginning of a journey is particularly pleasant – new impressions, fresh hopes....

P.G. A beginning may mean anything, but an end is bound to mean something. You see, I'm already in an argumentative mood! I hope we'll relish a good argument before the journey's end. I generally do.

R.S. Talking about beginnings and endings, you know, I've often thought that in music Bach is a beginning and Wagner an end. There now, does that whet your argumentative appetite?

P.G. The whistle's blown! We're away now! Round One of the tone-bout! I don't agree! In Bach the music of several centuries before him survives. An example is the tail-piece of the D Major *Prelude in the Dorian Mode* and the tail-piece of *the D Major Fugue in* the second book of *The Well-tempered Clavier.*

R.S. Well, I'll keep well-tempered. Especially as I don't particularly disagree. Neither do I think your statement denies my original one. Bach was something of a Janus of music: to say that he looked back does not mean he did not look forward. He did both. Another case of Bach's backward-lookingness is his indebtedness to Bernhardt Christian Weber, who in 1689 wrote a set of preludes and fugues entitled precisely *Das Wohltemperirte Klavier* – 33 years before Part I of Bach's identically entitled work, and 55 years before Part II! And

[38] *Cf.* Letters 21–24 and 26, pp. 103–109 and 110, above.

Bach's literary preface is almost verbatim the same as Weber's.[39]

P.G. Are you agreeing with me?

R.S. Hardly! Bach dwarfed his predecessors. He became a symbol to posterity: the emancipator of music from the yoke of the old system. Technically, Bach's premonitory importance, as I see it, is in his role as prime champion of the innovation of equal temperament. True, this innovation dates from before Bach, from the speculations of Marin Mersenne in his *Harmonie universelle* (1636) and of Andreas Werckmeister in his *Musikalische Temperatur* (1691). But they remained theorists. Bach put their theory into practice, and nobody did it better. We know that, as the new tuning became accepted and composers began to explore key-relationships other than the tonic-dominant hierarchy of fugue, music very soon – within Bach's lifetime – became transformed. From the linear art of counterpoint it became the art of the broad brush-stroke of block harmony. It is ironic that Bach, champion of the new, within his lifetime, came to be known (even to his sons) as 'the old Periwig': a relic of a rapidly achieved antiquity. But the Old Periwig was the master of a school far greater than that of St. Thomas at Leipzig: his disciples have numbered Mendelssohn, Brahms, Reger, Busoni, and Hindemith, among others. Wagner has not even the beginning of such a lineage.

P.G. Well, there was Richard the Second – Strauss, of course. But about harmony and counterpoint: I for one have always deplored the eighteenth-century submergence of old counterpoint.[40] Counterpoint remained swamped in the nineteenth century, but it's gradually coming back into its own in the twentieth. The fellow-feeling of the Church and the guilds of the Middle Ages was expressed in counterpoint. In the eighteenth century, when Europe was half populated by lackies bowing to petty princes, the fellow feeling disappeared. So did counterpoint. But I think we are achieving a measure of democracy these days. And counterpoint is the essence of democracy in music: every man-jack singing out

[39] Stevenson's note: antecedence of Bach's by Weber's '48' is disputed and considered disproved by some authorities. The MS of the Weber in the Brussels Conservatoire is [wrongly] dated 1698.

[40] Here P.G. has crossed out the word 'counterpoint' in the typescript and written 'polyphony'. He also writes: 'I never have cared much for counterpoint. What I swear by is many-voicedness (polyphony) (German: Mehrstimmigkeit). That is where I heartily disagree with both Reger & Busoni'. –RS

for himself, all pulling together. Remember too, Wagner was a consummate contrapuntist.[41]

R.S. But surely you don't disparage harmony per se? Goethe apostrophised Bach as 'the great harmonist' – which isn't really as paradoxical as it sounds, if we think of his preludes rather than his fugues. Add to the preludes the fantasies and toccatas.[42] They look forward to new freedom in forms, the antithesis of the strict spiritual exercise of that sonnet form in music, the fugue. And in his Passion music, Bach's recitatives became (much more than, say, those of Schütz) an expression of humanity, not merely declamation observing the rules of music and of prosody. And these recitatives were either melodic or harmonic, or both – never contrapuntal!

P.G. For me, the best harmony is the sum total of the counterpoint.[43] But about Wagner's school: how can he be an end if his influence is found in his followers? Apart from my quotations of Strauss, examples of Wagner's copiedness by his successors are: Grieg's *Evening in the High Hills*; and Delius's *On hearing the first cuckoo in Spring*. Wagner's English horn solo in *Tristan* leads to Grieg's *Evening in the High Hills*, in my opinion, and also to the wonderful opening of *The Rite of Spring*. Also, if I may say so, to my *Hill Song* for 22-some wind-stringband, with its fierce double-reed sonorities.

R.S. Aren't those echoes of mood? Of a certain exquisite voluptuousness or of a remote primeval strangeness of sound? I can't believe they are cases of technical evolution. Surely it is impossible to travel further along Wagner's road because it was the cul-de-sac of absolute chromaticism? Perhaps Schonberg has discovered an abyss at the end of the cul-de-sac.

P.G. No! Wagner made innovations in sound. Not in advocacy of new tonal systems, but in orchestration.[44] The solo English horn in *Tristan* in the mid nineteenth century – remember Rossini was still alive! – must have sounded as strange as the bassoon in *The Rite of Spring* in 1913. And Wagner was the first to realise orchestral sonority to the full. His frequent 'doublings' in his orchestration have been criticised, but they do make the music resound much more than any music that came before. Wagner, too, was an innovator in musical form. Before him it was in corsets! He took music out of the stays of sonata and symphony. He exploded the old

[41] P.G.: 'Polyphonist, not contrapuntist in my opinion'. –RS

[42] P.G.: 'I don't know the Fantasias and Toccatas'. –RS

[43] P.G.: 'Polyphony'. –RS

[44] P.G.: 'Remind me to enlarge on Bach's 'organ-register'-type of orchestration'. –RS

fallacy that music is architectonic, which it can never be, because it does not exist in space and time. He revealed music's nature as a flowing unfoldment – like a ribbon rolled out on the floor.

R.S. I'll think about that. It sounds convincing.

P.G. You know, I take a very narrow-minded view of music. For me music should be melody of one kind or another, and above all: music should not be florid. I do not say that my anti-florid view is a right one. I merely say that I cannot help feeling that way. That is why I love Bach and hate Mozart. That is why I enjoy Schoenberg and *musique concrète.*

R.S. ! ! ! But I think I see what you mean. Bach is not florid because he is not the Bacchus of music. That is Wagner! Wagner is for ever pouring out his music as if it were gallons of Rhine wine – or the Rhine itself! It goes on and on like the Rhine. I think, if Wagner's music-drama achieves immortality, it will be because it goes on for ever. But Bach is all muscle, no flabbiness. No – as you say: not florid. With him there is properly no ornament: all is theme. Mozart, of course, is full of ornament.

P.G. Ah! you're coming my way, perhaps. Well, I'll come yours. I'll grant you one thing. In finding Bach a beginning and Wagner an end, it may be because you associate Bach – more than Wagner – with the present age. In some ways, music, for the present anyway, may have learned what it can from Wagner. In fact, from Stravinsky in the twenties, it has been time and still is time to learn from Bach. Not back to Bach, but on from Bach. I'm sure if old Bach came back now, he would give us everything rolled into one: Strauss, Stravinsky, Schoenberg, Bartók, Hindemith and all the rest,[45] in a great unexpected and wholly refreshing play of counterpoint with jazz and folk elements, *musique concrète,* electronic music – just everything. In the twenties I asked, 'What's all this bug-a-boo about jazz?' Surely by now it has been absorbed in the main stream of music. What is certain is that we are now in an epoch which is not dissimilar from that which confronted the world at the time of Bach. That is, a vast horde of musical influences of great complexity seem to be coming together. We need a new composer large enough to embrace them all, large enough to 'contain multitudes', a Walt Whitman of music. I guess he may come from a new country: America, perhaps. Just as the States are the melting-pot of nations, so maybe the States will also be the melting-pot of music – of many musics.

[45] P.G.: 'I (personally) would not talk of such 'foreigners' as Stravinsky & Bartok when we have greater geniuses who are Nordic: – Cyril Scott, Sparre Olsen, etc.' –RS

R.S. Where are we? No, I don't mean the station. Our argument. I find myself agreeing with you.

P.G. And I find myself holding firm. I emphatically disagree that Bach was a start and Wagner a finish. Only in a dictionary of music is that so, and only because of an alphabetic accident. It is not a case of alpha and omega. You see that river there? Look through the window! The river running parallel to this rail-track? That's old Bach! And this great railroad car is Wagner! Very different, but both heading for the coast just the same. That river has been flowing on to the ocean for centuries before this train sped toward it; and the river is still there. The new music has been prophesied for centuries....

R.S. Yes, Caccini wrote his *Nuove musiche* in 1602, wasn't it?

P.G. ... and music all the time has been throwing up, Vesuvius-like, all sorts of possibilities, *von innen heraus.* Music, from obscure beginnings, has come more and more into the open. Sometimes, it is true, it has begun in the open – in the literal fields of folk-song – and finished in the study stifled. The air must be there all the time. And remember the word 'air' is an element of both nature and music. Man dies when deprived of air: and music dies when it too is deprived of air and melody.[46] Both Bach and Wagner were great melodists. And something more. They were foretellers of new music, of free music.

[46] P.G.: 'Yes!' –RS

Grainger and the Piano

From *The Percy Grainger Companion,* edited by Lewis Foreman, Thames Publishing, London, 1981, pp. 113–22.

Percy's 'Graingerness' was first manifested in a piano piece he composed in Frankfurt on 24 July 1898, at the age of sixteen. Its title is the first of his Graingerisms: *Saxon Twi-Play.* Whether that refers to the street sword-play of German youths or to the 'chopsticks' play of two hands on the keyboard is open to conjecture. Though the title is in English (if idiosyncratic), the tempo and interpretative directions are in Italian (albeit just as idiosyncratic). In the unpublished manuscript[47] I consulted in the Grainger House White Plains, N.Y., in May 1976, there is a unique marking in the last section of the piece: *excell al presto.* The 'excell' is obviously a mis-spelling of *accel*: Percy had so little feeling for Italian that maybe it's just as well he chose to use colloquial English for tempo and expression markings on his later compositions.

There is no reason why an English-speaking composer should not use English expression-marks (Britten, for instance, probably taking Grainger's lead, used them increasingly), any more than Beethoven should not use German directions, as he did in his late piano sonatas. But British snobbism is such that Beethoven's German (sometimes drawing on a vocabulary unfamiliar to non-Germans, as in the word *ermattet* –'exhausted', in Op. 110) is revered, whereas Grainger's English is deemed 'funny'. Racy it certainly is. In the very year that Grainger wrote his *Saxon Twi-Play,* MacDowell published his *Sea Pieces*; and they employ English very freely – for instance, 'well bound' for *legatissimo,* 'hold' for *tenuto,* and so on. MacDowell's example may have encouraged Grainger to use English terms instead of Italian – though, paradoxically, in the unpublished manuscript of Grainger's transcription of Byrd's *The Carman's Whistle* (made between 1942 and 1951) he employs a good many Italian expressions.[48] (Grainger was nothing if not paradoxical.)

[47] It has since been published by Bardic Edition.

[48] *The Carman's Whistle* has also now been published by Bardic Edition.

His first employment of his idiosyncratic English in published music was in his *Paraphrase on Tchaikovsky's Flower Waltz* (published in London in 1905) which includes such Graingerisms as 'harped' for *arpeggiando* and 'louden lots' for *crescendo molto*; and, at the end, bears the characteristic legend '20.4.04. S.S. "Sophocles"'.[49] But what a Graingeresque slip of the pen – a *glissando* rather than a slip! – to write 'excel to presto', for that is what he was doing all his life.

Grainger's unique contribution to the concert platform and to its repertory was that he brought the outdoors spirit into it. How did he do this? A curious thing is that, alone among the great composer/pianists, apart from transcriptions, he never wrote anything initially for piano. All his best-known compositions were originally conceived for other instrumentation. He claimed that he made piano versions only at the behest of his publishers. I suggest that he brought the open-air spirit into the concert hall because he was the only concert pianist who made music in the same way that a folk-singer makes his: naturally, untrammelled by notation.

Indeed, he once applied the same method to his own piano-playing as he did in recording folk-singers on the Edison phonograph, and then notating their performance. He improvised his *Lullaby* from *Tribute to Foster* on a Duo-Art Pianola and notated the rendition, thereby reversing the usual procedure of performing from a slavish reading from the printed page. In his notes to this published piece he states his objective of 'preserving, as it were photographically, all the rhythmic irregularities of an individual rendering' and adds that it is 'not intended to be followed slavishly, note for note, by other players'.

But it wasn't only in rhythmic freedom that Grainger's pianism emulated the folk-singer's; I believe he based *every* aspect of his playing and piano-writing on the folk-musician's model. In his essay 'The Impress of Personality in Unwritten Music'[50] he writes of the 'non-legato tendencies of folk-singers, who 'use their breath, more as some birds and animals do, in short stabs and gushes of quickly contrasted, twittering, pattering and coughing sounds which (to my ears, at least) are as beautiful as they are amusing'. He noted similar tendencies in British and Scandinavian folk-fiddlers, 'who are as fond of twiddles and quirks as are the old singers, and do not try to exchange the

[49] Grainger completed the scoring of his *Paraphrase of Tchaikovsky's Flower Waltz* while on a tour of South Africa in 1904. When touring in foreign parts he often waited until he was aboard ship to add the finishing touches – in this case the steamship Sophocles bound from South Africa to London in April 1904.

[50] Percy Grainger, 'The Impress of Personality in Unwritten Music', *The Musical Quarterly* I (July 1915), reprinted in Teresa Balough (ed.), *A Musical Genius from Australia, op. cit.*, p. 69.

Clarity at the keyboard: Grainger in 1920

"up and down" physical nature of the bow for the attainment of a continuous tone'.

Like the folk-musician, Grainger sought to *speak* in music. Indeed, it would be true to say that he was the only concert pianist who was also a folk-musician. Röntgen described him as 'a folkloristic genius'.[51] Grainger had absorbed so much folk-music that he was a folk-musician. So he articulated as a folk-musician does. In the piano, despite his love-hate relationship with it, he had in some ways an ideal medium, because it is essentially a *non-legato* instrument.

Grainger's folk-like articulation was often achieved, especially in passages marked 'roughly', by unusual fingering, such as what he termed 'bunched' fingering, meaning the use of the middle finger with the index finger wrapped over it and supported by the thumb under it, for increased strength. On a black key, four fingers would be used. Another unorthodox technique to achieve greater articulation was the use of uniform fingerings for double sixths (e.g. $\begin{smallmatrix}4 & 4 & 4\\ 1 & 1 & 1\end{smallmatrix}$ in the right hand). In the note to his arrangement of *Shepherd's Hey* he demonstrates his opposition to the Matthay 'relaxation methods' by urging the student to practice in 'the most mercilessly energetic, taxing and exhausting way possible' and claims that 'if the attack of double notes (sixths and octaves) is energetic enough, the relaxation (between attacks) would look after itself.' He adds, 'you do not have to tell a man to sleep who has just walked 65 miles without stopping'. The instruction for the double sixths is to play with 'stiff fingers, stiff wrist'! All this does not deny that Grainger could be as elegant as any pianist when he chose; just as his wardrobe contained Savile Row suits, however much his preferred garb was an open-neck blue shirt, white 'duck' house-painter's trousers, a sports jacket and his old army boots.

In his published *Guide to Virtuosity*,[52] we see how other aspects of his pianism were based on the human voice. His phrasing, for instance. He advises that, to compensate for decrease of intensity of tone towards the keyboard treble, a *rising* melody should be played *crescendo*, a *falling* one *diminuendo.* Short pauses on melodic climaxes – especially in *pp* – should simulate the singer's *mezza voce* or *falsetto.* Grainger achieved dynamic contrasts through *quantity* of tone, not *quality*. (Here he agrees with Sir James Jeans in asserting that if a note is played by 100 different pianists with the same tone-strength it will have the same quality). His speciality was what, in the *Guide to Virtuosity*, he calls 'simultaneous tone-strength differentiation': the bringing out of middle melodies. More of this later.

The *Guide* also presents his ideas on pedalling. He had many uses of the damper-pedal. Apart from 'syncopated' pedalling (probably the invention of Anton Rubinstein), he frequently used half-pedalling for clarification of harmony through partly sustained tone – like the sun

[51] *Brieven van Julius Rontgen*, H. J. Paris, Amsterdam, 1934, p. 251. –RS

[52] Schirmer, New York, 1933. –RS

bursting through a mist. And he often employed *vibrato* pedalling – a 'fluttering' of the foot on the damper pedal – to achieve a graded *diminuendo.*

He is unique in having used the middle, or *sostenuto*, pedal in *all* his piano-writing – even in song accompaniments. This enables a single note or a single chord to be sustained while other notes are played without pedal or with the damper and/or the 'soft' pedal. Thus, bass notes in the middle pedal function as the organ pedal-board; or, if in the middle register, they function as sustained horn-chords, increasing the quasi-orchestral possibilities of the piano. The *fons et origo* of Grainger's use of the middle pedal was Section 4 of the First Appendix to Volume I of the Busoni edition of Bach's *Well-tempered* Clavier:[53] 'On the Transcription of Bach's Organ-works for the Pianoforte'. In the summer of 1903 Grainger studied Bach-Busoni transcriptions with Busoni in Berlin, and the use of the middle pedal would certainly be an integral part of those lessons. Grainger was the only Busoni pupil who developed his master's technique of middle-pedalling.[54]

In the Grainger Museum in Melbourne in June 1980, I discussed with Libby Wright her researches on Grainger's re-workings of Bach transcriptions by Tausig and by Busoni. The Bach transcriptions Grainger played were really Bach-Tausig-Busoni-Grainger. To make a generalisation, I would say that Busoni's transcriptions were like Rembrandtesque engravings from a master painting, whereas Grainger's were like the painting made into a poster. One style employed finesse, elegance: the other, the broad brush stroke. Busoni's transcriptions sound splendid (unless you disagree with his aesthetic) in such a hall as London's Wigmore (seating about 500); Grainger's would sound sumptuous in a large American amphitheatre. And yet Grainger described himself as 'a pianist for the village hall' and Busoni as 'pianist for the metropolis' (but that was when Grainger had abandoned any ambition he ever may have had as a virtuoso, totally at loggerheads with the streamlined concert-world of the Horovitzian era).

Grainger used the 'soft' pedal not only in *piano* but in *forte*, just as Grieg achieved repressed passion in writing for string orchestra by using the mutes in *forte* passages. Grainger used the three pedals often simultaneously: the 'soft' and middle pedals pedipulated by the left foot, slewed round so that the toe worked the middle pedal and the heel the 'soft' pedal.

[53] Schirmer, New York, 1894. –RS

[54] *Cf.* Ronald Stevenson, 'Busoni – Doktor Faust of the Keyboard', *Piano Journal*, European Piano Teachers' Association, Vol. 1, No. I, 1980, pp. 14–15. –RS

Grainger's two-piano edition of the Grieg Concerto[55] is an exemplary piece of editing. He prints Grieg's original solo piano part, with addenda, sometimes initialed 'P.G.' and sometimes 'P.G.—E.G.' – indicating either his own re-writings or re-writings that he discussed with Grieg and that had Grieg's approval. The arpeggio-passage beginning in the fifteenth bar after the '*In tempo I'* in the first movement's cadenza (after the last bass chromatic run) is a brilliant example of Grainger's pianistic invention. Grieg's original gives a four-note arpeggio to each hand alternately: Grainger's revision preserves the same text, note for note, but divides the arpeggi between the hands, each hand playing only one note at a time – single notes alternating in an electrifying cascade, suggesting a diabolical Hardanger fiddler's super-athletic bowing.

Grainger was so concerned with amateur music-making that he made many versions of his music for beginners, the more advanced and the really advanced: sometimes calling for three pianists at one piano (*Zanzibar Boat Song)* and four pianists at two pianos – what he termed 'piano team-work' (his transcription of Bach's A minor Fugue from Book I of the '48') These ideas of piano pedagogy were ahead of their time. They certainly were designed to inculcate the musicality that only ensemble-work can provide: a feature often absent from piano lessons. Sometimes, as in his 'Children's March' *Over the Hills and Far Away* (which he described in his summer-school teaching-lists as 'easy'), he overestimated the tyro, as did Villa-Lobos, occasionally, in his *Guia Prático.* This was why I welcomed the commission to edit *The Young Pianist's Grainger* for Schott.[56]

In my researches in the Grainger House, White Plains, in 1976, I unearthed a piano-solo version by Grainger (dated 2 July 1901, London) of *The 'Rag'-Time Girl.*[57] This was based on an American popular song sung to Grainger by his Frankfurt friend Carlo Fischer. It was the first of a number of compositions based on, or influenced by, Black American music. From 1903 to 1909 he worked intermittently on another such popular song of the time, *In Dahomey* (still in manuscript[58]). In 1905 Stanford suggested to his former

[55] Schirmer, New York, 1920. –RS

[56] The Teresa Balough *Complete Catalogue of the Works of Percy Grainger,* University of Western Australia Press, Perth, 1975, erroneously states (footnote, p. 104) that my arrangements in *The Young Pianist's Grainger*, Schott, London, 1967, are 'more difficult' than those in the unpublished *Easy Grainger.* The reverse is true. –RS

[57] Published in *The Grainger Journal,* Vol. 3, No. 1, August 1980, pp. 14–15. –RS

[58] Not now: this 'Cakewalk Smasher', as Grainger described it, has since been

student Coleridge-Taylor that he send his *Twenty-four Negro Melodies* to Grainger. The first all-negro vocal ensemble to tour the world were the Jubilee Singers of Fisk University, Nashville, Tennessee. Their history and repertoire was published in London.[59] Towards the end of the last century they spread the fame of the negro spiritual. But neither their published songs, nor Coleridge-Taylor's piano transcriptions of spirituals, reproduced the vocal registration of the negro performance-style. In 1911 Grainger *did* reproduce that style in his (still unpublished) *Who built de Ark?* for 'leader' (rich middle voice), three accompanying male voices and guitar. Grainger's friend (and fellow Busoni student) Natalie Curtis Burlin was the first to record, on Edison phonograph, traditional old plantation songs as sung by negroes. From these recordings she made as exact a music notation as possible. These were published as *Negro Folk-Songs.*[60] They show how the 'lead' voice was never on top but, pitch-wise, in the *middle* of the ensemble–just as in Grainger's *Who built de Ark?* Now in the very year that Grainger wrote that spiritual-setting (1911) he published two piano pieces – *Irish Tune from County Derry* and *Sussex Mummers' Christmas Carol* – which both put the tune in the tenor, embedded in the harmonic texture in the same way as a negro's 'lead' voice in the vocal ensemble. My contention is that the negro style of harmony influenced Grainger's characteristic layout of keyboard texture: which means that not only his phrasing and articulation were based on folk performance practices but so was his *harmonic thinking.* Interesting that he told Natalie Curtis Burlin that he considered Black American harmony 'the most perfect part-singing in the world'.[61]

In 1913 Grainger made a concert tour of Russia. The Liszt pupil Siloti conducted for him and programmed Grainger's newly published string-orchestra version of the *Irish Tune from County Derry.* Siloti liked it so well that, not knowing Grainger had himself published a piano version of it, he published one of his own. The difference between the Grainger and Siloti versions is revealing: Siloti puts the tune on top throughout; Grainger's harmonisation is pure 'negro spiritual' (I mean in layout; I don't of course mean the *melodic* material sounds 'negroid').

---

published by Edition Peters.

[59] J. B. T. Marsh, *The Story of the Jubliee Singers including their Songs,* Hodder & Stoughton, London, 1899. –RS

[60] Four books, Hampton Series, Schirmer, New York, 1918–19. –RS

[61] Quoted in Natalie Curtis Burlin (ed.), *Negro Folk-Songs,* Hampton Series, Book I, Schirmer, New York, 1918, p. 9. –RS

Grainger's most sumptuous piano work is his *Ramble on the Rosenkavalier Love-Duet.*[62] This employs the full range of his pianism. It is the most fastidiously notated piano-writing in the whole virtuoso literature. (Yes, it even exceeds the fastidiousness of Godowsky, for Godowsky never notated such detailed pedalling as Grainger and never notated for middle pedal.) If the performer follows all the instructions faithfully – fingering, dynamics, phrasing, pedalling – he will not need to seek for an interpretation. The interpretation in this case *is* the notation.

There is so much to say about Grainger's piano-writing that I had better give a brief résumé of his pianistic innovations, rather than get lost in the thicket of his numerous works. He innovated direct contact with the piano strings in his *Pastoral;*[63] he specifies a marimba mallet to strike a bass string at the end of the piece – thereby making the so-called *avant garde* of half-a-century later seem the *derrière garde* they were (and are).

Use of the *fist* was another innovation. Near the end of the concert version of *Country Gardens*[64] he calls for the right hand to be clenched in a boxer's 'fist', the thumb-knuckle playing B flat and the little-finger knuckle playing the E flat a fourth higher, to get the hammered sonority he requires, which fingers alone could not achieve.

I have a photocopy of Grainger's working copy of the first edition of Cyril Scott's Piano Sonata. At the black-key *glissando,* Grainger has added a self-instruction: to pin a silk handkerchief on an elastic band into his breast pocket; to whip it out and play the *glis* with the handkerchief over his fingers, then release it and the elastic would return it to the pocket! Funny – yes, Harpo Marx-like – but *practical.*

His 'orchestration' of piano-writing is richly colourful. In *Blithe Bells*[65] (a free ramble, or fantasy, on Bach's *Sheep May Safely Graze)* he imitates sheep bells in high treble tenths. His transcription of Gershwin's *Love Walked In*[66] evokes musical glasses by two-note treble *tremoli,* containing the tune and a descant – the *tremoli* termed 'woggles'. His American folk-dance *Spoon River*[67] captures the 'seesaw' of folk-fiddle bowing in the chopped-up interplay of the two hands. A fife-and-drum band is strongly suggested in his Scots folk-song

[62] Furstner/Schirmer, Berlin/New York, 1928. –RS

[63] Schirmer, New York, 1916. –RS

[64] Schirmer, New York, 1918. –RS

[65] Schott, Mainz [London and New York], 1931. –RS

[66] Chappell/Gershwin Pub. Co., New York, 1946. –RS

[67] Schott/Schirmer, [London/New York], 1922. –RS

setting *O gin I were where Gowrie rins:*[68] the fife simulated by 'twiddly' ornamentation. The manuscript of this piece is a re-working of one of his Scots folksong settings of 1900, as he writes in his note 'remembered (no doubt inaccurately) Oct. 21, 1954'.

Another seven years and Grainger was dead – if one can say that about such a spirit. As he wrote on that early piano piece *Saxon Twi-Play,* he did indeed 'excel to the end'.

[68] Published in *The Grainger Journal,* Vol. 1, No. 2, December 1978, p. 2. –RS

Grainger: A Celtico-Nordic Alternative to Graeco-Roman Aesthetics

Conference paper presented at the Percy Grainger Centenary Conference at the University of Melbourne on 5 July 1982

It was another Percy – the poet Shelley – who declared 'We are all Greeks and Romans'.[69] But Shelley didn't know Grainger. It's true that the classics are, or were, the crux of the Oxbridge axis; and it's true that English law is based on Roman law. But it's also true that England's greatest dramatist confessed that he had 'little Latin and less Greek'.[70] Grainger had neither.

During the pregnancy of Rose Grainger, she kept at her bedside a reproduction of an ancient Greek archetype of male physical beauty. In Percy Grainger she actually *materialised* this image. He coalesced the beauty of Apollo with the athleticism of Mercury. But Grainger left the gods running – left them like broken icons in the desert; like Shelley's Ozymandias.

The Romans spoiled the Greeks in every sense. With them, the Attic drama became debased into the sickening spectacle of sacrifice – as entertainment in the Coliseum. The Romans, enjured by Brutus to lend him their ears, were apostrophised as citizens. They were the civic pillars of city society. They represented civilisation. But a civilisation that included the Coliseum ritual carnage was no more a civilisation than a society that attempts to rationalise nuclear suicide.

Civilisation means urbanisation. Grainger was an enemy of both. His *Kipling Jungle-Book Cycle* bears the dedication 'against civilization'. Grainger stood for culture, not civilisation.

Roman roads were arteries which, congested, caused the coronary occlusion of cities. Along those roads marched the gladiatorial armies, pioneer imperialists whose descendants march over the globe in our own century. But the Power of Rome was halted at Hadrian's Wall; its tide stemmed by a small nation, the Celtic Scots. Already two millennia

[69] In his introduction to *Hellas.*

[70] In fact, that assertion was made by Ben Jonson in the prefatory verse he contributed to the First Folio of Shakespeare's plays in 1623, 'To the Memory of my Beloved, the Author Mr. William Shakespeare and what he hath left us', which claims that 'thou hadst small Latine and less Greek'.

ago the Celtic alternative to Imperial Rome was adumbrated. The Roman march was militarism in full panoply. Against that, remember that the Celtic early Christian missionaries were the only ones who never shed blood.

Now, Grainger wrote only three original marches: the *Gum-suckers*, *Over the Hills and Far Away* and the *Marching Song of Democracy*. The *Gum-suckers* was his tribute to his fellows in the State of Victoria. It's a hiker's – not a soldier's – march. 'Gum-sucker' referred to the hiker's sucking a eucalyptus leaf for refreshment in hot summer weather. *Over the Hills and Far Away* is subtitled 'Children's March'. And the *Marching Song of Democracy* is described by Grainger in his preface to the score like this:

> it typifies the buoyant on-march of optimistic humanitarian democracy in a musical composition in which a forward-striding host of comradely, affectionate, athletic humanity might be heard 'chanting the great pride of man in himself'; the underlying urges to be heroic but not martial, exultant but not provocative, passionate but not dramatic, energetic but not fierce, athletic but not competitive.

His original plan was to write it for voices and whistlers only and have it performed by a chorus of men, women and children singing and whistling to the rhythmic accompaniment of their tramping feet as they marched along in the open air. Later he scored it for the concert hall. But he underlines that an athletic out-door spirit must be behind the piece from start to finish.

What's the difference between a military march and a non-military march? I'll tell you. The military march puts rhythm before melody: it chops the music up consonantally – that's why Germany, with its heavily consonantal language, has so many military marches; no accident that the Prussians emblazoned their helmets with the Roman eagle – instead of allowing music to course like a vowel-rich language. The military march puts deadly earnestness in the place of a spirit of play. Aldous Huxley wrote about the relationship of spectators at a bull-fight being comparable to that of a concert audience's reaction to the agony of, say, a Gustav Mahler; and adds that if a greater measure of social justice is ever achieved in the future, such agonisings will appear to belong to a pre-history in the arts. In a serialised article, 'Melody versus Rhythm' in the American journal *The Music News* on 29 September 1933,[71] Grainger wrote (in his ingenuous way):

> Rhythm is a great energizer; a great slave driver; and the lower types of mankind (the tyrants, the greedy ones, the business-minded people)

[71] *Cf.* note 39, p. 54, above.

> haven't been slow to sense the practical advantages to be drawn from rhythmically regular music as an energizing, action-bearing force. When these hard-headed, practical people want young men to go out and get themselves killed, they play marches to them. And they encourage sailors and roadworkers to sing at their jobs in order that the maximum of hard work may be forth-coming as economically as possible.

Bartók was interested enough in these views of Grainger's to reply to them in a later issue of the same magazine, opining that his view – Bartok's – held rhythm and melody in equipoise. Grainger felt that melody was a more exalted expression than rhythm; more of a spiritualising force.

In an interview Grainger gave to the Melbourne *Herald* newspaper on 10 September 1938, he shows how he doesn't want melody to be war-like either. He states there that 'German music of the 15th and 16th centuries contained no warlike message. Thereafter it became an essential part of it'. He excepted Bach – his favourite composer: surely feeling, as Kodály did, that Bach had distilled the whole of German folksong. If we pause and think about all this, we realise that the significant politico-historical event of the seventeenth-century Germany was the Thirty Years' War which populated the German landscape with human scarecrows. And, assuredly, the prevailing music would be the recruiting bugle. This got into Austro-German symphonic music, beginning in the musically Czech-Teuton-dominated Court of Mannheim in the mid-eighteenth century in the symphonies of the school of Stamic or Stamitz. The thematic bugle-call was known as the 'Mannheim rocket'. It then got into the music of the Viennese classics. Grainger's interview goes on: 'A simple test is to see how their motives suited instruments like the trumpet and the bugle. Most of them would be found to be based on the open notes of brass instruments. There are countless examples'.

PIANO SOLO: Examples Performed

To Grainger (who had heard much of the world's treasure trove of folk-song) bugle-call motives weren't melody at all. They were glorified harmony. He felt that the lovely contours of *The Irish Tune from County Derry* based on vocally grateful step-wise progression sometimes twining round a harmony but not becoming harmony – and with a beautifully-placed high note and a final sinking down – all this which made the tune the resonance of a human heart, this was infinitely more melodic in its very nature (and in its spiritualising influence) than a belligerent fanfare, however ingeniously it might be tossed to and fro in symphonic development.

These reflections of Grainger's are those of a largely self-educated composer, music's natural man. He only had three months formal, general education – three months' schooling – in his life: a circumstance that inevitably had the defects of its merits. But its main merit was that he came to music with a mind like a blank slate, a *tabula rasa*. If the classics – whether Greek or Roman or Viennese – had been inculcated into him, like so many others (like the great Sir Donald Francis Tovey, for instance) genuflection before the altar of the classics would have prevented Grainger from taking a peep over the shoulders of the classics to see and hear the peasants in the fields. (Of course, the Elysian Fields weren't supposed to be peasant-infested.) Sometimes Grainger overstates his case. But maybe there are enough connoisseurs of English good taste and understatement. But he had to overstate in order to get people to re-think at all. And even now, as I speak, I guess that some of my audience will be bringing the guarded prejudices of their own classically trained background to bear on the argument.

The point is that the classics of Vienna or of antiquity have little relevance to Grainger. He is a new type. Though he admired all of the repertoire he played, he realised that some of it was artistocratically rather than democratically oriented. For Grainger, music with one melody-line on top and only block harmonies underneath it, was an expression of aristocratic autocracy of one melody over all the other aspects of music. There is much piano music like that – nearly all the works of one of the greatest piano composers, Chopin: the E flat *Nocturne*, the G minor *Ballade*, the C sharp minor – oh, there are hundreds of examples.

For Grainger, the best harmony was – is – the by-product of polyphony: melody in all voices: tune multiplied to the *n*th degree. That's why he was often asking the pianist to bring out what he called a 'middle melody'; and one finds the instruction 'bass hugely to the fore.' Orchestrate this, and everybody in the band gets a try of the tune, instead of chugging along on repeated notes whose effect is like taking a tranquiliser. Grainger was especially interested in folk-polyphony which is never found in Latin or Teutonic countries but in Wales and in the heterophonic psalm-singing in Scots and Irish Gaelic still to be heard today; in Georgia in the U.S.S.R., in Bulgaria's Rhodope mountains and in Polynesian folk music; and in Black American improvised part-singing.

I have dealt with Grainger's attitude to each element of music – rhythm, melody, harmony, polyphony – what about his attitude to form and medium and the social aspect of music. His ideal was the tribal one of everybody participating. He believed in the axiom 'Doing is Learning. He wanted more and more people to make music – two minutes' silence to the memory of a great man would be totally unfitting in Grainger's case: it would have to be two minutes' pandemonium! His dream of street music on a mass scale (as in his original idea for his *Marching Song of Democracy*) is as yet unrealised. It would take music to people, instead of a comparatively few people taking themselves to music.

The place was important to Grainger. The ideal place was outdoors – the natural habitat of folk music. Hence his love of the wind band. But if indoors, preferably in a home with everybody participating – if some folk can only grunt instead of singing, why then, they can whistle. And to use the instruments easily to hand: hence his pioneering of the guitar – the instrument *par excellence* of today's youth. And if it's *got* to be a big concert hall, then, let's have audience-participation, which he also pioneered in his *Tribute to Foster* – even if it's only a snatch of a chorus. People feel elated after participating.

But the places he wasn't interested in were opera houses, cathedrals and ostentatious concert halls. To him, they were symbols of the Establishment, urbanisation. Therefore, the forms of music begot by such architecture were alien and antipathetic to him, even though he recognised past achievements in these forms. He was all for decentralisation of culture. In that, too, he was a pioneer. He didn't believe that skill (which threatens more than ever in a technocratic age) should be in advance of feeling, but should serve feeling.

He believed that Nordic culture produces composers rather than virtuosi. In the *Herald* article I quoted, there's a snatch of an interview with him. After this last assertion about Nordic culture producing composers, not virtuosi, his interviewer asks:

– 'But Germany?'

– 'Well, name one great virtuoso!'

–'Why, Schnabel.'

– 'An Austrian Jew.'

– 'Busoni?'

– 'An Italian.'

– 'Backhaus? Gieseking?'

– 'Yes, admitted, but there's no German cellist to equal Casals.'

Grainger is performing there, provoking. But he goes on to explain: 'Generally it's the musically underdeveloped countries which produce the most virtuosic virtuosi, as Hungary gave us Liszt, or Spain Sarasate, or Russia Anton Rubinstein. Many of the greatest are Jews'.

This view of the Jewish contribution to the history of virtuosity should counter-balance some of Grainger's other wild generalisations.

Grainger's view of the evolution of music is outlined in an article he wrote for *The Etude* magazine published in the States in August 1943, an incidental passage in an essay on Grieg:

> Freud's psychoanalysis, Einstein's relativity, aeronautics and the quest for speed are all manifestations of the same urge: to know nature better and, if need be, master her. Musical history clearly shows us the path from superstition and the propitiation of hostile forces (so-called primitive music and much folk music) through the conception, in religion, of a beneficent deity (worship-music, from Perontinus to Palestrina) on to the fearless, all-embracingness of science.

Grainger's experimental beatless, gliding free music was a first step in this direction. His Free Music was indicated by his predilection for quasi-improvised fantasy-variation form, which he termed the ramble. He was a rambler in nature and in music.

Constant Lambert, in his book *Music Ho!*, says there is nothing a composer can do with a folk-tune, except repeat it louder.[72] Precisely. But the conclusion I draw from that is that folk-music's natural form, when extended, is variation-form. Listen to the twentieth-century Irish composer Seán Ó'Riada on this, in his recently published book *Our Musical Heritage*[73] (meaning the Celtic, specifically Irish, heritage) and relate it to Grainger:

> Traditional Irish art never adopted the Greco-Roman forms spawned by the Renaissance, which have become the basis of European art. Take the European notion of 'development': a development which moves in a crescendo of tension ending in a crisis the resolution of which produces catharsis. In any Beethoven symphony, a movement will start off with two contrasting musical ideas. These are developed, played off against one another, given new significance by being led through a series of different keys. This creates a gradually mounting tension until a climax is reached. At the climax the tension is resolved, producing a feeling of release, or catharsis, and the original musical ideas appear transfigured, as a result of what has happened to them. It is the same in Sophocles' 'Oedipus Rex'. At the beginning, Oedipus is already doomed without knowing it. As the play proceeds, event after event brings him closer to realisation, and the tension mounts to a climax, with his realisation of his doom. The end follows quickly. This is the graph of a play by Shakespeare, of a Verdi opera, of a Hollywood film. It is the basis of

[72] Faber & Faber, London, 1934 (p. 146 in the 1966 edn.).

[73] Ed. Thomas Kinsella, The Dolmen Press, Dublin, 1982, p. 21.

European art. And it is quite foreign to traditional Irish art.

The simplest picture of traditional Irish art is the ancient symbol of the serpent with its tail in its mouth: 'In my end is my beginning'. It is essentially a cyclic form. You might represent it by drawing a curve, beginning at point A, widening out to form a series of almost-circles which overlap each other, and which themselves follow a circular path, so that the end of the last curve returns to the starting point at A.

This graph or curve seems visually complex but is fundamentally more realistic than the European graph, since it more truly corresponds with real life. It is, in fact, the graph of real life. Every day the sun rises, every day it sets. Every day possesses the same basic characteristics, follows the same fundamental pattern, while at the same time each day differs from the last in its ornamentation of events. The particular events of each day are, to the basic pattern of days, as the particular ornamentation of each verse of a song. This is the idea that has lain at the root of all Irish traditional art since pre-Christian times. It is represented in the carved stones of the great burial-ground at Newgrange, in the curvilinear designs of the Book of Kells, in the old mythological stories, episodic and cyclic in form, in all Gaelic poetry – even in James Joyce's *Ulysses* and *Finnegans Wake*; and in the *sean-nós* singing which still survives as an art-form today.[74] The basic pattern of the song remains in each verse, but the events, the ornaments, vary. This does not necessarily mean that the musician who does not use variation is a bad one; he is a passive holder of tradition. The musician who makes good variations is, on the other hand, a creative contributor to the tradition. He makes it grow and develop.

As a symbol of all I've been trying to say, I'll play my very recently made transcription of Grainger's full score *The Power of Rome and the Christian Heart.* The preface reads:

So Grainger's predilection for variation-form unites him with the Ur-Celtic art structure. To his well-known Nordic affinities – Grieg, Sandby, Sparre Olsen – are fused Celtic influences. They coalesce as they do indeed in Scotland.

His actual first encounter with a Celtic country took place when he visited Scotland at eighteen in 1900. He later described it to K. K. Nygaard as his 'artistic liberation'. The 'soul-shattering hillscapes of Argyll' suggested his *Hill-Songs.* In a letter to Karen Holten in 1909 he says he is learning the Scots Gaelic language. Some of his best known music has a Celtic base: *Scotch Strathspey and Reel, The Two Corbies, Lord*

[74] *Sean-nós* ('Old Style') is a highly ornamented style of traditional singing found in Gaelic, and particularly Irish, cultures. It is typified by rhythmic and ornamental variation with each successive verse.

Maxwell's Good Night, Molly on the Shore, Irish Tune from County Derry; and his *Scotch Folksongs* (twelve for voice and piano, two for choir and three for piano), composed between 1900 and 1954. In a letter to Basil Cameron in 1952 he writes of his 'adoration of Celticness', so it was a life-long love:

> This work is a protest against the Roman Empire conception of life – a privileged few catered to by a host of slaves – which spread from Rome to France, from France to England, and from England to America. The composition is the unfoldment of musical feelings started by thoughts of the agony of individual souls in conflict with the Powers-That-Be – as when the early Christians found themselves at strife with the Power of Ancient Rome.
>
> Percy Grainger

So Grainger's road is not the *Roman* road but Walt Whitman's *open* road:

Afoot and light-hearted I take to the open road,
Healthy, free, the world before me,
The long brown path before me leading wherever I choose.
Henceforth I ask not good-fortune, I myself am good-fortune,
Henceforth I whimper no more, postpone no more, need nothing.
Done with indoor complaints, libraries, querulous criticisms,
Strong and content I travel the open road.
Camerado I give you my hand!
I give you my love more precious than money,
I give you myself before preaching or law;
Will you give me yourself? Will you come travel with me?
Shall we stick by each other as long as we live?

PIANO SOLO: *The Power of Rome and the Christian Heart* Grainger/ Stevenson

Grainger's Transcriptions

Published in the Australian journal *Studies in Music* No. 16, 1982, an issue dedicated to Percy Grainger.

This subject is an uncomfortable one for a university publication; but there is no point in whitewashing Percy Grainger academically – it would only make him appear all the more as the cultural aborigine he was and wanted to be. Grainger refused a number of honorary doctorates because he felt that to accept would have been to deny his nature, which he knew to be that of a savage in civilisation. In High Academe, transcription is anathema; the essential Grainger, taboo. The friction of the two produces fire. But this fire sheds light, maybe even enlightenment.

Recent years have witnessed the phenomenon of extremely diverse and isolated music 'industries' such as, on the one hand, 'historicity' – the quixotic search for authentic performances of old music on instruments contemporaneous with its composition, with all the concomitant paraphernalia of correct ornamentation, a cultural immaculate conception – and, on the other hand, electronic music. These are the new academic fashions. Practitioners of both these cults seldom show interest in the art of transcription, generally thinking of it (if at all) as a nineteenth-century aberration, a fall from grace, a lapse of taste. Here I am reminded of an adage of the Scots poet Hugh MacDiarmid: 'Watertight compartments are of use only to a sinking ship'. Grainger was an all-round man in an age of specialists.

Grainger advised his musician-friends (myself included)[75] to study Arnold Schering's *Geschichte der Musik in Beispielen* (History of Music in Examples) (Leipzig, 1931). This contains, in its 313 complete compositions from a Greek ode to a Gluck aria, Caccini's solo madrigal *Amarilli, mia bella,* published in Florence in 1602, followed by Peter Philips' transcription of it for virginals which appeared in London in 1603 – a transcription far freer than any by Liszt. If one considers this Philips transcription and then Bach played on the Moog synthesizer, one sees that the worlds of old and new music are not worlds apart,

[75] In 'The Culturizing Possibilities of the Instrumentally Supplemented A Cappella Choir', *Musical Quarterly,* XXVIII/2 (April 1942), pp. 160–73; reprinted in Balough (ed.), *A Musical Genius from Australia, op. cit,* pp. 114–24.

but are part of the continuum that is music-history. And Liszt belongs to it also.

In the summer of 1903 in Berlin, Grainger took a concentrated course in piano from Liszt's heir apparent, Busoni. They studied the Bach-Busoni transcriptions. At that time Busoni was preparing his opuscule *A New Aesthetic of Music,* which appeared in 1907 (Trieste) and was later translated into a number of languages; the English translation by Theodore Baker (New York, 1911) was reprinted in recent years (New York, 1964). In this visionary essay Busoni considers, among much else, the art of transcription. He conceives notation of music, in itself, a transcription of an idea. From 'scription' to *tran*scription is only a step. Busoni adds that it is odd how variation form is esteemed by *Urtext*-fetishists, although variations on a borrowed theme produce a whole series of transcriptions which are least faithful when most ingenious. So, to purists, transcription is not good because it *varies* the original, while variation form is good, although it *transcribes* the original. It is folly to differentiate too finely between variation, transcription and composition. Every good transcription varies an original and is a composition in its own right.

Writing in the magazine *The Australian Musical News* (Melbourne, 1 April 1927), Grainger reaffirmed Busoni's statement: 'Busoni once very cleverly said: "All composition is always transcription". That is fundamentally true'. Grainger invokes the names of master composers who practiced the art of transcription and asks: 'Why should the smaller flight, who really hardly know anything at all, make such an uproar against arrangements and transcriptions?'

Grainger's practice of elastic scoring, which he more and more applied to his compositions, carries transcription further than any other composer has carried it. His foreword to his *Jutish Medley* (Schirmer/Schott, 1928, 1930) explains the principles of elastic scoring, which is the scoring of a work so that it can be performed by any medium from a solo instrument to a massed orchestra or wind band, using any *ad hoc* instrumental combinations. He writes:

> I do not care whether one of my 'elastically scored' pieces is played by 4 or 40 or 400 players, or any number in between; whether trumpet parts are played on trumpets or soprano saxophones, French horn parts played on French horns or E flat altos or alto saxophones [...]. This 'elastic scoring' is naturally fitted to musical conditions in small or out-of-the-way communities and to the needs of amateur orchestras and school, high school, college and music school orchestras everywhere [...]. It is intended to encourage music-lovers of all kinds to play together in groups, large or small, and to promote a more hospitable attitude towards inexperienced music-makers.

As I understand it, the purpose of Grainger's transcriptions is eight-fold:

1. To encourage more performance rather than only more listening to music, that is, to encourage active rather than passive music-making;
2. To increase dissemination of music otherwise unheard or heard only infrequently;
3. To enrich the repertoire of one instrument or ensemble by borrowing from the repertoire of another instrument or ensemble;
4. To bridge the gap between the musics of different ages;
5. To bridge cultural gaps;
6. To bring amateur and professional closer together;
7. To provide musically educational material;
8. To bring music to a broader social spectrum, rather than to treat it as a preserve of the few.

Many examples could be given of each category. Space and time allow only a few.

The need for active rather than passive music appreciation has been made more clamant by the gramophone. The danger with recordings is that they 'mummify' music in one performance, to the extent that other performances may be unfairly criticised from a position of bias. Grainger made many transcriptions of well-known music – such as Brahms' *Cradle Song*, Handel's *Hornpipe* from the *Water Music*, his own *Country Gardens* and *Shepherd's Hey* and many others (sometimes in versions ranging from very easy to perform, to very difficult, to provide for all stages of ability). He did not deny the role of the gramophone; he made many records himself. But he wanted as many people as possible to *make* music. And the majority of people will, of course, want to play something popular – hence his attention to popular music.

On the other hand, there is much fine music that receives infrequent performance, for instance, the songs of Fauré, which are still regularly sung only in France. Grainger made beautiful piano transcriptions of two of them: *Nell* and *Après un Rêve*.

With Arnold Dolmetsch, Grainger edited early chamber music. Dolmetsch edited the scores for consorts of viols by such masters as Alfonso Ferrabosco, John Jenkins and William Lawes; Grainger rescored the same works for violins, violas and cellos. Knowing the relative scarcity of viola-players, Grainger wrote a third violin part or an extra cello part to take the viola line. He also made woodwind versions of the same material. Transcribing old music such as this for modern instruments is a way of bridging the gap between the music of different ages by making it more accessible, for it is not everyone who has a consort of viols at his disposal, however much the purists may regret the fact.

In his piano transcription of Dowland's lute ayre *Now, o now, I needs must part,* Grainger gives one verse in Dowland's original harmony and adds a second verse in Graingeresque harmony. In a private recording *(Grainger at home,* held in the Grainger Museum, University of Melbourne, and in the Harvard University Sound Archives) he plays this piano version and extends it to a free improvisation, exploring still more adventurous harmony. This is another way of bridging music history and demonstrating historical perspective.

Grainger's transcriptions for tuneful percussion, strings and piano, of Ravel's piano piece *La Vallée des Cloches* (The Valley of Bells) is an example of (to use a neologism) 'pre-transcription', in the sense of something like a compositional 'pre-echo'. The influence on Ravel in this case was Javanese gamelan music. Here Grainger seeks to restore Ravel's music back to its source by making tuneful percussion approximate the bell sonorities of the gamelan ensemble. This is an example of soldering cultural divisions.

Grainger was a pioneer in piano teamwork. Group piano-teaching is a recent development that is a natural consequence of his teaching in the Chicago Music College in the 1920s. A major part of this work was his Bach transcriptions, particularly the version of the big A minor Fugue from Book I of the '48', transcribed for two (or more pianos, eight (or more) hands. This fugue requires stamina and endurance when played by a solo pianist; even to a virtuoso the part-playing at *tempo allegro* presents difficulties. The coda contains a pedal-point which is impossible to sustain on the harpsichord. Both the Busoni and Bartók editions suggest ingenious methods of sustaining it on the piano, neither of which is totally successful. These factors alone justify Grainger's idea of transcribing the fugue for two or more pianos, the point being that eight (or more) amateur hands in ensemble can certainly match – and even eclipse – the prowess of a solo virtuoso. And the pedal-point is easily sustained when allotted to one player. Thus the chasm between amateur and professional is leapt across with typical Graingeresque athleticism.

Any student who sets himself the joyous task of studying all the published Grainger transcriptions, with their copious footnotes (suggesting many further sources of study), would equip himself with a music education second to none that could be provided by any university in the world. It would also encompass ethnic music, a subject still absent from the curriculae of many music faculties.

The range of music encompassed in Grainger's transcriptions extends from early Mediaeval music (the *English Gothic Music* collection of choral music which he edited in collaboration with Dom Anselm Hughes) to piano transcriptions from Gershwin.

When Grainger transcribed for two pianos Richard Addinsell's *Warsaw Concerto* (music for the Second World War film *Dangerous Moonlight*) it was part of his social interest that also embraced British Music Hall songs. A popular promenade concert given by Grainger with the Toronto Philharmonic Orchestra in the University of Toronto Arena (Canada) on 21 May 1946 included both a group of Grainger's orchestrations of *English Gothic Music* and the *Warsaw Concerto* for piano and orchestra (the original version), among other items. In his programme note Grainger describes the 'outer guise' of the *Warsaw Concerto* (acknowledging its indebtedness to Rachmaninov) as 'Slavic, but with an inner message which is unmistakably English'. (He regarded music's national and race traits as basic to its interpretation.) In the same programme note, dropping a typical Graingeresque 'clanger' into the politeness of Academe, he typifies the Addinsell piece as 'a genuine contribution to the heart-throbs of music'. (Perhaps here I should supply a plentiful stock of exclamation marks!)

Grainger knew that such music as the *Warsaw Concerto* was a way of bringing lay music-lovers to higher things in music. It was surely for that reason that he made abridged solo-piano versions of selected movements from piano concertos by Grieg, Rachmaninov, Schumann and Tchaikovsky (published by Schirmer). These are no mere potboilers. Grainger was incapable of potboiling. If he addressed himself to such a task – or any task – he took it seriously. One can learn much from these abridgements. They are supplied with footnotes which are a mine of pianistic information. The version of the first movement of thc Gricg Concerto, for instance, contains footnotes not included in Grainger's edition of the complete work (in its version for solo piano and orchestral reduction on second piano). Grainger's abridged transcription of the finale of Rachmaninov's Second Piano Concerto evinces a much finer style of piano-writing than the original. That statement will be doubted by readers who have only a generalised idea that Rachmaninov was a great pianist and therefore must have written superbly for piano. But in an interview given to *The Etude* magazine in 1923 in America, and reprinted in part in his biography by Bertensson and Leyda (New York, 1956, and London, 1965), Rachmaninov was candid enough to admit that his Second Piano Concerto was 'uncomfortable to play'. This was in the context of Rachmaninov's admiring remarks about Grieg's *Klaviermässig* style. The Grainger re-writing of Rachmaninov affords, when compared with the original, a master lesson in piano-writing.

Those abridged versions of popular concertos were not merely intended for amateur pianists but for public performance. Grainger played his abridged version of the Tchaikovsky Concerto (No. 1) in a benefit concert by the Oratorio Choir of the First Baptist Church of White Plains, New York, on 27 November 1950, following it with his transcriptions of the Love Duet from *Der Rosenkavalier* and Tschaikovsky's *Flower Waltz*. In that kind of semi-amateur/semi-professional concert, some members of the audience would be hearing the Tchaikovsky themes for the first time and might have enlarged their interest in music as a result of that very concert; so what is the point of an academically trained musician taking a superior view of Grainger's popularising activities?

Grainger was also a pioneer in being the first concert pianist to perform in cinema and revue (as distinct from the pianists who accompanied silent films). He played the first movement of the Tchaikovsky B flat minor Concerto with the orchestral part played by himself on a Duo-Art piano roll in the Capitol Theatre, New York (the then 'world's largest theatre') every day – four times a day! – in the week 17–24 April 1921, sandwiched between Lyman Howe's famous *Ride on a Runaway Train* (a Screen Novelty) and a new Mack Sennett comedy *Officer Cupid*. And in the week commencing 29 March 1926 we find him again playing, in Keith-Albee's New York Hippodrome, Liszt's *Hungarian Fantasy* (with the theatre orchestra) and then, as piano solos, *Country Gardens* and Nathaniel Dett's 'Juba Dance', on a bill that began with a film lesson on dancing the 'Charleston' and included: an Icelandic skating club; Elsi Janis, mimic; Will Mahoney, humorist; a film of 'Our Gang' in *Monkey Business*, a 'smart Hispano-American Revue', *Spanish Dreams*; and much else. Here the concert pianist seems to have made a transcription of *himself*! A veritable Harry Houdini escapologist, freeing himself from the fetters of prim concert etiquette.

The ultimate significance of Grainger's transcriptions is that they apply to concert music the same principle that underlies folk music. Every folksinger makes a borrowed folk-song his own by adding his own 'twiddly bits' or by changing a phrase by a note here or there. In a 28-page letter[76] to the Scottish music-critic D. C. Parker Grainger writes: 'Later on I hope to publish my sketch books with free permission for anyone to use my themes, chords, ideas, etc. I should like to see every man tinkering with every other man's art; what kaleidoscopic, multitudinous results we should see!' Those words were penned on 23 August 1916; they are still futuristic.

[76] Published in *The Grainger Journal*, Vol. 4, No. 1, October 1981, pp. 4–10. –RS

I am reminded of a passage in Hugh MacDiarmid's long poem *In Memoriam James Joyce,* where he recalls some lines of the Irish poet Aodhagan O'Rathaille (1670-1726) from his great *aisling* or vision poem *Gile na Gile* (Brightness of Brightness):

> Oh, Aodhagen O'Rathaille meets again
> The Brightness of Brightness in a lonely glen
> And sees the hair that's plaited
> Like the generations of men.

This vision of the Gaelic Muse, whose hair is 'plaited like the generations of men', is a fitting symbol for both the folk-singer's art and for the composer's art of transcription. Grainger, as both master folklorist and master transcriber, has plaited generations of men in his work. He took strands of peasant and of aristocratic culture and twined them into the emergent culture of our age, the age of gestant democracy. His unique contribution deserves to be braided into the future.

In Dahomey: An Editorial Note

Stevenson contributed this Editorial Note to the publication by Peters Edition of Grainger's 'Cakewalk Smasher' *In Dahomey* in 1987.

Grainger's *In Dahomey* is a concert rag. It belongs to the masterpieces of ragtime, together with those of Eubie Blake and Scott Joplin. An even better comparison might be with the Creole rag-composer Louis Chauvin, Joplin's friend; because Chauvin mingled black and white heredity, just as Grainger mixes Cook's black music and Pryor's white in a process of acculturation. It has waited unpublished for 78 years — more than a lifetime. But its lifetime is Methuselan (and remember that this seventh in descent from Adam bore the name of the 'man of the javelin', a javelin thrown into the future!). Grainger's rag is published at a time when the efforts of such advocates as Joshua Rifkin and William Bolcom have done much to secure ragtime full musical citizenship alongside the masterpieces of European piano literature.

Two manuscripts (the only available, perhaps the only extant) were consulted:

(a) Grainger's original, kindly supplied by Mrs D. Hammond of Aylesbury, Buckinghamshire (UK), into whose possession it came through the family of the composition's dedicatee, Grainger's friend W. G. Rathbone. It is written in blue-black ink with some passages, which may be omitted by the performer, written in red ink. In the present edition, these optional cuts are indicated by alphabetical letters in bold type, A-AA, etc. Grainger's manuscript paper bears the imprint of S. Marshall & Sons, Adelaide, No. 1. Bars 31–33 are written on a different paper and glued as a palimpsest, obliterating an earlier version;

(b) a photocopy of an anonymous copyist's script, kindly supplied by Dr Kay Dreyfus, Archivist and Curator of the Grainger Museum, University of Melbourne. Dr. Dreyfus conjectures that the hand may be that of the composer's mother, Rose Grainger. Though the script does have features in common with other examples of Mrs Grainger's calligraphy, the editor thinks it is most probably in another hand.

Three inspirational sources gave rise to Grainger's *In Dahomey*, two of them musical, the other ethnographic:

1. *In Dahomey*: a Negro Musical Comedy / book by Jesse A. Shipp / lyrics by Paul Lawrence Dunbar and others / music by Will Marion Cook / produced at The Shaftesbury Theatre, London (UK), 16 May 1903 (an all-Black cast) / copyright 1902 by W. M. Cook, New York/ vocal score published by Keith Prowse & Co. Ltd., London 1903;

2. *A Coon Band Contest*: jazz fox-trot by Arthur Pryor / copyright [N.Y.?] 1899, by Arthur Pryor / piano score published by Emil Ascher, N.Y. 1918 (the subtitle 'jazz-fox-trot' was added to the edition of 1918 and is stylistically an anachronism relative to the edition of 1899);

3. The Imperial International Exhibition, London (UK), 1909. This featured a reconstructed Dahomey village with adobe huts and wrestling demonstrations by Black Africans in tribal costume. Grainger purchased a postcard from this exhibition. Dahomey (French *Dahomé*), formerly an independent kingdom, was a French colony in 1909 in West Africa.

The editor is indebted to Mr Don Gillespie for supplying photocopies of title-pages and specimen pages of printed music of the published piano scores of the first two sources listed above.

W. M. Cook (1869–1944) was a Washington-born ragtime composer, son of a Black professor of law at Howard University. He studied violin at Oberlin Conservatory and later with Joachim in Berlin and Dvořák at the National Conservatory, New York. He trained an all-Black band in New York in 1905 and the American Syncopated Orchestra which toured the States and Europe. He composed an operetta *Clorinda or The Origin of the Cakewalk* (Broadway, 1898) and an opera *St. Louis 'Ooman.*[77]

Arthur Pryor (1870–1942) was a white American musician born in St Joseph, Missouri. He founded his concert band in 1903 when he relinquished his position as first trombone and assistant conductor of Sousa's band. He recorded *A Coon Band Contest* in New York on 17 October 1905 (Victor 4069).

Grainger's *In Dahomey* quotes (opening measures and elsewhere) the chorus of Cook's *Brown Skin Baby Mine* (words by W. M. Cook and Cecil Mack):

> She ain't no violet,
> She ain't no red, red rose ...
> But 'mongst de flowers fair
> Kaint non compare
> Wid brown skin baby mine.

[77] *Cf.* John Tasker Howard, *Our American Music*, Cromwell, New York, 3rd edn. [1946] consulted. –RS

Pryor's *A Coon Band Contest* is quoted by Grainger, beginning in bar 34.

The syncopation basic to ragtime (as it is to all Black music) originated, according to Natalie Curtis-Burlin,[78] in the black slave's heroic attempts to learn the alien English language. Natalie Curtis-Burlin instances the accentuation of 'Go Down Moses'. (Curtis-Burlin was a friend of Grainger and, like him, a fellow-student under Busoni.)

Grainger's subtitle to *In Dahomey*: a 'cakewalk smasher', invokes the dance of black American nineteenth-century origin, popularised in imitations in 'black' minstrel shows, vaudeville and burlesque, especially in 'walk around' finales. It originated in parodies of white slave-owners' genteel manners and dances. The name may derive from the prize of a cake given to the best slave dancers. Even before the 'Nineties, 'cakewalk contests' were organised at public entertainments in northern areas of the USA. Its improvised choreography featured arm-in-arm strutting and prancing with bowing fore and aft, high kicks and salutes to spectators. Its most celebrated imitation in piano recital literature is Debussy's 'Golliwogg's Cakewalk' from his *Children's Corner Suite* (1906–8). The cakewalk tempo (like all ragtime) was very moderate. Listen to Grainger's recording of the Debussy (a collector's disc: matrix and take number 81323-3; catalogue number [USA] 3002-D; subsequent US numbers 2001-M and 183-M; recorded 31 October 1923). Grainger's tempo is exemplary and suggests a preference for the most moderate tempo of *In Dahomey*. Grainger's Debussy is also characterised by rhythmic 'commas'. His *In Dahomey* extends these commas to semi-colons. Are they related to elisions in Black speech (as in W. M. Cook's operatic title *St. Louis 'Ooman*)?

As to the other word in the subtitle – 'smasher' – it is justified by the cataclysm of virtuosity in the piece. This is at its most frenetic in the innovations of fist and back-of-hand *glissandi* – pre-echoes of Grainger's 'Free Music'.

What of Grainger's other connections and affinities with Black musicians? They were many: his collaborations with R. Nathaniel Dett, Duke Ellington and J. Lawrence Cook. The Black composer who had most in common with Grainger was surely Joseph Boulogne, Chevalier de Saint-Georges (1739–99), born on the Caribbean island of Guadeloupe of a French father and black slave mother. He studied violin with Gossec but plied rapier as deftly as bow. Sprinter, bareback equestrian, skater, swimmer, crack pistol-shot, as well as symphonist and quartettist, here indeed was a brother of Grainger across the centuries!

[78] *Cf. Negro Folk-Songs*, Hampton series, Books I–IV, Schirmer, New York, 1918–19. –RS

Dr Kay Dreyfus communicates this amusing comment from Grainger's letter to his Danish sweetheart Karen Holten, from N.D.L.S.S. 'Seydlitz', 1 June 1909:

> I have completed writing out *In Dahomey*, with the exception of 2 notes which I will write in Colombo harbor so that I can sign the piece on English-owned earth. (Ceylon belongs to us, you see.) I won't sign anything on a German ship. In the worst case I write 'At Sea'.[79]

He added the two notes in Aden Harbour on 12 June 1909.

A few editorial notes may be presented in briefest form:

Grainger's fingering is non-italic.

Editorial fingering is italicised.

Grainger's Pedaling: Ped. *

Editorial Pedaling: 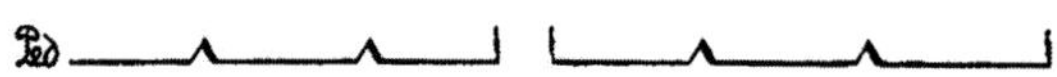

Editorial suggestions in square brackets: [ ]

Grainger's crossbeams often separated: 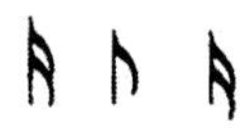

Editorial crossbeams joined to clarify rhythm: 

Editorial fingering of left-hand arpeggi follows Grainger's advice as given in his master lesson on Grieg's *Norwegian Bridal Procession* (Theodore Presser, New York, 1920); the point being to relieve hand tension by dividing a wide-spanning arpeggio into smaller hand positions.

Grainger's multiple *ossias* (alternative, variorum readings) render many different versions of the piece possible: a democratic principle, allowing performer's choice. This procedure was also practised by Boulez and others with a delay of something like a half-century. But these *ossias* create legibility problems and do not economise on paper. The editor has accordingly had recourse to Liszt's practice of notating two hands on one stave (as in the opening measures).

[79] Nonetheless, this letter does not appear in Dr Dreyfus' edition of Grainger's letters, *The Farthest North of Humanness* (Macmillan, London, 1985).

Thoughts on Whitman and Grainger

Before our second interview together in the summer of 2005 (*cf.* pp. 213–52), Stevenson found his thoughts often wandering to the work of Walt Whitman and the influence the poet had exercised on both himself and Grainger. Knowing that we would be discussing the work of the great poet, he decided to write down some of his thoughts on the two men. This note is dated '12 July 2005, West Linton'.

> The top shelf of my library is devoted to Walt Whitman: many editions of *Leaves of Grass*. My favourite is the edition of 1888 (Ferguson Bros. & Co., Printers, Philadelphia). Mine is No. 536 of an edition of 600 copies. In his 'Note at the End' he writes:
>
> > I have wanted to leave something markedly *personal*. I have put my name with pen-and-ink with my own hand in the present volume. And from engraved or photo'd portraits taken from life, I have selected some, of different stages, which please me best, (or at any rate displease me least) and bequeathed them at a venture to you, reader, with my love.
> >
> > W. W. Nov. 13, '88

Percy Grainger's major tribute to Whitman is his *Marching Song of Democracy*. Its dedication reads: 'For my darling mother, united with her in loving adoration of Walt Whitman: begun 1901, continued 1908, 1915 and finally scored 1915–17'. The preface to it begins with a quote from Whitman's 'A Backward Glance o'er Travel'd Roads' (*Leaves of Grass*): 'of the great poems receiv'd from abroad and from the ages, and to-day enveloping and penetrating America; is there one that is consistent with these United States, or essentially applicable to them as they are and are to be?' Grainger's original plan was to write that music 'for voices and whistlers only (no instruments) and have it performed by a chorus of men, women and children singing and whistling to the rhythmic accompaniment of their tramping feet as they marched along in the open air'. But he later scored it for the concert hall. He added: 'An athletic out-of-door spirit must, however, be understood to be behind the music from start to finish'. The vocal parts are not set to a poem but are sung to 'nonsense syllables […] such as children use in their thoughtless singing.' So the 'text' reads 'Ta da di dara da da' – and so on.

He adds a detailed note on the pronunciation of the nonsense syllables. Ultimately he added an orchestral accompaniment, but I personally appeal for an enterprising choral society to restore a performance to the composer's original idea without orchestra (*a cappella,* as musicologists name it).

Grainger, who always discussed his enthusiasms, was surely influential in encouraging his friends Delius and Vaughan Williams and the Dane Herman Sandby to compose works in tribute to Whitman. I myself have set to choral music *To the Unknown Region,* the same Whitman poem that Vaughan Williams set; and I've included in it an English translation of a Horace Ode, *Eheu Fugaces* ('Swiftly they pass, the flying years') which Vaughan Williams made.

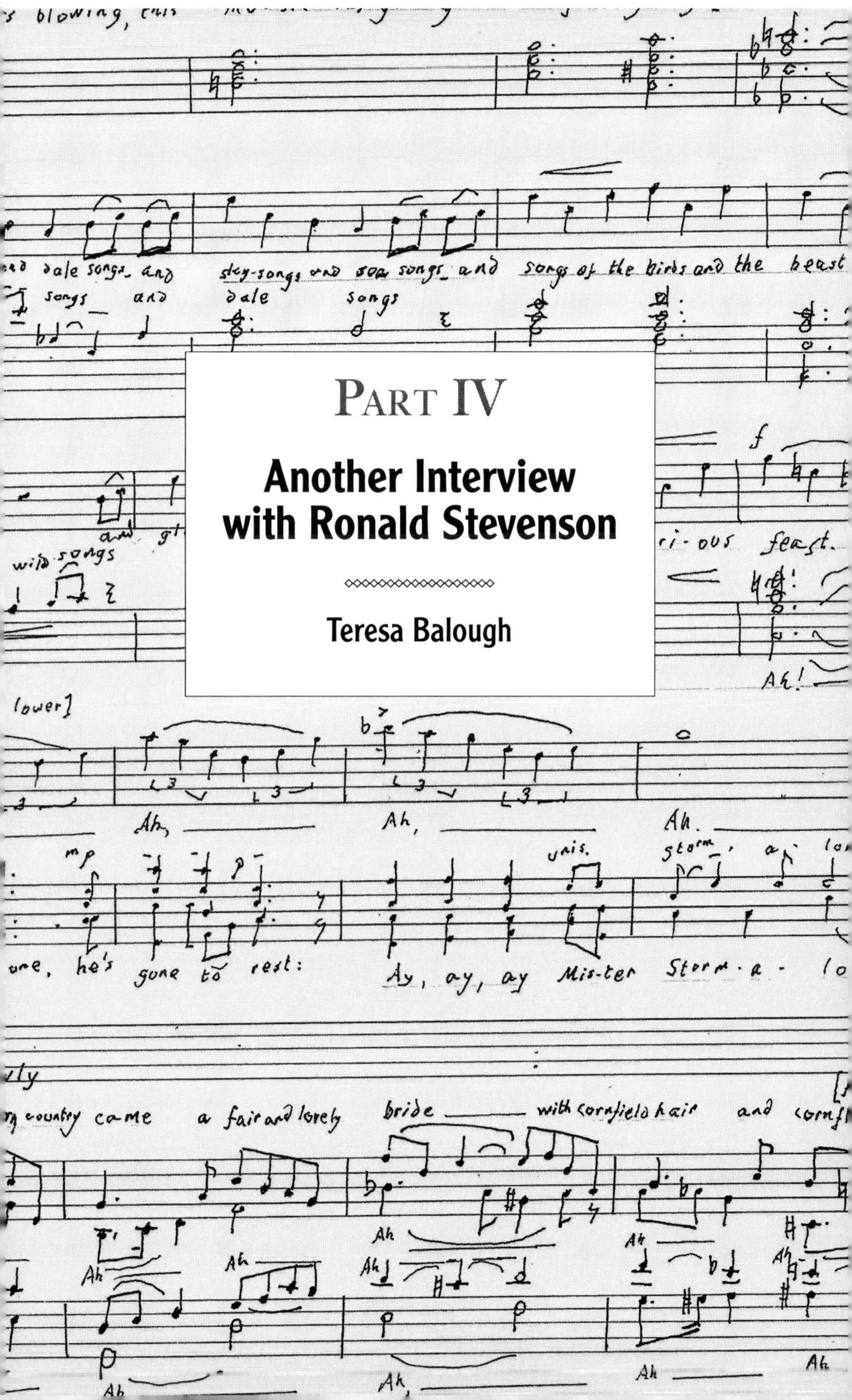

Part IV

Another Interview with Ronald Stevenson

Teresa Balough

Well, Terry, I'm delighted that we're here in my music room and we're going to talk about Percy Grainger.[1]

One of the things that you have in common with Grainger is your mutual love of the American poet Walt Whitman. When did you first come to know his work?

When I was a student in Manchester. It was really through my study of Delius, I would say, and his setting of Whitman. Whitman spoke to me in a way that no other poet did. He spoke directly. I was very enthusiastic about the music of Delius, mainly because, not only because but *mainly* because Delius was from the north of the British Isles, from the north of England and most of the famous British composers have been born in the midlands, as Elgar was, or south of the midlands. So Delius was unique in that respect, and that appealed to me very much. I identified with that. It was a delight to realise that Whitman meant so much to Percy Grainger. That came later; I realised that later. My first knowledge of Percy's music came also simultaneously, on the same day or evening, I can't remember which now, in a radio broadcast, a very primitive radio from about 1934, I think, and I'd be about six. It's amazing really because I remember this from the age of six. It surprises me now. You see, my maternal grandfather was a bargee on the Leeds Liverpool Canal, and he had a primitive gramophone phonograph on his barge, and he also had a radio; and I remember very clearly hearing Percy Grainger's inevitable *Country Gardens* from that radio. That impressed me very, very much. I loved that music and especially coming over the water. And then I heard a recording on the same program of Delius' *Summer Night on the River* which, of course, I realised as a child that there was an agreement with the actual happening, what I was hearing and seeing; it was the river. It was a canal, actually. So that was the first time I heard Delius' music, and I loved it immediately. I thought there was something very special about it, and it's so touching that it was in relation to Percy Grainger. No doubt some highly intelligent broadcaster had decided to unite these in one programme. So I heard that, and it was across the water that I heard that sound; and it was magical.

[1] Recorded on 15 July 2005.

So when you were about six years old you first heard Grainger and you had come to Walt Whitman through Delius.

Yes, that's right. I know it must have been then because there was the announcement of Delius' death about that time, yes, if not on that very day. It's strange; I was walking with my father in the countryside around Blackburn, which is very industrial but there's beautiful countryside around there, and I had the *Serenade from Hassan* on my mind at this time, you see. I kept hearing this, remembering it, I mean. We had no radio then, at that particular time anyway. And when we arrived home, Delius' death was announced on the radio, the same day.

Do you remember how old you would have been then?

Well, quite young. Delius died in 1934, didn't he? I was born in '28, so I was six.

It's interesting because, of course, Delius loved Walt Whitman so much, too. You all have that in common.

Well, I think that was the approach to Whitman, hearing Delius works, particularly *Sea Drift*. That impressed me deeply.

Even as a very young boy you felt this connection?

Yes, and I was able before I saw the score even, I was able to play on the piano the *a cappella* passage 'Oh rising stars, perhaps the one I want so much will rise again with some of you', and I was filled by this second chord in the progression [goes to the piano and plays the four opening chords of that section of *Sea Drift*]. That to me was a new magic: the openness [plays the fourth chord again]. Those separate notes give that openness of the open air [illustrates the four separate notes of the chord followed by the four chords of the passage again] and the night sky.

And, of course, that's Whitman!

Yes, yes; indeed, yes. That is a very, very deep impression from my childhood.

So the first impression that you recall of introduction to Whitman came through Delius and all tied in with your first hearing of Percy as well. That's a wonderful trilogy.

That's the way it worked out. I didn't know how much had to come from that into the future of my life. I'd no idea.

It's interesting you have these roots in your early childhood just as Whitman had roots in his very early childhood and Percy did, too.

I remember also the death of George Gershwin. May I just insert this? This was later in the '30s, I think, a little later,[2] and this again was a kind of strange impression. I was on the site of a dump, a dumping ground, for rubbish. Industrial towns have this, had it even then. Amid all that rubbish I saw, unbelievably, a red rose, a fresh rose, a full rose; and I (this is a strange thought for a young child to have), I thought, 'that is George Gershwin'. I can't remember now whether the death had been announced or the death was announced afterwards. But it was the same evening as the death of Gershwin and I had that insight that this is like the music of Gershwin, the rose among the rubbish! I mean, set against, I'm sorry to say this, but a great deal of what – especially when I was very young I thought this – so much rubbishy music from America, this so exquisite music came like that rose. Those are some, James Joyce would have called them 'epiphanies'. I had, I think, about six of them when I was very young. But I'll not go into the others now.

Maybe we can go into that later. That sounds fascinating.

If I remember them all now. It's some time since I (I should have written them down), it's some time since I have thought about them, about this, actually. But I remembered these two incidents very clearly.

That's really quite amazing.

Well, being so young I think it is, it was. I think I was, what should I say, I was older than my years in some ways, in some ways.

You had an older soul. It's fascinating how you came to the work of Whitman and of Delius and of Grainger all together, as it were.

[2] Gershwin died on 11 July 1937.

And then I heard a good deal of Percy Grainger broadcast. At that time a great deal was broadcast by the BBC, that time being the late '30s.

Would that be the folk-music settings primarily?

Yes, I think so, yes. I came to, should we say, the more serious things later. Which is right. It's very good that I did that. It has to have the folk root.

So even from your very early childhood these men have had a great influence on you.

Oh, very great, very great, greater than I realised at the time. I've only realised this in perspective.

Of course, that's the way we all do. We look back and see the pattern. What would you say, thinking back, has been the greatest significance to you of Walt Whitman on your life and on your work?

Well, I think of that line of Whitman addressed to the reader, 'He who touches this, remember this is not a book, you are touching a man'.[3] Now this meant so much to me. It spoke really very directly to me. I'd never read any other writer who spoke like this, whose voice I could hear, as it were, addressing me personally, very personally. It meant so much to me, and I've only tried to set to music one poem of Walt Whitman, which I can play for you later I think, some of it anyway. And Percy only set what he called 'nonsense words', I think, to his 'In Memoriam, Whitman',[4] didn't he.

Yes, that's right. He used the nonsense syllables in the Marching Song. *It goes beyond words.*

Not words, but syllables. I think he encouraged others, too, in their

[3] 'Camerado, this is no book, Who touches this touches a man', from 'Songs of Parting' in *Leaves of Grass* by Walt Whitman.

[4] Grainger's *Marching Song of Democracy* (1901, 1908, 1915–17) for mixed chorus (singing nonsense syllables), orchestra and organ, later revised for concert band, was inspired by 'A Backward Glance O'er Travel'd Roads in Whitman's *Leaves of Grass* and bears the inscription 'For my darling mother, united with her in loving adoration of Walt Whitman'.

interest in Whitman, including Herman Sandby[5] who wrote a work to Whitman, at least one. I also loved the freedom in Whitman's writing. This was probably the first free verse in English, I should think, or some of the first. I think musically the sense of rhythm, the wide-open spaces in the lines, the same as in Delius' chord that I played, that wide open space, that meant a great deal to me.

I began in my setting to music with the influence of my father, who sang Irish and Scottish songs mainly, almost exclusively, and a little opera, a little light opera as well. Therefore, the first songs that I wrote were really very much influenced by my father's singing, what he sang, the kind of text that he sang. And I chose a poet (no advice from school or anything like that) entirely on my own, I chose Sir Walter Scott, 'The Violets'. That was, I think, the first song. Also I was very intrigued by George Gordon, Lord Byron, who wrote 'So we'll go no more a-roving so late into the night'. That is actually an Aberdonian folksong, and Byron took it over. So that was one of my first influences: 'So we'll go no more a-roving So late into the night, Though the heart be still as loving And the moon be still as bright'. Now I don't know what a boy of fourteen or fifteen was doing entranced by such words. I suppose I loved the sound of them. I couldn't, I think, at that age in those days, adolescent boys being much younger then than now, I don't think I could understand the implication of the words; but I loved the sound of the words. Byron was, you see, a Scottish poet. Many people don't realise that. He was brought up in Scotland, in the Gordon family, Aberdeen. It's interesting, I think, from the influence of my father's singing, which was mainly as I've said of Irish and Scottish songs, that I chose Byron and Sir Walter Scott. I came to that entirely on my own. Nobody had introduced Scott to me at all. That was 'The Violets', and I've been recently trying to recapture that mood in these very recent late years of setting other Scots music. His poetry is almost unknown. The Waverley Novels are very well known but not the poetry. The poetry was what interested me very much. And Scott didn't write very much in Lowland Scots; he wrote a little in Lowland Scots. After all he was a Borderer. He lived in the Scottish Borders not very far from here. The kind of association with Scotland he had, I felt, was mine, living in the Borders from my father's background, so I identified with that very much.

It's no wonder that you were also in love with Percy's folk-music settings too. It's a part of that. It follows along naturally.

[5] *Cf.* pp. 171–72, above.

Yes, indeed. Another influence was Edward MacDowell,[6] and there I realised that here was a connection again with Scotland and Ireland. And I felt it was very near to Percy Grainger, although I think Percy only played one work of MacDowell, one short piano piece, 'To a Water Lily'.[7] Later I realised that MacDowell had really done something which Percy did in a way. Perhaps he got it from Percy. I've no proof of this. He identified with Scandinavia. MacDowell was a friend of Grieg's, correspondence friend; and he wrote a wonderful *Keltic Sonata*[8] which I've played in public a number of times. I love it. It's not very well known, and I think that was something very new that MacDowell should have [identified with] Ireland and Scotland, because practically no body else was doing that since John Field,[9] the Irish composer. Nobody had really done that very much. I value that in MacDowell.

It's interesting how these composers that you value so much have the nationalist roots, the Celtic roots, and yet spoke to this broader audience, much like Whitman with America.

That's what I feel. Yes, thank you. That's a good insight; that harmonises what I feel very much!

Well, speaking of Whitman and Grainger, when I think about them I often think that they seem to be two sides of the same coin. One side is musical and the other side is poetic, and thinking about their lives, of course they had very different lives in many ways, but there are some amazing parallels.

Tell me, please.

I'm thinking of, for example, the fact that Whitman wrote his Leaves of Grass *at a fairly early age.*

[6] Edward MacDowell (1860-1908) was an American Romantic composer and pianist born to a Quaker family of Scottish descent. He is considered to have been the first American composer to become well known abroad. Much of his music, such as *Woodland Sketches* and *The 'Indian' Suite*, is characterised by a lush, out-of-doors quality.

[7] No. 6 of MacDowell's ten *Woodland Sketches*, Op. 51, of 1896.

[8] Piano Sonata No. 4 in E minor, Op. 59, written in 1900.

[9] John Field (1782–1837), the prolific pre-Romantic Irish pianist and composer, pioneered the lyrical piano solo as an accepted concert style and was best-known for introducing the compositional form for piano known as the 'Nocturne', of which he wrote eighteen; they were an appreciable influence on Chopin.

Thirty-three, I think.

Yes, I think so, and then from there on he refined that work. He spent the rest of his life working through the Leaves of Grass, *adding to it, refining it, creating more beauty; and when we think about Percy, of course, we know that he did a similar thing. He started as a very young child, actually, composing in a burst of creativity up to his twenties and then spent a great deal of time refining piece after piece.*

Yes, well perhaps that's true of myself, if I may bring myself into context. When I presented my *Passacaglia,* which is my best-known work, to Dimitri Shostakovich at the Edinburgh Festival in 1962, the Chairman at that meeting was the Scottish poet Hugh MacDiarmid. At the end of that meeting we walked along George Street in Edinburgh, the central part of Edinburgh. MacDiarmid had a kind of Whitmanesque way with him, very old-world really, very different from what young people think today. He put his arm in mine as we walked along George Street; and that was an old-fashioned thing to do, a wordless symbol of friendship. We were walking along George Street in Edinburgh and he said, 'now you're interested in epic work'. (And I'm coming back to the point you've made just now.) He said, 'I have a suggestion to make to you: there is a Scottish poem with the title 'Ben Dorain' (the 'Ben' for a mountain), and it's a poem of 555 lines. The poet was blind so it had to be memorised. The poet was Duncan ban MacIntyre. There are a number of translations. I've attempted a translation, a version in English, not in Lowlands Scots, in English; and you could perhaps give this a little thought about another epic work'. Well, of course, the same evening I began, and I'm now in the final stages of it.[10] So it's lasted, what, fifty years is it? Yes. The Edinburgh Festival in 1962, I think it was. So I'm working on that now, and I'm very glad that it has taken this time because I've made other discoveries about this poem *Ben Dorain.* For instance, I met a wonderful lady who wrote about Percy Grainger to me as 'a golden glory', 'Percy was a golden glory'. She was an old American lady. I think the most important folklorist in Scotland, who learned the Scottish Gaelic language. I only met her later. Marjorie bought me her book years ago, in the 1960s; and it's gone into a second edition later. This is Margaret Fay Shaw,[11] a

[10] Stevenson's *Praise of Ben Dorain* – for orchestra and chamber orchestra, chorus and semi-chorus – was premiered on 19 January 2008 by the BBC Scottish Symphony Orchestra and 'a chorus assembled by Scottish Opera' which included the Chapel Choir of the University of Glasgow and The Edinburgh Singers, conducted by James Grossmith.

[11] Margaret Fay Shaw (1903–2004) was an American-born photographer and

major figure. She died very recently. I had this book from Marjorie in the 1960s, and it's my favourite book of folksongs. It's *Folksongs and Folklore of South Uist*; and she adds a dimension that I believe no other folklorist has added to her research, which is to take photographs of the folksingers, her own photographs, very wonderful photographs.

A holistic approach.

Yes. So I only got to know her in the last years of her life, and she invited us to the Isle of Canna in the Hebrides. Marjorie and I had two or three wonderful days with her. She gave me *carte blanche* to use her book, make versions of the folk melodies from South Uist just as I liked. And I discovered in that collection a Ben Dorain song. Now Ben Dorain, of course, was celebrated by a poet from the Isle of Skye. Now this [version] wasn't [from] the Isle of Skye you see, this was [from] another Hebridean island [South Uist]. I've researched more and discovered there is a Canadian version of Ben Dorain; and I weave this in as well, you see, because it really is an epic in conception. The poet thought of it as an epic, and there's no reason why I shouldn't extend it to this. That's from Nova Scotia. I've discovered that. I've done this research on it very recently. So I'm glad that I've taken about fifty years because through that time span I've discovered other things that I didn't know years ago.

I think in conception it's a very Graingeresque work. I've used the forces, if that is the word appropriate to the structure. I've taken the original Gaelic language and I've begun it with two children's voices, first of all the girl's voice and then a boy's voice. The young boy treble can go higher and stronger than the young girl and, therefore, he goes to higher notes in the prefatory few bars. Then the choir *a cappella* is introduced, that is the full choir singing the original language, the Gaelic language. Then I've used an accompaniment of a full orchestra for the full choir; and I've also used, for the translation into English, a chamber choir and a chamber orchestra from the front of the stage. So that is what I've been doing recently.

Isn't it rather unusual for composers to do this, to take the work of their early years and continue developing it for years and years and years?

---

collector of Gaelic song and folklore most well known for her *Folksongs and Folklore of South Uist* first published by Routledge and Kegan Paul in 1955. She made her home in the Hebrides of Scotland from 1924, living on South Uist, Barra, and from 1938 the Isle of Canna which she and her husband, the folklorist John Lorne Campbell, bought and gave to the National Trust of Scotland.

It's a very Graingeresque thing.

It's a marvellous thing that you all three [Stevenson, Grainger, and Whitman] have in common. Usually people are running from one thing to the next, but you're developing more and more.

That's right, especially with this work, but with other works as well. *Ben Dorain* has a very special place, especially as Marjorie bought this wonderful book. She began it in a sense about Margaret Fay Shaw.

That's a marvellous story. Well you know that both Whitman and Grainger (and obviously yourself) felt that the impulses you have in childhood are very important. Some people dismiss their childhood.

I couldn't possibly do that.

They didn't do that either, nor do you.

Especially my father [was], you see, a very, very deep and high influence in my life, especially his singing of Scottish song and his encouragement of my music. He was a railway worker. He was not the highest-paid railway worker. He was not a driver of trains, railway trains. He was a fireman who was paid less than the driver. He did pass his exams to be a driver, but his health prevented that.

This is my father in the First World War as a young sailor [indicates a photograph on the mantelpiece]. I'm so moved by this photograph because he looks so, if I may say, virginal. A strange word to use with a man, but I feel that; and there he's dressed in the uniform of murder, really. I love that photograph. Here he is later on in life as a railway worker [indicates another photograph], lighting his lamp.

Those are wonderful photos.

I feel this very strongly about the (I'm sorry to usc the word, a rather uncomfortable word) 'class,' the 'class struggle,' the working class, the middle class, the upper class, all these horrible phrases. I still consider myself a member of the working class because I work with my hands as a pianist. The working class work with their hands; and I owe so much to my father, to his singing, to his love of song. When I was, I think, about seventeen I went with him to Manchester for an examination towards a scholarship; and I was so touched (more touched in memory than I was at the time even) that my father said, 'I want you to do your best to get this scholarship because I'm sorry to say that I can't afford to pay for you to go'. Well, I did get the scholarship.

Then I had a Russian teacher, Iso Elinson[12] (the Biblical name Esau); and he was a student, he had been a student of Blumenfeld,[13] the teacher of Horowitz in Russia. He was helped very much by Glazunov.[14] He said Glazunov was so kind to him because he [Glazunov] put up posters for him for his concerts. He himself climbed up ladders and put up posters; and one of the posters listed, among other works, *The Earl King*, the Schubert song transcribed by Liszt, which Iso was going to play. A young Russian Red Guard came up and said: 'We can't have any kings here; this Earl King we can't let him in'. So Glazunov had to explain what this was. Glazunov toured with Iso Elinson. Well, Elinson, through Glazunov, actually was allowed to leave what was then the Soviet Union. Very strange: he went to the beginning of Nazi Germany. It was a very odd thing; I don't think he knew anything about it, about politics. He met a young characteristic Aryan lady who was the daughter of one of the leaders of music in the Nazi party,[15] and he fell in love with her. They came to Britain and married, and he was the teacher of piano at the Royal Manchester College of Music. His wife was also a teacher there. Iso Elinson, although he didn't know about Percy Grainger (he didn't know about Busoni either, really), he suggested that I play Bach, which was both Graingeresque and Busonian, the 48 Preludes and Fugues. It was a wonderful idea, a wonderful basis for all my work at the keyboard.

I remember there was a very fine musician on the staff of the Royal

[12] Stevenson studied with the Russian-Jewish emigre virtuoso Iso Elinson (1907–64) at the Royal Manchester College of Music.

[13] The Ukranian pianist and composer of Polish extraction Felix Blumenfeld (1863–1931) taught piano at the St Petersburg Conservatory, numbering Vladimir Horowitz, Simon Barere and Heinrich Neuhaus among his pupils.

[14] The famed Russian composer Alexander Glazunov (1865-1936) was a professor at the St. Petersburg Conservatory and its director from 1905-28.

[15] Iso Elison's wife, Hedwig (1907–83), born in Jena, Germany, was the daughter of Fritz Stein (1879–1961), who became director of the Hochschule für Musik in Berlin after the National Socialists came to power. Stein, who was also president of the Reichsbund für Evangelische Kirchenmusik during the Nazi period, wrote both a biography of Reger (whom he had known), published by Athenaion, Potsdam, in 1939, and a pictorial biography, *Max Reger: Sein Leben in Bildern*, Bibliographisches Institut, Leipzig, 1941. Peter Gellhorn, a Jewish student at the Hochschule at the time, was at pains to exculpate Stein and Clemens Schmalstich, seemingly another Nazi placeman: Stein 'behaved very well indeed, and I have only very pleasant memories of him and of Schmalstich. One could hardly refuse the jobs they were offered, but they didn't approve of what was going on' (Martin Anderson, obituary of Gellhorn, *The Independent*, 21 February 2004).

Manchester College of Music called Frank Merrick,[16] from Percy's time, really. I remember one day when I was playing Beethoven Opus 101 in A Major. I was very touched that Iso Elinson contacted Frank Merrick in the hall, in the concert hall of the college, and I could hear him saying, 'Listen to this, listen to this cantabile'. I think it was through Elinson that I acquired that touch. Perhaps Percy had the same. Of course, he had a Russian-inspired teacher didn't he: Pabst[17] in Australia who later went to Russia. So I think it may have been this same touch that was taught at that time. The quality of touch, that's the most valuable thing, to make the piano sing. Well, Iso Elinson said to me at one stage, 'what kind of piano have you got?' Now I had a miserable upright piano. Not all upright pianos are miserable by any means, but mine was very ancient; and I said to Iso Elinson, 'it's an old piano, difficult to get it tuned.' Then he said, 'you should have a grand piano'. Now I thought that was a very senseless thing, a very unaware thing for him to say. It meant that he'd no idea of my family background to request a grand piano from a railway worker. I didn't tell my father this for some time. But then the piano was misbehaving even worse than ever. About a fortnight later than that, I did tell my father; and my father's reply was just to say, 'oh, yes'. He didn't go into talking about it; but a few weeks after that he said to me one Friday evening, 'I want you to get ready tomorrow morning because we're going to town centre'. And we went into a shop that sold pianos. Now you can't find such a shop these days in the north of England or in Scotland. You simply cannot find them; they have television sets instead of pianos. We went into this piano shop. It was very interesting what my father said. He said, Try the pianos and tell me the one you like best,' an extraordinary thing to say. Many parents would, I think, first of all have inquired about prices. He didn't: 'the one that you like best.' His boy had to have the one he liked best. I tried the pianos, and I told him. It wasn't a Steinway, it was a Goerz and Kalman, a famous German make. It was a boudoir grand piano, a little larger than a baby grand but not a full grand. Then my father went to the manager of this shop and asked him how much it was. I always get it wrong how much it was, but it was an astronomic price. Marjorie thinks I

[16] Frank Merrick (1886–1981), best known as a composer and pianist, studied with Theodor Leschetizky and taught at the Royal Manchester College of Music from 1911 to 1929. He entered – and won a heat of – the competition launched by the Columbia Graphophone Co., in 1928 to mark the centenary of Schubert's death with a completion of the 'Unfinished' Symphony. Ronald Stevenson has transcribed the slow movement of Merrick's Second Piano Concerto for solo piano.

[17] *Cf.* note 5 on p. 11

exaggerate in my memory, but to me the thing was an exaggeration as a young lad. My father said, 'we're having that piano, so deliver it'. And that was a grand piano delivered in a working class area. Of course, the neighbors thought that my father was above his station. 'What is Stevenson doing? Who does he think he is' kind of approach. My father didn't bother about that, so I had this piano. What he did for me in music.

When I was at the Royal Manchester College of Music, somebody was supposed to be teaching me composition who later taught Maxwell Davies[18] and others. There's no need to mention his name.[19] His only comment to me was: 'your music is not discordant enough to be modern'. How simplistic can you get? I've never heard of anything like this. But I remember one Sunday evening in the silence of the Sabbath trying to produce as much discord from that piano as I could. My father came into the room as though he'd been shot out of a cannon. He said: 'Now what are you doing to that piano?' I told him what my teacher had said, and my father's reply was one of the best lessons in composition that I've ever had. He said: 'Try to think of a tune. If you can play a tune on the piano that is a good start'. Advice from a very simple man, speaking the direct truth about music. So I went on from there you see, and I accompanied him in mainly Scottish and Irish songs. He was too shy to sing in public. He had a light lyric tenor voice, a beautiful voice. He loved these Irish and Scottish folksongs and some light opera by, for instance, Balfe,[20] the Irish composer; and I accompanied him.

He had one friend called Bob Johnson who used to come on a Sunday evening, one major friend really. In the 1930s I would take tea in to them. My mother would say: 'Take the tray in with the tea'. I remember as a child (it would be about 1938) taking the tea through I heard them speaking names, foreign names, which became historical. I heard them speak about Hitler and Mussolini. My father had been a sailor in the First World War. He was convinced that war was coming, absolutely convinced. He was very interested in the Soviet

[18] Peter Maxwell Davies, English composer and conductor born in 1934, studied at the Royal Manchester College of Music and with fellow students Harrison Birtwhistle, Alexander Goehr, Elgar Howarth and John Ogdon formed New Music Manchester, a group supporting contemporary music.

[19] Though anyone familiar with this period of British music will recognise an allusion to Richard Hall.

[20] The Irish singer and composer Michael Balfe (1808–70) was the composer of 28 operas, including the popular *The Bohemian Girl.*

Union. Other people – Bertrand Russell,[21] for instance – visited the Soviet Union and thought that war would not come. But my father, a working man, was convinced that war would come.

I think the working people often have more wisdom and understanding. They're more in connection with life.

And my father, who had been in the navy in the First World War, supported my pacifism. You see, my first grand tour was as a pacifist, not as a concert pianist. I was only seventeen years and nine months of age and I had to register for the call up, the military service it was called. It can't be service because service is given freely. This was conscription; one was forced to do this. I'm not saying that I was right, on looking back on it. If I had known in the 1930s about Hitler and Mussolini, I may have joined the forces. Retrospectively I'm thinking this. What I did know as a young man, especially in my knowledge of Ireland and Scotland, what I did know was that the British army, some sections of the British army were being sent to Ireland against the Irish Independence Movement. I knew that, I knew enough about that. My father didn't talk about that very much; but I did know that, and I refused to join up. So I had my first grand tour with the hospitality of His Majesty (it was at that time King George). In other words, I was imprisoned. That was the grand tour. I began in Preston and Liverpool and Birmingham. I was what is called a 'first offender'; and I was an offender in civil law, not in criminal law. Legally I should have had a prison cell to myself, which I did in Preston and Liverpool; but then when I got to Birmingham I discovered that there were so many prisoners there, not pacifists, criminals, minor criminals very often (they would smash a window, a post-office window or something like that in order to get the hospitality of His Majesty in order to have a free winter in prison with a little warmth perhaps, not much but a little), and I shared a cell with six hardened criminals in Birmingham, in Winston Green Prison. They had no idea what a young concert pianist was; they'd never heard of it, never heard of such a person. At that time I had long hair, very long hair, in the tradition of the concert pianist. There was this ceremonial barbering of my hair, and I think this was already in Liverpool or maybe Birmingham. I can't remember, but it doesn't matter. It was in one of the first prisons I attended. The prisoners were brought in to observe this ceremonial cutting of hair to embarrass me amidst shouts of 'Lady Godiva'. Then

[21] Bertrand Russell (1872–1970) the British-born populariser of philosophy and mathematics, was also well known as a pacifist and anti-war activist.

I went to, after Winston Green, I went to one of the major prisons in London; and I met a fellow pacifist there. [There were] a number of pacifists in the London prison. This was a student from Cambridge University, a Biblical student actually. I'm still friendly with him after all these years, a man called Victor Perry. Vic Perry and I were given the job of sweeping up this particular wing of the prison, sweeping the floors. There were many chairs. One day the screw (the screw was the prison officer) who had the key for the door (that's why he was called the 'screw' in this kind of comical language for prison officers, or used to be, anyway) said to Victor Perry: 'Pick up those chairs and bring them over here'. So Vic piled them all up. He said: 'Bring them all over', so Vic piled them all up and they all fell. The prison officer said: 'Do it again, Perry'. So he did precisely that again! And that was spirited; that was wonderful. And we still are great friends.

You spent how many years in prison?

Oh, no, no, it wasn't years, it was months, three months.

It must have seemed like a long time.

Oh, yes. I had to have three months. I was told by a pacifist lawyer before all this took place, I was told that I should actually request three months because then I could appeal. If I didn't have three months, I couldn't appeal; with less than three months I couldn't appeal. And so I appealed before the Appellate Tribunal, and a Quaker who had befriended me came to speak for me to attest to my sincerity. The Appellate Tribunal could have done one of a number of things. I could have gone into coal-mining, work of national importance, or agricultural work, or the Royal Army Medical Corps. So I chose agricultural work, and I did ditching and draining, the most fundamental thing in farming. The land has got to be ditched and drained before you can grow anything.

How long did you have to spend doing that?

Eighteen months, the same as the call-up, the same period as I would have done in the army.

I see, but then you couldn't practice or compose or anything during that time?

Oh, I could compose. I composed a great deal. First of all, I worked on a pacifist farm. I wrote to Michael Tippett, who was a pacifist and had been in prison; and he gave me the address of a pacifist farm in the south of England which was run by, I could almost say, a disciple of D. H. Lawrence, [someone who] had been a great friend of D. H. Lawrence. I worked on that pacifist farm for a time, and I composed some music for the little choir to sing. I did something very illegal: I left the pacifist farm because I witnessed (can you imagine on a pacifist farm), I witnessed a fox-hunt. I actually think I heard the kill, I heard the screaming of this animal; and I thought to myself: 'Right, I'm leaving tomorrow'. I thought if they needed a sermon about a fox-hunt, a so-called pacifist needed that, then that was very poor. So I didn't even mention why I was leaving, I just said, 'I'm leaving'. I'd no right to leave legally; I could have been put into prison again because it was directed labour, you see. So I then quickly went to the north of England, and I had to very quickly find other work in farming, on the land, to finish that period, the legal period. I worked with a bunch of Irishmen, and I was a vegetarian. I used to take a can of what was called 'nut meat'; and one of the Irishmen said (when it was time to have something to eat we had to provide our own sandwiches or whatever), 'Jesus, Mary and Joseph, what is that you've got there?' And I said, 'well, I've got an uncle in South Africa' – total lie – 'who has a snake farm. This is snake meat. Would you like some?' He said: 'No, that's the very devil! I'm not having that!' We were rained off because you can't work on farm land, ditching and draining, when it's pouring down. So we were what is called 'rained off,' so we went to a shippen[22] where the cows were, a beautiful experience, the breath of the cow and the quietness of the cow. I did a lot of composition there. I composed *Songs of Innocence* of William Blake, nineteen songs of William Blake composed under those circumstances. Of course, the Irishmen thought this was very strange. What was I doing? They'd never seen anything like this, putting little black dots on paper.

Well we've been talking about your father and the wonderful influence he had on you, and it makes me think also of Whitman and Grainger and their reverence for their mothers in their case. It seemed to serve a similar role.
Well, I also revered my mother, of course.

I'm sure, yes. I came across a quote by Whitman in which he said of himself that 'I was well-begotten and raised by a perfect mother'. It reminds me of Percy's attitude towards his own mother.

Yes, I like that. It's true. In my case it was more my father, I would say.

[22] A cow barn or cattle shed.

Yes. One of the other things that I think of that is similar between Whitman and Grainger is they were self-educated, at least in the sense that neither went to college; and I've read that Whitman self-educated himself by becoming a printer, by reading constantly and collecting bits of information. And, of course, Grainger was self-educated in the sense of his languages, his philology, and so forth, that he garnered for himself.

About four months' schooling wasn't it![23]

Right. That's right. I thought that was interesting, that connection as well. What do you think of this, how it makes them independent thinkers in a way by not having a regimented education?

Oh yes, I do believe this. I think that my father was a much more active influence on my education than any school was.

I'm remembering when I first heard Percy Grainger's piano-playing. It was the amazing recordings he made of the Chopin B Minor Sonata, and that was to be played at speed 80, not speed 78. There was an old record shop in Manchester which I used to visit with my younger student colleague Lawrence Glover.[24] They had a machine that could play speed 80, and they had the recording of the B Minor Sonata. Lawrence and I listened to it; and when we came to the finale, we looked at each other in total disbelief of what we were hearing. This was very, very great pianism; and, of course, Horowitz was all the rage at that time. Lawrence said, and I confirmed, I agreed with him, 'You know, Horowitz is nothing on this'. The sense of rhythm, the live rhythm, went even through *ritardandi*, of which there are not many in this movement. That was a big moment in my pianistic career to hear that playing. Many people don't realise what a truly great pianist Percy Grainger was.

Marjorie was just mentioning yesterday that many people, aside from you, don't realise the connection with Busoni that Percy had in his interpretations and his use of the piano pedals. The pedalling was something that none of Busoni's other students took that up as Percy did.

Yes, that's right, that's right. Percy used the middle pedal, the third pedal in everything, even in piano accompaniments for songs, which is extraordinary. Certainly that was from Busoni. There's no doubt

[23] As a young boy, Grainger only spent a total of about three months in school. Otherwise he was taught by his mother and by tutoresses.

[24] *Cf.* note 13, p. 34, above.

about it at all. Whilst we're on the subject of Busoni, I would like to show you a passage which to my knowledge has never been quoted, Percy on Busoni from an American newspaper. It's a very rare passage I've never seen quoted anywhere from *The Public Ledger*, Philadelphia, Pennsylvania, 28 March 1915. Quotation:

> Percy Grainger, who was a pupil of Busoni, went with him last Saturday to hear the first American performance of his [Busoni's] *Indian Fantasy* by the Philadelphia Orchestra under Stokowski. After hearing it, he [Percy] wrote to a friend:
>
>> It is a fascinating work. It had a great success and made a genuine impression in Philadelphia. The work pulsates with real nature and, it seems to me, real prairie feeling. The Indian themes in themselves are very striking and Busoni has used them in a very unconventional way producing great natural flow of form and introducing many shimmering, sensitive and subtle color effects and polyphonic treatments.

That's wonderful! I've never seen that. Where did you come across it?

I can't remember.

I do think there was a deeper connection between them than many people have given credit for.

Yes, it was 1984 I put that in. I discovered that, but I can't remember how I came across it. There it is [shows the article]. That is a photocopy of the actual music [illustrating the article]. So that is original research and totally new.

We've just touched on Percy and Busoni. Percy and I were thinking along a similar line at the same kind of date. I've got a facsimile here, a photocopy of a manuscript of his transcription from William Byrd, 1947.[25] Now about that time, I made transcriptions as he has done from William Byrd, I made transcriptions from John Bull.[26] At the same time. Now it's interesting that this was an attempt to reassess or to bring to light again or to sound again music from a similar background as William Byrd and John Bull are, certainly. And I made piano transcriptions of three pieces of John Bull, *Pavane,*

[25] *Cf.* p 181, above.

[26] Stevenson transcribed a Pavan, Galliard and Jig from the English composer John Bull (1562–1628) as *Three Elizabethan Pieces after John Bull* for piano solo in 1950. In 2004 these were reworked and orchestrated as *John Bull Suite* for orchestra.

Galliard and Jig; and later I orchestrated them. So that's another link. I don't understand that Percy says of this work, *The Carman's Whistle* of William Byrd, Air and Variations for the Virginal,[27] 'for the 4-foot and 8-foot stops of the virginals'. Now I've never seen a virginal with (and it sounds plural but it's singular), I've never seen such an instrument with four-foot and sixteen-foot stops.[28] I've only seen an eight-foot one. I wonder. This may be a mistake of Percy's. I mean, he may be thinking of the harpsichord. Some harpsichords had four-foot and sixteen-foot stops. The sixteen-foot was unusual actually, but that's just kind of a little musicological point. I hesitate to criticise him because he knew far more than I did, and he may have known virginals with those stops.

On the other hand, he would probably applaud you for questioning that if it needed to be questioned.

Yes, he would want the truth. Of course, yes. He says that.

It's interesting that the two of you were composing, transcribing, arranging along similar lines.

At the same time.

And that's before you corresponded too, isn't it?

Yes, that's right.

About ten years before you start your correspondence.

Yes.

Well, to think back now to Whitman again, it seems to me that perhaps one of the things that drew Percy the most to Whitman was his love of democracy and his feeling that everyone was equal: the common man, the common person, the equality of experience. You've mentioned your love of Whitman's use of rhythm, his freedom of rhythm, and I'm wondering about the philosophy of how that affected you and your music. I'm also wondering if the free rhythm of Whitman's poetry suggested or was a kind of footnote to or encouragement for Percy's use of free rhythm.

[27] The virginal, a keyboard instrument that was popular in the sixteenth and seventeenth centuries, is a rectangular harpsichord with the strings stretched parallel to the keyboard.

[28] Stops are devices used to produce a special tone quality or alteration of sound.

I don't think anybody's written about that, about a possible source or encouragement in pursuit of this. I know that he listened to readings in Germany already, Percy did. I know that, but I'm wondering if there was a connection with Whitman too. Certainly it is an affinity whether there was a historic or biographical connection or not. It is an affinity.

It certainly is, and when you think about the freedom of rhythms somehow that, to me, ties in with a feeling of equality of all rhythms, equality of democracy. It all comes together.

Yes. Now let's get back to your other question. Please tell me again.

Yes, I was thinking of the feeling for democracy in Whitman and how that influenced you or mirrored, perhaps, your feelings when you came to Whitman.

Yes, well it didn't need translating for me. I knew it immediately. This was something that spoke to me, something which I felt very keenly. I did not really become politically aware until a bit later in my life, certainly in my twenties, I would say. But I don't like a narrow political viewpoint. Now K. K. Nygaard[29] told me that Percy Grainger was a one-time member of the American Communist Party.

Really! I didn't know that.

Well, K. K. told me that definitely and that Percy was disillusioned by it after awhile, came out of it.

That's very interesting.

He did have a friend who was a member of the American Communist Party who had a great deal of trouble, the composer who wrote for the piano strings.

Cowell.

Henry Cowell[30] was certainly a member of the American Communist Party.

[29] *Cf.* note 2, p. 27, above.

[30] The pioneering American composer of experimental music Henry Cowell (1897–1965) joined the Composer's Collective, an offshoot of the Communist Party's International Music Bureau, in the 1930s along with colleagues such as Charles Seeger, Aaron Copland and Marc Blitzstein.

And he had a lot of trouble, yes.

He had a very great deal of trouble and Percy befriended him and actually brought him to live in White Plains, didn't he?

Yes, he did.

So that is a fact that Cowell was certainly a member of the American Communist Party. There's no doubting that at all and had had work published in the Soviet Union quite early on.

Well that could possibly account for some of the difficulties, the political difficulties, that he experienced.

K. K. told me that Percy was convinced that Cowell had never molested children. That was the case made out against him.[31]

One has to wonder if that was not a frame or trumped-up.

I think we are probably dealing now in things that are unpublishable! (LAUGHTER)

Well, the next thing I'm going to allude to might be unpublishable too. But when we were talking about the similarities between two of your mentors, Grainger and Whitman, there's another thing that strikes me; and I want to see what your opinion on this is. You know, with his belief in democracy Percy was a very strong believer in personal freedom; and he once wrote that he felt that as long as people didn't impose their beliefs on other people, they should be allowed to do whatever they chose, anything that they chose; and I think he even said it would be a good thing in America if you had different states designated for people who wanted to do things in certain ways and they could go and live there.

Remind me later that I do have an article published in America in which Percy is quoted as being very pro-Soviet Union, and that was at a difficult time in the States.

That's very interesting, and certainly I'll remind you of that. *I'd like to see it,*

[31] In 1938 Cowell was sentenced to fifteen years in San Quentin Prison on a morals charge, the details of which were very nebulous. Grainger and other musicians supported him by performing his works, writing and visiting him; and in 1940 he was granted parole through Grainger's petitions and offer of employment and full board at his home in White Plains, New York.

Henry Cowell with the Graingers at their house, 1950s

but the one thing that has gotten Percy posthumously into as much trouble as anything else is his attitude towards sexual orientations and freedoms. What is interesting about this is he championed it verbally, sexual freedom, and this got him into a lot of trouble, not so much in his lifetime but afterwards with a lot of misunderstandings, putting a lot of emphasis on the wrong aspects of his life and so forth. But in reading about Whitman, isn't it true that this also caused Whitman a great deal of trouble because he was so explicit in celebrating the body and sexuality and so forth? I think it was the 1856 preface to Leaves of Grass *in which he stated, and I'm quoting, 'The most significant evil in the present deterioration of man in society is sexual denial and hypocrisy.' Now that sounds like something Percy could have written!*

Well, the top shelf in my library is Walt Whitman. The very top shelf. There was some assumption in America that Whitman was homosexual. His biographer, Gay Wilson Allen, perhaps an unfortunate first name, rejects this totally. I have that book, the biography by Gay Wilson Allen.[32] There is a similarity in the two men's desire for personal freedom and feeling really of almost the divinity of the body. And I

[32] *The Solitary Singer: A Critical Biography of Walt Whitman*, MacMillan, New York, 1955.

think about how, in reading about Whitman, how he was criticised, of course, during his era for this; and many people, even Emerson, put him aside because they could not come that far with him. I think about Percy and how in all the films and biographies and so forth this has been an aspect of his life that has been put under the magnifying glass to the exclusion of more important things. The interesting thing is that in reading about Whitman, it has also been talked about how his feeling for the body was almost a mystical, religious feeling for the body.

Even in considering the mortification of the flesh which so many religious aesthetics have practiced, we find that with Percy. We certainly find that, and it's not looked at in this way.

Yes, surely. I think I can understand that. If there were comparisons with my own life I would tell you, but there aren't any comparisons, I think, with my own life. I'm not being critical of Grainger. I wouldn't be, not at all. It's very much to do with individual conscience, I think. I don't like external disapproval from people who've never gone into the details and don't understand the background.

Absolutely. I remember your once talking to me about Percy's fascination with some of the practices that Native Americans undertook as a kind of a sacrifice really.[33]

Yes, and that was omitted by John Bird.[34] Not only John Bird. He sent the material to Benjamin Britten and Peter Pears; and I know because John showed me this correspondence, I know that Britten and Pears asked for this to be removed from the book.[35]

That's too bad. They didn't understand it.

No, they didn't. How much more interesting it would have been to have related it to some American Indian practices. How much more it would have told one about Percy.

I think so too. The Sun Dance in particular. It almost seems as though Percy had that sense without actually, perhaps, even knowing at the time what these practices were; but he had that feeling for attaching oneself to the divine.

[33] *Cf.* note 26, p. 46, above.

[34] *Cf.* p. 43, above.

[35] *Cf.* p. 44, above.

Remind me. I'm just making a footnote now, a verbal footnote. I do have some pages which I copied out from Australia, from the Grainger Library. I have one or two pages touching on this, very much so, which I haven't seen published anywhere.

I would love to see that.

They're in Percy's hand (I copied them out) on this point about the Amerindians.

As far as I know, you're the only person that seems to understand this about Percy's philosophy, this connection with the sacred, with Native America, rather than it being some kind of aberration that either needs to be dissected or covered up, one or the other.

Well, there is also a dream that he had which was omitted from the book, from John Bird's book, which I think is a very good book but it's a pity that these things are missing. There is a dream which could really have been written by an American Indian. One of Percy's dreams. But we'll come back to that later as well; I need to check.

Going back again to the relationship between Grainger and Whitman, both of them loving the common person, I remember that Percy used to say that he would look at the little cottages from the train as he passed by, the working men's houses, and wish that he could be a part of that world rather than the high society that he lived in.

I have thought of that when I've passed such houses on the train. Those words have come to mind.

At any rate, there is Grainger's love of the music of the people, the folk music, and Whitman's love of every person, really of every common person, all of whom he found beautiful. No matter what they looked like physically, he found a beauty within them. But then also through this, there is this almost international embrace of humanity. I think of Whitman saying, and I'm quoting him, 'My spirit has passed in compassion and determination around the whole world. I have looked for equals and lovers and found them ready for me in all lands'.[36] *And I think again how that must have influenced Percy, who embraced the world, and yourself with your wonderful Passacaglia*[37] *and*

[36] Walt Whitman, 'Salut au Monde!', in *Leaves of Grass* (1892 edition; Bantam Books, New York, 1983, p. 118).

[37] 'The work is written in an international (but not cosmopolitan) spirit, and

many of your works that embrace all countries, all peoples. So this mystic kind of union appears again.

Yes. In my own case I would add to that a book by the Scottish poet Hugh MacDiarmid, his *In Memoriam James Joyce.*[38] The subtitle is *From A Vision of World Language.* The book is (this is very funny in a way, what I'm saying, it's true and funny) non-academic. The academics would love to go into this very deeply, but actually it isn't academic at all. MacDiarmid said, 'I have written this book in twenty languages', not one of which he knew, including English! Now this is a great Scottish poet. Every letter to me is signed 'Love from Valda [that's his wife] and I'. I mean who can say 'love from I'? He thought it was bad English to say 'love from me, from Valda and me', you see. So this is amazing. There's a poet who somehow got hold of twenty languages, not one of which he knew (LAUGHTER), and made a book out of it, *In Memoriam James Joyce: From a Vision of World Language.* It was a blindness of language actually (MORE LAUGHTER), but things can happen like this in poetry or maybe in music, comparable things. And, in a way, it doesn't matter whether he knew the languages or not. He could use what he wanted. He could find somehow, or friends could find for him, in the case of MacDiarmid, what he wanted. But I do find that the vision of that, the ideal wish for all that, is very much related to Whitman and to Grainger. Now I remember when I first met the poet MacDiarmid, or Christopher Murray Grieve to give him his real name, on a bus from Edinburgh to the Scottish Borders (we lived near to each other, fairly near, just a few miles away). We got into conversation, and I mentioned Walt Whitman. He put his hand on my knee and he said very fervently, 'One of my gods'. Now for a man approaching seventy to make such a statement argues for a very youthful spirit. His work, MacDiarmid's work, his best is very near to Whitman, very, very near. I think probably the nearest and, incidentally, I don't know how he did it, but he manages in *In Memoriam James Joyce* to quote Busoni extensively, the only poet I know who has ever quoted Busoni's literary writings. (LAUGHTER) Somebody must have put him up to it. Somebody must have suggested this, you

---

includes, within the larger framework, dances from many countries': Ronald Stevenson in an address to Shostakovich on the presentation of the manuscript of *Passacaglia on DSCH* to him in 1962. Stevenson's Violin Concerto is written in a similar 'internationalist' spirit. On the *Passacaglia on DSCH cf.* Ateş Orga, 'The Piano Music', in Colin Scott-Sutherland (ed.), *op. cit,* pp. 81–98; and on the Violin Concerto *cf.* Malcolm MacDonald, 'The Orchestral Music', *ibid.,* pp. 154–59.

[38] William Maclellan, Glasgow, 1955.

see. That's alright. Why not? In fact, it's an extension of folk-poetry collection, of folk-song collection isn't it that one can take advice, indications from friends, quite sophisticated friends, better educated formally than one is oneself. Why not? That's what MacDiarmid did, and I respect that.

We never discussed Percy Grainger. I don't know if he would have extended to knowledge of Percy Grainger, Hugh MacDiarmid. Though it was amazing to what his knowledge did extend.

How old were you when you met MacDiarmid?

Oh, how old was I. I must have been in my late twenties, I think.

So you were still quite young.

Yes, yes, and we had an all-night discussion here with John Ogdon.[39] I don't know if you know about this. Well, you see, MacDiarmid was very friendly with a Parsee composer called Sorabji,[40] and I have a letter somewhere from Sorabji to Percy Grainger.

Do you? Oh my goodness.

Yes, this isn't known. This isn't known, in fact, it's highly improbable that Percy was interested in Sorabji or that Sorabji corresponded with him, which is more like it that Sorabji corresponded to Percy Grainger. But I have that facsimile somewhere. Make a note of it and remember: letter to Percy Grainger from Sorabji. It was the 1920s, I think, and Sorabji sent him some music.[41] I don't want to pre-empt the letter too much, but Percy says: 'I need to play it through on the piano before I can comment', because it was very complex music. And he's encouraging. That is an aspect of Percy that many people wouldn't think because Sorabji is connected more with Busoni and he's often thought of as a thundering intellectual, not an intuitive at all. That's what I value about Percy, that Percy held in balance the mind and the heart. He did, more than or as much as anybody I can

[39] A transcription of this conversation is published in MacDiarmid's *The Company I've Kept*, Hutchinson, London, 1966, pp. 38–70.

[40] *Cf.* note 85 on p. 120, above.

[41] Stevenson's copy is of a letter dated 20 February 1924 from Percy Grainger to Kaikhosru Sorabji of which an earlier copy exists in the Grainger Museum; in it Grainger thanks Sorabji for the gift of two of his works and promises to send some of his own works in return.

think of in music. Busoni also had something of that, but I think Busoni didn't have it in such balance. I think Busoni was a passionate intellectual and the intellectuality as far as communication with people was concerned outstretched his intuition. That's the trouble. Busoni was a man of feeling, but that small part of the music public who are interested in Busoni at all would not believe that. They would think that he was a dry intellectual. I would say he was a passionate intellectual. But we are talking now about Busoni; then it becomes too wandering. (LAUGHTER)

That's alright because this is wonderful to have taken down. Whatever you have to say is marvellous. Another thing that I think of in common with Whitman and Grainger is the belief not only in freedom of expression for individuals but also wholeness and ensemble, having people work together. Whitman said, and I'm quoting, 'I will not make poems with reference to parts, but I will make poems, songs, thoughts with reference to ensemble'.[42] *And, of course, Grainger believed so strongly in ensemble that he took piano music, as you know, and wrote it out for 'Piano Teamwork', so the pianists wouldn't have to be lonesome.*

Yes, indeed, wonderful. I love that. That's very true, a very, very good comparison. Perhaps Percy influenced Busoni in reading Whitman. There are references in Busoni's letters to having read Whitman, and I have the [listing of the] Busoni library, which was sold after his death, and certainly *Leaves of Grass* is there without a doubt.

I know that Percy encouraged Busoni to read Kipling and perhaps Whitman too, then.

Yes, yes, he did, and Mrs Busoni told me that Busoni went along with him, with his interest in Whitman, but not with Kipling. I can understand that, but the Kipling poems are really poems of the common man, aren't they, very often?

I think Kipling also has been greatly misunderstood.

Yes, so do I.

It's interesting to reflect that the three, or three of the people most admired, Kipling, Whitman, Grainger, at least by me, perhaps by you, I don't think people have understood entirely what they were saying.

[42] Walt Whitman, 'Starting from Paumanok', in *Leaves of Grass* (1892 edition; Bantam Books, New York, 1983, p. 17).

I think that's true. Yes, that can be the only answer to it, I think.

Going into a slightly different area, I feel and know that it's interesting to think that Whitman, of course, was a pioneer in formulating a new set of ideas about poetry, writing in this freedom of style that was totally different, a new poetics if you will, and Grainger also wrote about a music of the future that would be free of restrictions and so forth. I'm wondering what your insight into that would be, your feeling of the commonality again of their achievement.

Yes, oh, it's very true and it's parallel, it's certainly parallel. They speak with one voice really, two men speaking with one voice about that.

I was very excited to read that in Specimen Days *Whitman said that 'even as a boy I had the fancy, the wish to write a piece about the seashore.* [...] *nothing but seatossings in sight in every direction as far as the eye could reach* [...]. *I felt that I must one day write a book expressing this liquid, mystic theme'.*[43] *And that's very exciting when you think of Percy's desire to write 'Free Music' and one of the first ones being the* Sea Songs.[44] *It's amazing.*

Yes, yes, that's a very good comparison. That's a wonderful comparison. Now, there's another link between Busoni and Percy. K. K. Nygaard told me that he went to a concert in which the young, so-called *avant-gardist* music was performed from Germany and France in New York; and Varèse[45] was there; and Varèse and Percy were sitting next to each other. Now I don't know if Percy and Varèse had met before. Varèse was, of course, a great protégé of Busoni, and Varèse admired Stockhausen.[46] He admired this very much, and Percy went along with him. He agreed with this. I feel that that is a *cul-de-sac.* I'm not with them there, either of them. I think that Varèse is a hugely overestimated composer who had very few works. I mean, he destroyed huge works

[43] Walt Whitman, 'Sea Shore Fancies', from *Specimen Days* in *Walt Whitman Complete Poetry and Collected Prose* (The Library of America, New York, 1982), p. 796.

[44] Grainger's first written attempt at creating a beatless free-music style was his *Sea Song* sketched for three solovoxes operated by a paper roll running in a silenced reproducing piano, accompanied by reed organ, in 1907.

[45] The French-born American composer Edgard Varèse (1883–1965) was an early advocate of new forms in music, from the fiercely discordant to the use of electronic sounds and music on tape.

[46] Karlheinz Stockhausen (1928–2007) was a controversial German composer of electronic music and 'controlled chance' serial music (music which proceeds through the repetition of pre-determined sets of musical elements rather than inspiration).

early on in his life, literally destroyed them; but his fame rests on about sixteen opus numbers. Well, that doesn't matter in a way. There are one or two others in the history of twentieth-century music with whom one could make a comparison, but I do believe that genius generally likes to produce many works. There are some exceptions. Chopin was an exception; he produced very little compared to (say) Schubert. I think Percy was, strikes me as having been very agreeable with nearly everybody, I should think, and certainly with Edgard Varèse, you see. (LAUGHTER) I think he would want to go along with it. He would think this was a possible way into the future. Actually it didn't have anything like the value that Percy's ideas of 'Free Music' had. But he would go along with that, and Varèse was a very striking personality and very dominant, I think. Percy was not a dominant character, really, was he?

I don't think he was aggressive.

Not aggressively dominant.

He wanted to be kind to people, and I don't think he would be pugilistic with anyone over their ideas. He would write about it later and argue that way.

Yes, sure, yes. But that perhaps isn't generally known. K. K. told me this. He was at the same concert, I think. I think that's right that Varèse and Percy sat next to each other.

It's very interesting about Percy. One often thinks of him as being very argumentative, but I don't think he personally was, as you say. If he were with you he would want to embrace your, your freedom of expression certainly.

Yes, yes, yes. I think that socially Percy Grainger was not aggressive and opposite to anybody. I think he was socially very well balanced, but he would go home and think about it and write about it (LAUGHTER) and probably come to a totally different conclusion!

That's right. You're absolutely right. Maybe he had that in common with Whitman, too. Whitman seemed always to be a very agreeable kind of person.

Yes, that's the impression, yes.

But thinking these thoughts at the same time.

Yes, that's right, yes. They had that in common, I would guess.

I often think about what Burnett[47] *said about Percy which is that he would 'leap out' sometimes with these statements just to see what happened.*

Yes, oh yes.

He would on occasion make some really wild statement to see if someone would argue with him about it.

I wish Burnett had lived longer.

Yes. Don't we all? Well, he was the one who really knew Percy the best, wasn't he, he and K. K. and, of course, Ella. I think also of how Whitman used to write about what I think he called 'The Answerer', the poet who would help people to see a new way of doing things, to see really the divinity and creativity within themselves.[48] *And I think Percy used to talk about the 'Oversoul', Oversouls who helped people not by dictating to them what they should be doing but helping them to become creative themselves, to bring it out. It seems to me that in a lot of your works you do this too, that you in a sense invite your audience or your performers to be a creative part of this whole process.*

I take a different view, a different view from most people I've met about the development of music in the twentieth century. I don't think Percy would have agreed with me because he would have wanted to see development. I don't see it in the twentieth century. The twentieth century is, from my reading, the least developmental of recent centuries. I think the nineteenth century was much more developed, went through many more influences. One thinks of Haydn, still alive in the first decade of the nineteenth century and composing settings of Scottish folksongs commissioned from Edinburgh. I think he died in 1809, if I remember, and then soon after that, very soon after that we have three really significant composers born within a year: Chopin, Schumann and Mendelssohn. And Berlioz was still alive and still writing at that time, the beginning of the nineteenth century. I'm arguing the case of the nineteenth century being a very progressive period. Most people wouldn't say that; they would think that it wasn't half so progressive as the twentieth century. I'm arguing against the idea that modernism must have two factors: it must have discord and rhythm. Well, that was founded, that concept was founded, I think, by Stravinsky in *The Rite of Spring* in 1913 and

[47] *Cf.* note 5, p. 29, above.

[48] Walt Whitman, 'Song of the Answerer' from *Leaves of Grass* (1892 edn.; quoted as in 1983 edn., *op. cit.*, pp. 133–37.

it went on for the whole of the century – especially, I must say, in American universities and British universities, too. Stravinsky went on, of course, to do very different things after *The Rite of Spring*, very many different things. But it's *The Rite of Spring* that has stuck, especially with musicologists and composers indeed. So I think of the nineteenth century, Chopin, Schumann and Mendelssohn, three totally different composers. Mendelssohn was in a way a classic born after his time, very classically minded. The interesting thing is that the three of them admired Bach very much. The young Mendelssohn was the first to conduct the *Saint Matthew Passion.*[49] Then Schumann's great *Six Fugues on BACH* for pedal piano; they can be played on a piano actually, piano duet. They did have a piano at that time with a pedal board, which is like an organ; and he wrote these six fugues [on which] he spent a year of his life. He thought these were the best things he'd ever done, but they've gone into oblivion. Most people have never even heard of these *Fugues on BACH.* He devoted a whole year to it, you see. So a comparison between these three shows how it was not simply Romanticism, it was the neo-Baroque as well, you see. Then you had Brahms and Wagner, and even Mahler spent most of his life in the nineteenth century rather than the twentieth. He was born halfway through the nineteenth century and died in the first decade of the twentieth century.[50] So all that development is there, all that variety is there. But it's all written off as Romantic, and we can 'ignore' it. The twentieth century was experimental, but what about all those experiments? I think the twentieth century has had *experiment* without *experience.*

Is part of it, do you think, maybe the problem that the twentieth-century composers who were doing something vital, not just dissonance and endless rhythm change and so forth, didn't get the same opportunity to be heard that composers who were in this line in the nineteenth century had. Chopin, Schumann, Mendelssohn, they were heard; but in this century how much was Grainger heard.

Yes.

There was some hearing in the early part of the century….

Yes, that's right.

[49] That is, he was the first person to conduct the work since Bach's own lifetime.

[50] *Recte* 1911.

... and then you come up through yourself and, for example, not being heard at the Proms like you should be. That's not right.

I did give one concert, one Proms concert and one Proms concert in Glasgow as well. But I think that a composer has to make his or her own way. I don't think it always depends on, or shouldn't depend on, agents. And also finding one's way through like-minded musicians and music-lovers. One's way can be made with help from them. But I think that it's a different period now. Have you read a new book, fairly new, by Jacques Barzun?[51]

I know him, yes.

He's still alive, isn't he? Yes. I think, unless I'm imagining it, I think he was a hundred years of age very recently, and he's written an amazing book, *From Dawn to Decadence*.[52] And he believes (I have the book, a huge book), he believes that the arts are under a blanket as if of snow, that the arts are not going to be functional with intelligent wide publics for another fifty years. He believes that western art, especially music, has reached such a state that it is no longer really communicating with human beings, that it has no human content, the arts in themselves, no real human content. It really is a very important book. One can disagree with it, but that is his prophecy; it's almost a prophecy at the end of his life.

He's referring to the arts that are being heard, because there are some, such as yourself, with wonderful human content.

Yes.

But that's not basically what's being heard, what's being seen.

Yes, that's right.

There's a quotation of Whitman which I particularly love. It's from A Song of Occupations, *and he says, 'All music is what awakes from you when you are reminded by the instruments'.*

[51] The American writer Jacques Barzun (b. 1907) is the widely respected author of over thirty books on the philosophy of culture and ideas.

[52] *From Dawn to Decadence: 500 Years of Western Cultural Life, 1500 to the Present*, Harper Collins, New York, 2000.

You're not only quoting from Walt, you're quoting from Ronald Stevenson! (LAUGHTER)

There you go, you see I'm plagiarising you!

And there's another quote that can go along with that. This is my little book on music, music of the western world.[53] A very important passage comes from Robert G. Ingersoll[54] who gave the funeral oration for Walt Whitman. This is from that oration on Walt Whitman:

> I believe that certain feelings and passions, joy, grief, emulation, revenge, produce certain molecular movements in the brain, that every thought is accompanied by certain physical phenomena. Now it may be that certain sounds produce the same molecular action in the brain that accompanies certain feelings and that these sounds produce first the molecular movements and these in their turn reproduce the feelings, emotions and states of mind capable of producing the same or like molecular movements. So that what we call heroic music produces the same molecular action in the brain, the same physical changes, that are produced by the real feeling of heroism, that the sounds we call plaintive produce the same movements in the brain that grief or the twilight of grief actually produces. There may be a rhythmical, molecular movement belonging to each state of mind that accompanies each thought or passion, and it may be that music produces the same state of mind or feeling that produces the music by producing the same molecular movements.

I find that an astonishing passage. So that's page 9 of my little book *Western Music.*

So that when Whitman is conveying his poetry to us, we take it in and experience the same feelings.

Yes, yes. I added a footnote in a way which is not as poetically expressed. This has to do with science from *The Times*, the newspaper *The Times* from 1968, but I said it confirms Ingersoll's hypothesis: 'Electrical recordings taken from single cells of a cat's brain have shown the existence of cells that are active only during fighting. When the

[53] *Cf.* note 33, p. 20, above.

[54] Robert Green Ingersoll (1833–99), a Civil War veteran, orator and political leader, delivered his 'Tribute to Walt Whitman' on 30 March 1892, four days after the poet's death; collected in *The Enemies of Individuality and Mental Freedom* by Robert G. Ingersoll, Haldeman-Julius Co., Girard, Kansas, no date.

electrode is used to stimulate such cells, instead of to record from them, the cat hisses or makes aggressive motions'. I thought that was a footnote to Ingersoll really. But that doesn't answer your question. I can't remember what your question was.

It's really a wonderful quotation. And I think also of how that relates to what Percy talked about in terms of using music to raise consciousness.

Yes, this is *A Song for Occupations*: 'All music is what awakes from you when you are reminded by the instruments'. And then I comment:

> In other words it is not the instruments that matter most, not the performers, not even the composer, but all these factors taken together, projected onto the retina of music, the human brain. This is the very beginning of the listening experience, the root of music's meaning to human beings.

So there it is.

Do you know the work of John Blacking and How Musical Is Man*?*[55]

Oh, indeed I do, yes. It's a fine book.

He says something similar, I think.

There's a great deal about Percy in the book, isn't there?

In a later book there is, the one he wrote about folk-music, about Percy;[56] *but I'm thinking of the little book he wrote, just a little short book,* How Musical Is Man? *It's about his time spent with the Venda in South Africa and how music was a part of their lives.*

I think I have it from years ago. I had a little correspondence with Blacking.

I don't think aside from yourself and Percy and Blacking that most people pick

[55] John Blacking (1928–90) was an anthropologist and ethnomusicologist whose final academic position was at Queen's University, Belfast, Northern Ireland. *How Musical Is Man?* (University of Washington Press, Seattle, 1973) is based on Blacking's sojourn with the Venda people of South Africa and his observations of the place of music in their lives.

[56] John Blacking, *A Commonsense View of All Music: Reflections on Percy Grainger's Writings on Ethnomusicology and Music Education*, Cambridge University Press, Cambridge, 1987.

up on that use of music for raising consciousness in the sense of making us more aware, more alive; and certainly most music that we hear today is not aimed at that. It's aimed more at stimulation, I think, at the senses. It seems we need to come back to that.

Now, you did a Whitman setting.

One, yes, but I've also brought into it a poem by Vaughan Williams which he never set to music.

A poem he wrote himself?

Yes, well it's a translation from Horace. The Whitman poem that I've set was also set by Vaughan Williams.[57] [promises to look up the work and perform it at the piano later.]

Let's talk about your meeting with Benjamin Britten and your discussion of Percy.

I was told that Britten[58] only invited people for around fifteen minutes because he was not very well in health. It was towards the end of his life, and I said, 'Let's say something about Percy Grainger'. And we both exclaimed simultaneously, when I said: 'as a pianist', he said: 'the B Minor Sonata of Chopin and the last recording he made of the Grieg Piano Concerto, the last one'. I said: 'Yes, they didn't issue it because of wrong notes'. He said, 'It's my favourite recording of the Grieg Concerto'. Now I think that speaks volumes from a composer. I mean, who are the critics, who is the general public? Ben Britten has said this himself about this recording. I find it very, very moving that recording because he'd already had, I think, about a half-a-dozen operations. The last recording made in Denmark wasn't it?

With the Aarhus Symphony Orchestra. It was finally released on a long-playing record. Is that the one you mean?

But it was withdrawn.

[57] The words for *Toward the Unknown Region* are taken from Whitman's poem 'Darest Thou Now O Soul' in 'Whispers of Heavenly Death' from *Leaves of Grass*:

> Darest thou now O soul,
> Walk out with me toward the unknown region,
> Where neither ground is for the feet nor any path to follow?

Stevenson's setting is for *a cappella* mixed chorus.

[58] *Cf.* note 15 on p. 34.

It was withdrawn, but it's wonderful. It's wild.

Yes, I love it. Benjamin Britten thought that was the best recording that he'd heard, the best performance he ever heard of it, so who are the critics to mention disapproval? I don't know what I was going to say now, which subject.

We had been meandering.

Yes, that's good. That's a Whitmanesque thing to do. [LAUGHTER]

The 'Open Road'.

Yes.

Well, it seems as though it's a path that you certainly have trod.

Yes, I have tried, yes. Certainly. I've read Walt Whitman a very great deal, most of all in the open air. I've taken the book with me many, many times. 'Camerado, this is no book. He who touches this touches a man.' Marvellous. That word, 'camerado,' it doesn't exist in any language except Whitman's own language. (LAUGHTER)

I think he even calls God 'The Great Camerado'.

Marvellous! (LAUGHTER)

Didn't he say that his work needed to be read in the open air, not confined?

Did he say that?

He did say it. You've caught that. It's understood so much better.

That, by the way, [picking up a framed picture from the widow sill] is the original Gordon Craig[59] woodcut of Walt Whitman.

Oh, he's beautiful. That's in the book, yes.

And it's signed by Gordon Craig. That is the original.

How did you come by this woodcut?

[59] *Cf.* note 8, p. 14, above; Craig was also a talented engraver and classical artist.

Well, Marjorie found that in an old shop in Edinburgh, years and years and years and years ago, in the 1950s, I think. She knew how much I would value it. That's in the book. That's the original, yes.

Did you find the Whitman piece you've written?

Yes. I have it here. It's a rough manuscript: 'Darest thou narrow soul. Branch out with me toward the unknown region where neither ground is for the feet nor any path to follow. Then we burst forth, we float in time and space, o soul. Prepared for them equal ... o joy.'

Before we close, let's talk about how you decided to write to Percy, how you inaugurated the correspondence.

Well, it was for the wrong reason because I was inquiring about his time with Busoni. It was really for the wrong reason. Busoni was my interest at that time, you see; and then I realised a little later that Grainger was more important to me than I had realised, than I had thought. So we quickly got on to other subjects. It's a very poor reason for contacting him really.

I don't know. It seems like Busoni brought you together, which is very interesting if you think about it.

Yes, it is so. I think that Percy had changed his view of Busoni since the passage I read to him. I think he'd developed, he'd changed. And that interests me very much because these two influences in my life I think counterbalance each other. Maybe I'm repeating myself. Busoni was a passionate intellectual. Now I don't think that Percy would like to consider himself intellectual, but he was an aspirant intellectual. I think he aspired to read a great deal and to bring books to the table. He really was a guest. (LAUGHTER) Does that to some measure answer your question?

Yes, I think it does because you were corresponding with him to get information for your work on Busoni.

That's right, that's right. But I wanted to thank him for what his music had meant to me. Even in that first letter I'm sure I said that.

Yes, because you'd known his music since childhood.

Oh, yes. And it was a counterbalance to Busoni, I think. I mean Percy was the aspirant intellectual as well, but he was intuitive and that far more than Busoni was; and I think that that balanced it for me. That is why I was attracted to both of them.

Percy always brought that out-of-doors quality, the open-air quality.

Yes, oh yes. That I valued very much, and that I think I recognised from Whitman, very strongly.

Yes. It's really wonderful to see how the tapestry has been woven between all of you and come together.

Now I also wanted to ask you about Lawrence Glover. I know he's a very, very dear friend of yours. Can you give me any kind of biographical information for the general reader?[60]

Lawrence was from Ulster, from Northern Ireland, and he was a little younger than I was as a student at The Royal Manchester College of Music. He really was the pianist who succeeded John Ogdon more than anybody. He was, I would say, a great pianist. He was very modest and he only recorded some song accompaniments, I believe. I don't believe he recorded anything as a solo pianist. He was the principal piano teacher, piano professor at The Glasgow Academy of Music.[61] He became that. I gave a public concert and lecture on Percy, and he and I played a Grainger programme. We played, for instance, Percy's transcription for two pianos of the *Dance Rhapsody* of Delius, and we also played the *Hill Song*, the shorter version for two pianos of the *Hill Song*. Lawrence played some of his own folk-song transcriptions and I played some of mine and spoke to the audience during the recital, lunch-hour recital.

We went back to Lawrence's flat. (His wife was a fine musician as well. She died very recently.) And I had a strange feeling visiting that flat. I also met his son, who was really very like Lawrence was when Lawrence was young. It was like a double take really, and I had a very strange feeling. Mrs Glover and I stayed up. She was one of the comparatively few ladies who liked to drink whisky (she didn't overdo it), but we stayed up quite late having a drink or two or three perhaps (LAUGHTER); and I had a very, very strange feeling (nothing to do with the whisky). In that house I had (I can't describe it), I had perhaps a premonition. I don't know, but I didn't hear from them for a month or so, and then I rang to ask how they were. Well,

[60] *Cf.* also pp. 34 and 228, above.

[61] That is, the Royal Scottish Academy of Music and Drama, as it is now known.

the son had suddenly died. He was only a young man, you see. And I wondered if that very, very strange feeling I had that night was somehow something to do with that. I don't know. Lawrence wrote a piece in memory of his son, and we played that for piano duet, based on a Scottish folk-song, the folk-song 'The Bonnie Earl of Murray'. Marjorie and I visited Lawrence a few times. He lived just a few miles away towards Glasgow. I reminisced about our earlier days and tried to engage his interest. Of course, he was very immediately engaged. He was a very special figure in my life. We corresponded a good deal; and I tried to help him with the study of polyphony and he was very receptive of that. I think that Lawrence was two or possibly as much as four years younger than I was, and he loved Percy Grainger's music very, very much.

Would you feel like doing the Whitman now?

Yes. [performs his work based on Whitman's *Toward the Unknown Region* at the piano.]

Very beautiful, Ronald. It feels like it goes to the unknown region.

Thank you very much.

When did you write that?

11/7, I first wrote the day, not the month like the American way, 11/7/62.

Do you remember what was happening in your life that inspired you to create it at that time?

Yes, I do indeed. I had just finished composing my big *Passacaglia* for piano, and I wanted to re-address myself to the archetypal form of music, the human voice and the voice multiplying in choral music and, of course, my deep and long love of Walt Whitman.

Now this is for mixed chorus?

Yes, it is. That's right. I often read Walt in the woods. There are special places that I associate with him still, and this music came out of those readings in the open air. And I think there's something of the open air spirit about it, especially in some of the harmonies, I think, in some of the harmonies, I would say. For instance, this, I think is very open air harmony. [performs last few bars]

It is, and yet there's that element of the unknown with the slight clash. It's wonderful. Now does that have instrumental accompaniment, or piano, or is it a cappella?

A cappella.

It's beautiful, wonderful. I wish that this could be recorded.

So do I, yes. I must make a final copy of it.

I hope you will.

Yes, I will. Thanks to your encouragement I will.

Now this was '62, so it was just a year or so after Percy passed on.

Yes.

I think he would have loved this. He would have loved to know this piece.

I like to think he would. In fact, I couldn't think of writing a setting of Whitman without thinking of Percy. The two were almost synonymous for me. I realise that, that he was nearer to Whitman than any other musician I know, even nearer than Delius, I think.

Well he has that same open-air quality in his work that Whitman had in his writing. And that you've captured here.

Yes, yes. And I love the old word for melody, which is 'air', and we need air obviously! (LAUGHTER) Our music needs air; it needs melody. The 'Londonderry Air', as it used to be called, the Irish Tune from Londonderry, the 'Air on the G String', it comes a number of times in music. Thanks for asking me to play it.

Thanks for playing it. That was beautiful.

Appendix
Grainger in Ronald Stevenson's Output

1. RONALD STEVENSON'S TRANSCRIPTIONS, ARRANGEMENTS AND EDITIONS OF WORKS BY PERCY GRAINGER[1]

Australian Up-Country Song arranged for two recorders and piano (1965)
Bridal Lullaby edited for piano solo (Bardic Edition, 1990) (1987–summer 1989)
Green Bushes transcribed for piano solo (1963)
Hill Song No. 1 transcribed for piano solo (1960)
In Dahomey (Cakewalk Smasher) (Edition Peters, 1987) (MS. date unknown)
Kintra Gairdens arranged for highland bagpipe (1980)
Molly on the Shore arranged for flute and cello (1970)
'Northern March' from *Youthful Suite* transcribed for piano solo (1983)
Over the Hills and Far Away (Children's March) arranged for oboe, bassoon, violin and piano 3-some (c. 1966)
—— arranged for two recorders and piano (1965)
The Power of Rome and the Christian Heart transcribed for piano solo (1981)
The Power of Love arranged for tenor and harp, with English text by Grainger from Danish folk-original (1975)
'The Reel of Tulloch' from *Scotch Strathspey and Reel* arranged for flute and cello (1970)
Shepherd's Hey arranged for violin, treble (or tenor) recorder and anglo-concertina c. 1966)
Spoon River arranged for flute and cello (1970)
Three Scotch Folk-Songs
1. 'Will ye gang to the Hielands, Leezie Lindsay?'
2. 'Mo Nighean Dubh'
3a. 'O gin I were where Gadie Rins' (performing edition).

[1] Gleaned primarily from Scott-Sutherland (ed.), *Ronald Stevenson: The Man and his Music, op. cit.*, with further additions by Ronald Stevenson.

3b 'O gin I were where Gadie Rins' (simplified arrangement) edited for piano solo (C.F. Peters, 1984) (dated 1983)

The Warriors, transcribed for solo piano

The Warriors of Peace transcription for two pianos of *The Warriors*, Part II (2 November 1989)

The Young Pianist's Grainger

1. 'Country Gardens' (simplified edition by P.A.G.)
2. 'Shepherd's Hey' (simplified edition by P.A.G.)
3. 'Molly on the Shore' (abridged by R.S.)
4. 'Mock Morris' (easy arrangement by R.S.)
5. 'Beautiful Fresh Flower' (easy arrangement by R.S.)
6. 'Australian Up-Country Song' (edited by R.S.)
7. 'Irish Tune from County Derry' (edited by R.S.)
8. 'Walking Tune' (easy arrangement by R.S.)
9. 'Hill Song No. 1 (easy arrangement by R.S.)
10. 'To a Nordic Princess' (easy arrangement by R.S.)
11. 'One More Day My John' (edited by R.S.)
12. 'Spoon River' (easy arrangement by R.S.)
13. 'Blithe Bells' (easy version by P.A.G.)
14. 'Over the Hills and Far Away' (easy arrangement by R.S.)
15. 'Now O Now I Needs Must Part' (freely set for piano by P.A.G.) edited and with an introduction and explanatory notes (Schott, 1967) (1966).

2. ORIGINAL WORKS BY RONALD STEVENSON INSPIRED BY WORKS OF PERCY GRAINGER

Corroboree for Grainger for piano solo, wind band, and percussion. This is a radical reworking, with much new material, of Stevenson's orchestral work *Jamboree for Grainger.* Commissioned by Napier Polytechnic, Edinburgh (1960, rev. 1989).

Fanfare for Grainger for four trumpets in B flat with side-drum (1979).

Harlem (125th Street) Walkabout for piano solo. The first twelve bars are a completion of a 1919 Grainger sketch entitled 'A Little March Air'. It was renamed by a vote of the audience at its first public performance in White Plains, New York, 10 April 1987 (1987)

Jamboree for Grainger for full orchestra (1960–61).

—— for two pianos (1960).

A Wreath of Tunes in Memory of Percy Grainger for chorus (SATB) and piano with text by Ronald Stevenson to tunes by Percy Grainger (10–23 February 1961) – *cf.* pp. 257–61, below. *A Wreath of Tunes in*

Memory of Percy Grainger was begun shortly after Stevenson learned of Grainger's death, on 10 February 1961, and completed on 23 February 1961. In this homage Stevenson quotes five melodies either written by or of deep significance to Grainger. The work opens in the style of a sea chanty, quoting from 'Storm Along', a pumping chanty noted down by Grainger in 1906 and set by him for unaccompanied male chorus in 1907. Stevenson then segues into 'Waltzing Matilda' to celebrate the country of Grainger's birth, followed by musical quotations from Stephen Foster's 'Camptown Races' which Grainger's mother used to sing to him as a lullaby and which he immortalised in his own *Tribute to Foster,* composed in 1913–14. Stevenson then adroitly combines these two melodies while quoting Grainger's words to the refrain from *Tribute to Foster.* In recognition of Grainger's love for Scandinavia, Stevenson follows with a pastoral section from Grieg's 'Morning Song' from *Peer Gynt.* The penultimate selection quotes liberally from Grainger's *Bridal Song: To a Nordic Princess,* written for his Swedish bride Ella Viola Strom in 1927–28 and sets to the music the dedication with which Grainger prefaced the published edition of *Bridal Song.* Coming full circle, the *Wreath* then closes with another reference to the sea-chanty melody with which it opened.

3. RECORDINGS BY RONALD STEVENSON OF THE WORKS OF PERCY GRAINGER

Percy Grainger: 'Salute to Scotland' :
Hill-Song No. 1 (arr. Stevenson)
Songs of the North:

i. 'Willie's gane to Melville Castle'
ii. 'Weaving song'
iii. 'Skye boat song'
iv. 'This is no my plaid'
v. 'Turn ye to me'
vi. 'Drowned'
vii. 'Fair young Mary'
viii. 'Lizzie Lindsay'
ix. 'The women are a' gane wud'
x. 'My faithful fond one'
xi. 'Bonnie George Campbell'
xii. 'O'er the moor'
xiii. 'O gin I were where Gowrie rins'

xiv. 'Mo Ninghean Dhu'
3. *Three Scotch Folksongs* (edited Stevenson)
   i. 'Will ye gang to the Hielands, Leezie Lindsay?'
   ii. 'Mo Nighean Dubh'
   iii. 'O gin I were where Gadie rins'

Scotch *Strathspey and Reel* Ronald Stevenson, piano, Altarus AIR-CD-9040.

Ramble on Love, Percy Grainger's 'Ramble' (Fantasy) on the last Love-Duet from Richard Strauss' opera *Der Rosenkavalier* in *Twentieth-Century Operatic Fantasias* performed by Ronald Stevenson, piano, Altarus, AIR-CD-9042.

Stevenson's A Wreath of Tunes in Memory of Percy Grainger

2
In Melbourne town this boy was born
div.
Ah!
Ah!
Ah!
Hum
Mel-bourne, Melbourne.
Yes, right 'Down Under' that's where he's from
Mel-bourne, Melbourne town. His
Mel-bourne, Mel-bourne
Hum
Mammy sang that song when he cried: Doo-dah! Doo-dah! Doo-dah! That Foster song was his lullaby
pp
Hum
Ah!
La, La-la. la. La lala la lala lala lala lala la la etc.
(Gb) (F#)
unis.
Lightly Leggiero
La la
a2 unison forte
La-la-la
Gwine to still be sung As long as the world's hearts
div.
young, Just like the tunes that Grainger wrote, Gwine to still be sung.
Pastorale: Andante
mf
From mountains of Norway and meadows of England, This boy plucked his music like wild flowers like
Vocalise: Ah
Ah

3
wild flowers blowing, this mu-sic was growing and bur-geo-ning bright with sun and show'rs.
Hill-songs and dale songs, and day-songs and sea-songs, and songs of the birds and the beasts.
Wild songs and glad songs Made music a glo-ri-ous feast.
Sopranos (or an octave lower)
Grain-gert's gone, he's gone to rest: Ay, ay, ay Mis-ter Storm-a-long.
From a Northern country came a fair and lovely bride with cornfield hair and cornflower eyes;
+ Text by Percy Grainger

4
whose won-drous ra - - - - - - - - - - diance makes real the god-desses of the
Who but to be-hold who but to be-hold is to
unis. ALTO
div.
who but to be-hold but to be-hold is to
who but to be-hold is to love
love and loving ne'er know aught of death.
love and loving ne'er know aught of death.
love and loving ne'er to know aught of death.
SOPRANOS
ALTOS
TENORS
Humming
BASSES div.
Humming

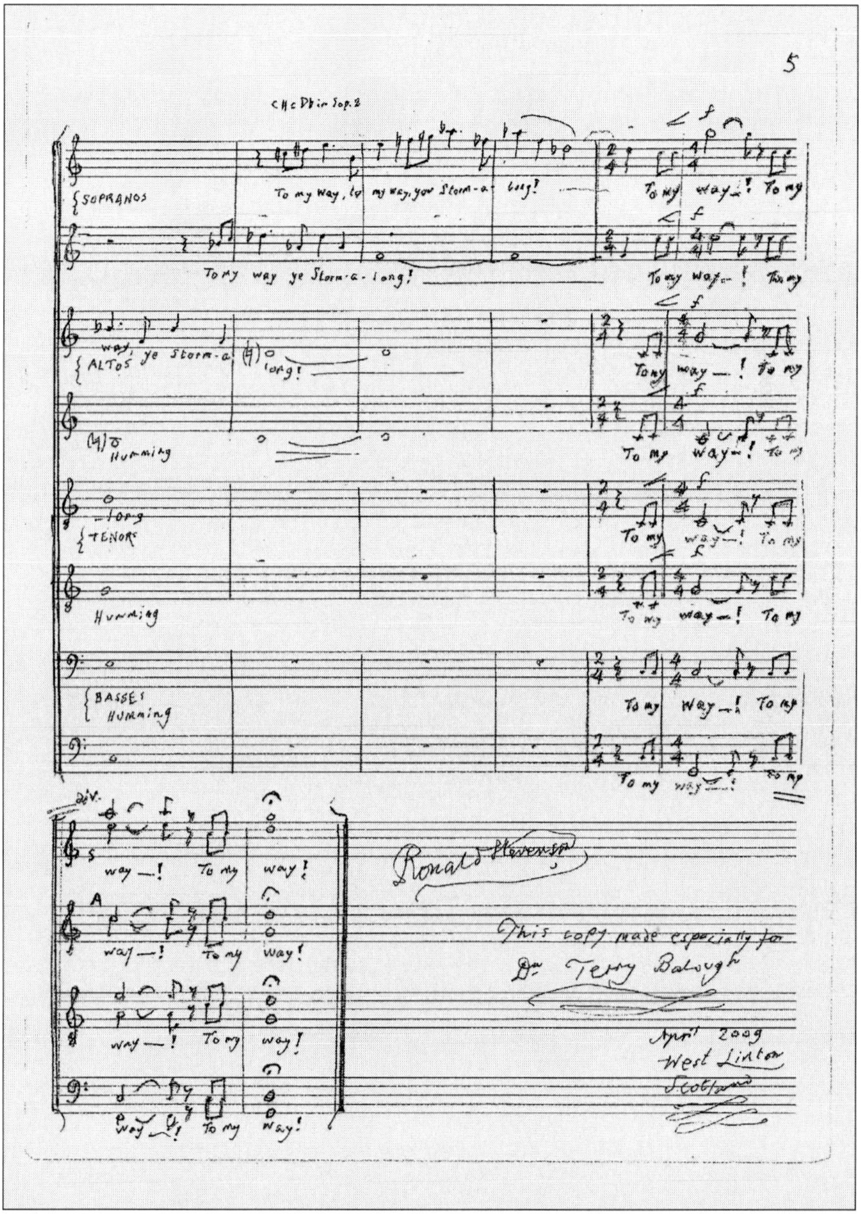
5
SOPRANOS
To my way, to my way, ye Storm-a-long!
To my way ye Storm-a-long!
ALTOS
way, ye Storm-a-long!
Humming
TENORS
Humming
BASSES
Humming
To my way—! To my
way—! To my way!
Ronald Stevenson
This copy made especially for
Dr. Terry Balough
April 2009
West Linton
Scotland

Bibliography

1. Writings by and Interviews with Percy Grainger

Anon., 'Percy Grainger's Fighting Creed: His Guiding Principles as a Composer', *The Australian Musical News,* 1 October 1924, pp. 17–18.

Teresa Balough, (ed.). *A Musical Genius from Australia: Selected Writings by and about Percy Grainger,* Callaway International Resource Centre for Music Education University of Western Australia , Perth, 1982; 2nd edn. 1997

Malcolm Gillies and Bruce Clunies Ross (eds.), *Grainger on Music,* Oxford University Press, Oxford, 1999

Malcolm Gillies and David Pear (eds.), *The All-Round Man: Selected Letters of Percy Grainger, 1914–1961,* Clarendon Press, Oxford, 1994

Malcolm Gillies and David Pear (eds.), *Portrait of Percy Grainger,* University of Rochester Press, Rochester, 2002

Malcolm Gillies, David Pear and Mark Carroll (eds.), *Self-Portrait of Percy Grainger,* Oxford University Press, New York, 2006

Percy Grainger, 'English-Speaking Music and the War Effort', typescript of a broadcast for the Australian Broadcasting Commission, delivered 21 October 1943; typescript held in the Grainger Museum, Melbourne

Edna Horton (interviewer), 'Rare Music of Early English Age Restored,' *Musical Courier,* 1 October 1939; reprint.

John Kennedy, 'Anybody Can Play the Piano: An Interview with Percy Grainger', *Collier's,* 24 September 1927, pp. 24 and 34

2. Writings about Percy Grainger

John Bird, *Percy Grainger,* Elek Books, London, 1976; 2nd edn. Faber & Faber, London, 1982

Eileen Dorum, *Percy Grainger: The Man behind the Music,* published by the author, Melbourne, 1986

Sparre Olsen, *Percy Grainger,* Det Norske Samlaget, Oslo, 1963

Cyril Scott, 'Percy Grainger: The Music and the Man', *The Musical Quarterly,* Vol. II, No. 3 (July 1916), pp. 425–33.

3. Writings by Ronald Stevenson

Martin Anderson (ed.), *Ronald Stevenson on Music and Musicians,* Vol. 1, *Busoni: Aspects of a Genius,* Toccata Press, London, forthcoming

Ronald Stevenson, *Western Music: An Introduction*, Kahn & Averill, London, 1971

——, 'Busoni – Doktor Faust of the Keyboard', *Piano Journal*, European Piano Teachers' Association, Vol. 1, No. I, 1980, pp. 14–15.

Chris Walton (ed.), *Song in Gold Pavilion: Ronald Stevenson on Music*, University of Pretoria Press, Pretoria, 2009

4. Writings about Ronald Stevenson

Alastair Chisholm, 'Stevenson's Soutar Settings in the Context of Some Personal Memories,' *Chapman*, Nos. 89–90 (double issue), Summer 1998, pp. 74–76.

Malcolm MacDonald, *Ronald Stevenson: A Musical Biography*, National Library of Scotland, Edinburgh, 1989

Colin Scott-Sutherland (ed.), *Ronald Stevenson: The Man and his Music*, Toccata Press, London, 2005

5. Other Publications Cited

Béla Bartók, *Béla Bartók Essays*, ed. Benjamin Suchoff, Faber & Faber, London, 1976

Jacques Barzun, *From Dawn to Decadence: 500 Years of Western Cultural Life, 1500 to the Present*, Harper Collins, London, 2000

John Blacking, *How Musical Is Man?*, University of Washington Press, Seattle, 1973

——, *A Commonsense View of All Music: Reflections on Percy Grainger's Writings on Ethnomusicology and Music Education*, Cambridge University Press, Cambridge, 1987

Natalie Curtis-Burlin, *Negro Folk-Songs*, Hampton series, Books I–IV, Schirmer, New York, 1918–19

Hugh MacDiarmid, *The Company I've Kept*, Hutchinson, London, 1966

——, *In Memoriam James Joyce: From a Vision of World Language*, William Maclellan, Glasgow, 1955

John Tasker Howard, *Our American Music*, 3rd edn., Cromwell, New York, 1946

Hendrik Willem van Loon, *The Arts*, Simon and Schuster, New York, 1937

Gay Wilson Allen, *The Solitary Singer: A Critical Biography of Walt Whitman*, MacMillan, New York, 1955.

Index of Grainger's Works

General Index

Audio CD: Ronald Stevenson's 'An Evening with Percy Grainger'

On the evening of 10 April 1987 Ronald Stevenson gave a lecture-recital entitled ' An Evening with Percy Grainger' in the Public Library in White Plains, New York. During the intermission, he presented Orrin Dow, then director of the library, with copies of the Grainger-Stevenson correspondence. Grainger lived at 7 Cromwell Place in White Plains from 1921 until his death in 1961, and the library is a short walk from his home. The lecture-recital was recorded on cassette by Burnett Cross and has been edited and abridged for CD by Richard Black.

1	Introduction: 'The Unknown Grainger'	5:40
2	'A Piece in Search of a Title'	2:44
3	'Percy Grainger the Reformer'	2:38
4	*Bridal Lullaby*: Introduction	4:57
5	*Bridal Lullaby*	2:33
6	*Gardineriana Rhapsody*: Introduction	3:48
7	*Gardineriana Rhapsody*	11:13
8	Presentation of Grainger-Stevenson Correspondence	5:36
9	Introduction: 'The Popular Grainger: The Social Sunburst'; *Country Gardens*	1:56
10	*Australian Up-Country Song*: Introduction	1:30
11	*Australian Up-Country Song*	5:57
12	*Spoon River*: Introduction	1:04
13	*Spoon River*	2:27
14	'Grainger and Folk-Song'	8:24
15	*Irish Tune from County Derry*	3:35
16	*Scotch Strathspey and Reel*: Introduction	3:01
17	*Scotch Strathspey and Reel*	4:27
18	Encore Introduction: *Three Scotch Folksongs from 'Songs of the North'*	1:13
19	'Will Ye Gang to the Hielands, Leezie Lindsay'	1:05
20	'Mo Nighean Dubh': Introduction	0:50
21	'Mo Nighean Dubh'	1:29
22	'O Gin I Were Where Gadie Rins': Introduction	0:46
23	'O Gin I Were Where Gadie Rins'	1:25
	Total timing	77:22